D1483579

Internationalization of Ethnic Conflict

ICES ETHNIC STUDIES SERIES

Published in the same series:

Robert B. Goldmann and A. Jeyaratnam Wilson (eds), *From Independence to Statehood: Managing Ethnic Conflict in Five African and Asian States*, 1984

Dieter Rothermund and John Simon (eds), *Education and the Integration of Ethnic Minorities*, 1986

R. Siriwardena (ed.), *Equality and the Religious Traditions of Asia*, 1987

Neelan Tiruchelvam and Radhika Coomaraswamy (eds), *The Role of the Judiciary in Plural Societies*, 1987

K.M. de Silva, Pensri Duke, Ellen S. Goldberg and Nathan Katz (eds), *Ethnic Conflict in Buddhist Societies*, 1988

Ralph R. Premdas, S.W.R. de A. Samarasinghe and Alan B. Anderson (eds), *Secessionist Movements in Comparative Perspective*, 1990

Internationalization of Ethnic Conflict

Edited by

K.M. de Silva
and R.J. May

INTERNATIONAL CENTRE FOR ETHNIC
STUDIES, SRI LANKA
in association with
FRIEDRICH EBERT STIFTUNG

 Pinter Publishers, London

First published in Great Britain in 1991 by
Pinter Publishers Limited
25 Floral Street, London WC2E 9DS

British Library Cataloguing in Publication Data

A CIP catalogue record for this book is available from the
British Library
ISBN 0 86187 093 X

Typeset by GCS, Leighton Buzzard, Bedfordshire
Printed and bound in Great Britain by
Biddles Ltd, Guildford and King's Lynn

CONTENTS

Dedicated to the memory of
Akira Nagazumi 1929–1987
Director, ICES, 1985–1987

NOTES ON CONTRIBUTORS

K.M. de Silva is Foundation Professor of Sri Lanka History at the University of Peradeniya, Sri Lanka, and Executive Director, International Centre for Ethnic Studies, Sri Lanka. His publications include *Social Policy and Missionary Organizations in Ceylon 1840–1855* (1965), *A History of Sri Lanka* (1981), *Managing Ethnic Tensions in Multi-Ethnic Societies: Sri Lanka 1880–1985* (1986).

Partha S. Ghosh is Director, Indian Council for Social Science Research, New Delhi, India.

Aruna Gopinath is Lecturer, Department of History, University of Malaya, Kuala Lumpur, Malaysia.

Shelton U. Kodikara is Professor of International Relations and Co-ordinator of the International Relations Programme of the University of Colombo, Sri Lanka.

Bertil Lintner is a journalist and specialist on Burma for the *Far Eastern Economic Review*.

R.J. May is Senior Fellow, Department of Political and Social Change, Research School of Pacific Studies, Australian National University, Canberra, Australia. He was formerly Director, Institute of Applied Social and Economic Research, Papua New Guinea.

S.D. Muni is Professor of South Asian Studies, School of International Studies, Jawaharlal Nehru University, New Delhi, India.

Ralph R. Premdas is Senior Fellow, Center for Developing Area Studies, McGill University, Montreal, Canada.

Rasul B. Rais is Visiting Scholar, Russian Research Center, Harvard University, Massachusetts, United States, and Associate Professor, Department of International Relations, Quaid-I-Azam University, Islamabad, Pakistan.

Tom Rogers is Fulbright Professor of International Relations, Area Study Centre, Quaid-I-Azam University, Islamabad, Pakistan.

Chaiwat Satha-Anand is Associate Professor, Faculty of Political Science, Thammasat University, Bangkok, Thailand.

Bhabani Sen Gupta is Professor, Centre for Policy Research, New Delhi, India.

PREFACE

Ethnic conflicts are no longer confined to the country of their origin. Driven by factors such as cross-border links between ethnic groups, quick global dissemination of news, international concern for human rights, international terrorism, and easy access to the international arms market, ethnic conflicts are increasingly getting internationalized.

There is a growing opinion that the international community should pay less heed to the traditional principle of sovereignty and more to the human rights of oppressed ethnic minorities. The predicament of the Iraqi Kurds in the aftermath of the Gulf War has given the UN itself an important direct new role in determining the future of minority ethnic groups embroiled in conflict situations. In short, ethnic conflict has introduced a major new element to the conduct of international relations. In such a context this monograph offers its readers some highly topical case studies that examine in depth the process of internationalization of ethnic conflicts in several Third World countries.

ACKNOWLEDGMENTS

The editors of this volume wish to thank the authors of the chapters it contains, and all other participants at the international workshop from the discussions of which it emerged in this present form. We are particularly grateful to Bertil Lintner who was kind enough to respond to an invitation by the editors to help fill a gap in our study by writing a paper for us at very short notice. We are very grateful to him for this. We have benefitted very much from the unstinted co-operation of the staff of the ICES. Ms Shamalie de Soysa organized the conference, ably assisted by Ms Eranganie Wijeratne and Ms Nalini Weragama. The production of the papers and the final text was, as usual, the work of Ms Sepali Liyanamana and Ms Bernadine Perera. Ms Kanthi Gamage had the formidable task of the proof-reading: of the articles, the revisions, and finally of this book. Our Accountant Ms Chalani Lokugamage stepped in whenever there were calls for assistance in the preparation of the book, while Mr Tilak Jayatilake and Mr Samarakoon Bandara helped in the running of the conference and in innumerable other ways. The ICES wishes to acknowledge with thanks the generous financial support we have had from the Friedrich Ebert Stiftung (FES) in these endeavours of ours, and the encouragement given by Mr Arnold Wernhoerner and his successor Dr Rheinhold Plate. K.M. de Silva's chapter in this volume is a revised and abridged version of his original paper. The research involved in the revision was funded in part by a grant from the U.S. Institute of Peace in Washington D.C.

K.M. de Silva
R.J. May

INTRODUCTION

K.M. de Silva and R.J. May

All the chapters, save one, in this volume are revised versions of papers presented at a three-day international workshop on the theme of Internationalization of Ethnic Conflict, organized by the International Centre for Ethnic Studies, in association with the Friedrich Ebert Stiftung, Colombo and held on 2–4 August 1989 in Colombo. The exception is Bertil Lintner's chapter on the internationalization of ethnic conflict in Burma, which was specially prepared for this volume at the request of the editors.

It was both poignant and appropriate that the workshop was held against the background of frenetic diplomatic activity and considerable bickering between Sri Lanka and India, on the speed and the timetable of the withdrawal of the Indian Peace-Keeping Force (IPKF) from the north and east of the island. Needless to say, the Indo-Sri Lanka imbroglio was one of the principal themes of the discussion with three papers dealing with it directly. All three papers are published here in a revised and shortened form. K.M. de Silva's chapter, which is the longest in this volume, is itself a substantially reduced version of a 20,000-word paper presented at the conference. There were other issues that received as much attention as this: Cyprus; the recrudescence of unresolved ethnic rivalries of the past in Central and Eastern Europe, in particular the plight of the Hungarian minority in Romania; and the problems of ethnic conflict in South and South-East Asia. This last theme included the problems of the Muslim minorities of Thailand and the Philippines, the case of the West Papua movement in Irian Jaya in Indonesia; and then the Punjab, Nepal, and the refugee problems of Pakistan—the Afghan refugees living within Pakistan, and the Pakistani minority living in Bangladesh and intent on securing repatriation to their 'homeland'.

In a search for greater cohesion in the preparation of this present volume, and for considerations of space, it was decided to restrict the scope of the volume to the internationalization of ethnic conflict in South and South-East Asia, where the theme can be studied in all its various forms and ramifications. The conflicts reviewed in this volume, with the exception of that in Thailand, are all post-colonial ones. In so far as Malaysia is often drawn into the conflict in Thailand, even the latter has some peripheral link with colonialism.

Ethnicity in South and South-East Asia is both a powerful constructive force and a potent destabilizing element. In alliance with nationalism it was one of the principal driving-forces in the struggle for independence against colonial rule. As an integral part of the historical anti-colonial revolutions of the post-World War II era ethnicity was much more than an emotional or cultural bond: its dynamism and intensity found support and legitimacy in the ideology of nationalism as the accepted basis of the modern state. Ethnicity is also a major, if not the principal, source of internal tensions and conflicts in Third World societies newly emerging from colonialism, through the rivalries of different ethnic groups living within the boundaries of the new states. The political establishment in post-colonial states—though not only in post-colonial situations—is often embroiled in protracted social conflicts with ethnic and religious groups that resist the expanding powers and demands of the state. Every chapter in this book provides examples of these.

The strength of powerful forces like culture, religion and ethnicity stemming from pre-colonial times puts tremendous pressure on the state in post-colonial societies. The state is often a colonial inheritance, a structure seized through successful rebellion or, less frequently, won after prolonged negotiation, from the colonial powers. The processes of post-colonial consolidation and expansion, and of state-building as pursued by the new rulers, often disregard indigenous forces such as language, culture, religion and ethnicity with the same insouciance as that of their colonial predecessors. The successor states, intent on preserving their inheritance unchanged, confront separatist forces immanent in these powerful but contradictory processes. Thus separatism is as much the result of imposing colonial rule in these regions, as it is a consequence of the re-emergence of powerful pre-colonial forces seeking a political identity coincident with language and culture, or with religion, in a post-colonial setting. It is not unusual for a minority ethnic resistance to seek the creation of a new state if it could convert itself into a majority.

Quite often post-colonial states have artificial boundaries, but their new rulers are intent on protecting them at all costs. Where inherited and often artificial, national and internal, boundaries devised by colonial rulers separate people of the same ethnic group, as in the case of Thailand and Malaysia, frontiers and boundaries are disputed and the resulting potential for violence is very great. Any adjustment of the boundaries is seen to be inherently subversive—because it is intrinsically destabilizing—of the integrity of the post-colonial state system no less than of the individual state or states concerned. Separatism could be and is a powerful destabilizing force. It has generally been held at bay by that even more powerful force—Asian nationalism embodied in the post-colonial state system of Asia. Separatist movements in the Third World, in general, find that the great obstruction they face is a widespread hostility to disturbing the status quo. Because practically everyone is vulnerable to the pull of indigenous—and often, external—separatist forces, it is seen to be in everyone's interest to help existing post-colonial nation-states resist threats to their integrity from indigenous as well as external separatist forces.

A general reluctance to disturb the status quo embodied in the boundaries of the post-colonial state system, however, does not prevent or even inhibit involvement in ethnic conflict in neighbouring states—India's involvement in Sri Lanka's ethnic conflict is a typical example—or as in the case of the Islamic world and the conflicts within Thailand and the Philippines, in distant parts of the world. In an age of instant transmission of information through modern communication technology, few ethnic conflicts remain localized for very long.

The key to understanding the strength of separatist forces in South and South-East Asia is a knowledge of the way or ways in which the colonial empires of these regions were built. The British in India were in the first instance the successors of the last great Muslim dynasties who dominated Northern India for a thousand years—the Mughals. But the empire they constructed was larger than any the Mughals had ever controlled, encompassing as it did present-day India, Pakistan and Bangladesh together with Burma (a link between South and South-East Asia). The raj incorporated within its borders peoples and territories which Indian rulers of the past had seldom been able to control, among them the peoples of the north-east and north-west frontiers of the raj. The conquest of Burma, and the subjugation of the Sikhs from which spring some of South and South-East Asia's most troublesome separatist movements have their roots in this relentless expansion of the raj.

By one of those curious accidents of history, or to be more accurate, one of those quirks of British administrative policy—or lack of it—Sri Lanka or Ceylon as it was then called, did not form part of the British raj, except for a brief period of three years in the earliest phase of British rule of the littoral when there was an experiment in dual control between the Madras government of the East India Company on the one hand and Whitehall on the other. There was a major rebellion against that administration in 1797 and 1798, and the lesson that was learned from it was the need to have a separate administration for the island, that is to say, separate from the East India Company's territories in India. Whitehall's control over Sri Lanka (or Ceylon) was through the institutional framework of the Colonial Office; over India, it was through the English East India Company till 1858, and then the India Office. Each protected its turf from interference by the other with a zeal that would have done credit to pre-independence and post-independence politicians of the two countries. How different was the fate of Burma, swallowed in three large gulps between 1824 and 1886, and generally ruled as part of the East India Company's possessions and from the 1850s as part of the raj, until 1937 when it was, at last, separated from the raj.

II

Ralph Premdas' chapter on 'The internationalization of ethnic conflict: some theoretical explorations' seeks to identify some typologies for understanding the links in the process of internationalizing an ethnic conflict. These include the ethnic affinity link provided by diaspora groups, often the products of overseas migrations resulting from episodes of, or prolonged periods of, ethnic conflict; the political power links associated with ideological support; the economic link stemming from common and endangered commercial and financial interests; and what may be termed ethical linkages, based on the interest shown by governments and non-governmental organizations in human rights violations. Internationalization of a conflict confers visibility and therefore a great or greater measure of protection where a minority faces repression, deportation or even extermination. In this way internationalization provides new sources of sympathies, material resources and even organizational skills to the affected minority groups.

The consequences of internationalization of an ethnic conflict are not necessarily those which the affected parties generally anticipate; nor are they wholly beneficial, as demonstrated in the case of the Tamils of Sri Lanka and the Indian involvement on their behalf. On the contrary, internationalization often helps to prolong a conflict and makes parties to the conflict more intractable; again, when larger regional or global powers enter a domestic ethnic dispute, playing the role of sponsors and suppliers, the original issues in the conflict may be superseded by the interests of the external contenders. On the other hand, through a process of conciliation the external powers may also become a moderating factor in conflicts, helping to bring the contending parties to the negotiating-table and even imposing a settlement on them.

The other chapters of this volume are case studies of the internationalization of ethnic conflict. They exemplify the operation of what we call the second law of ethnic conflict, that once such a conflict breaks out, sooner or later, indeed sooner rather than later in this era of instant communications, it will be internationalized. There are several agents of internationalization quite apart from affected minorities seeking and obtaining support from their diaspora groups in other parts of the world, especially the developed world. There are predatory regional powers who capitalize on opportunities to intervene diplomatically or militarily: indirectly through arms supplies and by facilitating the training of guerrillas, and on rarer occasions, directly, either on their own initiative or with the consent of one or all of the contending parties; and non-governmental organizations such as the Minority Rights Group, Amnesty International, and the International Commission of Jurists operating on their own or through UN agencies.

Three chapters by K.M. de Silva, S.U. Kodikara and S.D. Muni deal with the complexities of Indo-Sri Lankan relations and the internationalization of Sri Lanka's ethnic conflict. From the mid-1970s Indo-Sri Lankan relations were dominated by Indian responses to Sri Lanka's ethnic conflict, Sinhalese versus Tamils. The mid and late 1970s saw the beginning of the second phase in ethnic violence in the island. The first phase had been in the mid and late 1950s. At that time India had shown much less interest in it; indeed it was treated as a matter of Sri Lanka's domestic politics and not for India's diplomatic or political intervention. The situation changed in the 1970s. After its successful intervention in East Pakistan and the creation of Bangladesh, India was in a more self-confident mood. The débâcle of 1962, when China had inflicted a demoralizing defeat on India, had long been forgotten. The other factor which influenced the relationship between the two countries was the Tamil Nadu connection and its impact on the Sri Lankan situation. The rise of the Dravida Kazhagam (DK) and later the Dravida Munetra Kazhagam (DMK) in the early 1950s, reviewed in some detail in Kodikara's chapter, represented the same powerful force of linguistic nationalism that had transformed the politics of Sri Lanka in the same period. Between 1952 and 1967 the DMK had risen from challenger to the Congress to be the ruling party in Tamil Nadu. The DK and DMK were far more conscious of the rights of Tamils in South Asia than the Congress-dominated governments of Madras had been, and acted with much less restraint in demonstrating their concern about these. Very soon Tamil politics in South Asia had a regional rather than a purely local impact.

The chapters on Sri Lanka distinguish the main phases in the development and expansion of India's involvement in Sri Lankan affairs over the 1980s, till it reached its apogee in the Indo-Sri Lankan peace accord of 1987. India was drawn into the conflict as mediator but eventually became a combatant. She had other roles as well in the process of internationalizing the conflict, especially through the use of her diplomatic missions in Western capitals to espouse the cause of Sri Lanka's Tamils, and in initiating or lending support to moves at the United Nations and in UN subcommittees designed to embarass the Sri Lanka government on this issue. This was apart from assistance, moral, financial and military—through the provision of training facilities and the supply and shipment of arms—to Tamil separatist groups.

K.M. de Silva's chapter draws attention to the hard lesson that emerges from India's mediation and interventionist role in Sri Lanka's ethnic conflict: that most outside powers have less to offer by way of example in their own political system and political experiences than they think they have. To be drawn into an ethnic conflict in a neighbouring state is the worst folly for a regional power no less than for a superpower, as Israel and Syria have learned and are still learning in the Lebanon, and India has learned in Sri Lanka.

Outside intervention in a civil conflict can take many forms. First of all, the intervenor may begin by giving aid to one or other of the participants, or cutting off such aid. This assistance may be to encourage the continuation of the struggle, to compel or persuade one or other of the participants to alter its or their strategy, or even to encourage a settlement. Second, the intervenor may try to resolve the conflict itself, by acting as a mediator, applying sanctions to one, some or all of the parties, or underwriting a settlement. Third, the intervenor may become a common enemy of all or some of the warring factions. The Indian intervention in the Sri Lanka conflict has taken all these forms.

India confronts problems in two strategically important border areas: the north-east and the north-west. Of these one is underdeveloped and the other, the Punjab, is one of the most highly developed agricultural regions of the whole subcontinent. The Punjab situation demonstrates a very significant point: that economic prosperity does not guarantee political quiescence if other factors, especially political or religious, or a potent combination of both, emerge to spark off a separatist movement. Bhabani Sen Gupta shows how the Sikh diaspora has been critically important in the internationalization of the problem through financial support, publicity and political pressure in the United Kingdom, United States and Canada, while Rasul Bux Rais assesses the charge levelled by the Indians that Pakistani support is a significant aspect of the military strength of Sikh separatists through the provision of safe areas for training, the obtaining and transfer of arms, and the provision of a refuge for activists on the run.

Tom Rogers deals with an important aspect in the internationalization of ethnic conflict: the flow of refugees. He documents the case of Afghan refugees in Pakistan fleeing a violent civil war. It has drawn international attention through the sheer size of the refugee influx. The presence of Afghan refugees in Pakistan in such large numbers creates political difficulties for the host society, and complicates the already difficult relations among its own peoples divided by ethnicity in a polity that was constructed to demonstrate the strength of religion as a cohesive force.

Bertil Lintner looks at the contemporary situation in Burma and the processes of internationalizing that country's ethnic conflicts. The complexity of Burma's current ethnic problems can only be understood against the background of the manner of its absorption in the raj. One stream of political evolution emphasized Burma's distinct identity within the raj; a second stream of political evolution strengthened the forces of ethnic separateness within Burma, between the Burman majority (generally the more advanced people of the plains and the Irrawady delta) and the minority peoples, the Karens, the Shans, the Kachins and others.

The Burmese 'empire' had been on the crest of a wave of expansion since the late eighteenth century when the Burmese had inflicted a crushing defeat on their Thai rivals. But their defeat by the British in 1824 meant that the Burmese rulers did not have the time to consolidate their conquests, and to absorb the various groups of peoples who were part of the Burmese kingdom before the latter was absorbed by the British. The processes of conquest by the British served to emphasize the differences between the peoples of Burma, its minority groups and the Karens in particular, and the Burman majority.

The turbulent politics of the last phase of British rule in Burma, followed by the shattering impact of the Japanese conquest accentuated these differences. Aung San, the one Burmese leader who could have held the ramshackle post-colonial Burmese state together, was tragically assassinated at the very moment when he was poised to take power in an independent Burma. Ever since then Burma has seen no peace, and no political stability. Separatism became a way of life, and a civil war which pitted the Burman majority against the minorities has been a grim and seemingly permanent reality. As Bertil Lintner puts it: 'The union of Burma has had not only 42 years of independence from Britain, but also as many years of civil war, strife and insurgency.' His chapter traces the course of events in that unhappy country since the crushing of Burma's version of the pro-democracy movement in 1988. He delineates the peculiar features of the internationalization of Burma's ethnic conflict, and argues that the Burmese state seems to be on the verge of a decisive victory over the Karens, something that had eluded it for the last forty years.

In her chapter Aruna Gopinath deals with the problems posed by two Islamic minorities, one the Malay Muslims of the four southernmost provinces of Thailand, and the Moros of the Philippines. Both conflicts have a long and turbulent history, and both have been internationalized in the context of world-wide Islamic resurgence. Chaiwat Satha-Anand's chapter gives us a glimpse of a rarely explored facet of the internationalization of ethnic conflict, the world-view of a minority under pressure—the Thai Muslims.

Internationalization of these two conflicts takes two forms: moral and political support in the councils of the Islamic World, and the supply of financial assistance and arms to the guerrillas. The Moro guerrillas have been more successful in this regard than the Malay Muslims of Thailand. Indeed Thailand's diplomats have succeeded to a far greater extent than their Filipino counterparts in blunting the political challenge posed by efforts on the part of their recalcitrant Islamic minority to internationalize the issue through the support of the Islamic World.

R.J. May's chapter 'Sources of external support for the West Papua movement' deals with the ethnic conflict which stems from Indonesia's absorption of part of the huge island of New Guinea. It provides an example of ethnic conflict in which internationalization has been thwarted so far, but in which the potential for it nevertheless remains, incipient rather than dormant. The Indonesians have succeeded in imposing their rule on West Irian almost on their own terms. There have been serious violations of human rights in the process but despite the airing of these abuses through organizations such as the Minority Rights Group, Amnesty International and Survival International, there has been little or no international support for the Irianese people in their resistance to Indonesia, and much less for their demands for a Free West Papua.

R.J. May concludes his chapter thus:

> The fact remains that the countries most likely to be able to influence the situation—the United States, Australia, and perhaps Papua New Guinea—themselves have strong strategic and/or commercial reasons for maintaining good relations with Indonesia. And these are seen to outweigh the interests of West Papua's Melanesian population.
>
> Consequently, the West Papuan movement within Irian Jaya has had to rely essentially on its own, meagre, local resources, mobilizing the local population against a militarily vastly superior and generally repressive regime in Jakarta. In this context, achievement of a Free West Papua seems an impossibility, though the struggle is likely to continue for years to come. For the West Papuans the harsh reality has been that it is difficult to internationalize an issue, however just, when the strategic interests of potential supporters are best served by ignoring it.

1 THE INTERNATIONALIZATION OF ETHNIC CONFLICT: SOME THEORETICAL EXPLORATIONS

Ralph R. Premdas

Among the few particularly potent factors that may trigger intense mass conflict engulfing significant parts of the world in war is domestic ethnic strife. Internal disturbances that are deep and divisive, persistent and impoverishing, tend to attract external predators and opportunists who, for reasons of their own, exploit internal rifts, adding fuel to the fire. Ethnic strifes tend to be deep and divisive, and readily combust into wider conflagrations in a world of power struggles and self-interested intervention. The pervasive incidence of cultural pluralism and multi-ethnicity found among the world's 160 states provides potentially the flammable raw materials for conflict; their permeable borders facilitate widening involvement with dire and destructive consequences. Rapid means of mass communications, wide diffusion of transistor receptors to the farthest ends of the earth, and easily accessible weapons arsenals add to the scenario of ethnically-ignited strifes becoming contagious and uncontrollable. Irreconcilable ethnic strife is the stuff that feeds international power struggles, threatening world stability and mankind's future. Often kindled in a remote corner of the world within the dark hate-filled hearts of ethnic communities, ethnic conflict in the modern world can spread rapidly to other places within a state, then across borders, embroiling and accumulating antagonists and strange bedfellows, thereby growing larger and more irrationally out of control. Lebanon and its regional neighbours as well as Sri Lanka and the Indian subcontinent point to the unbridled destruction and entangling international alliances that domestic ethnic strife fosters.

The Arab–Israeli conflict in the Middle East, perhaps more than any other, illustrates the destructive dimensions of the internationalization of ethnic conflict. Ethnic strife that bestrides borders now stalks the world with nuclear teeth. The South African case, like the Arab–Israeli, also demonstrates the potential threat to world peace posed by the incandescent and amply armed ethnic conflict. Strategically located and abundantly endowed with vital mineral resources, South Africa with its struggle between 'blacks' and 'whites' has provided inviting waters in which the big powers fish. Bullets and bombs that explode in Soweto echo in the living-rooms of 'blacks' and 'whites' in the United States, Western Europe, Southern Africa, and the Caribbean among other places. The permeable international system permits rapid diffusion of domestic ethnic strife which in turn finds new identifiers and participants in distant lands, offering funds and moral support, thereby enlarging the conflict, often prolonging and intensifying it, threatening international peace and security.

The multi-ethnic and unintegrated structure of most states both in the developed and less developed world; the permeable and open borders of the international state system; the wide diffusion of rapid means of communications across the globe; the widespread concern for human rights; and the migration and diaspora of many nationality groups to other parts of the world—all of these factors have promoted the spread of ethnic conflict internationally. There cannot be any doubt about the potential of ethnic conflict to engulf entire regions, thus threatening peace and security in a fragile world. What we lack is systematic knowledge and reliable explanations of the role of the ethnic factor in international frays. How many international conflicts are ethnically instigated? Does an ethnic conflict assume a distinctive character separate from other conflicts? How do domestic ethnic conflicts cross borders? When an ethnic conflict becomes internationalized and involves the big powers, does it assume a new form? Does it necessarily become more complex and intractable? Does it become more intense, prolonged and destructive? In effect, are there patterns in the internationalization of ethnic conflict? In this chapter an attempt is made to probe these questions. A typology of ethnic conflict is offered and several factors that tend to feature in the internationalization of ethnic strife are identified with a view towards generating hypotheses to explain the phenomenon of internationalized ethnic strife generally.

1. A typology of links to the international system

When fed into the international system, domestic ethnic strifes avail themselves of several conduits for expansion. The most obvious is the ethnic affinity link where the same ethnic community straddles the borders of two or more states. This feature offers the most natural means by which an internal ethnic struggle is internationalized. The Basques straddle both Spain and France; Tamils dwell contiguously in both Sri Lanka and India; the Kurds are dispersed adjacently in Turkey, Iran,

Iraq, Syria and the Soviet Union; the Irish occupy Northern Ireland and the adjoining Republic of Ireland; Yorubas live in both Nigeria and Togo. The list is seemingly endless. On every habitable continent, artificial map-drawn borders do not coincide with human social solidarity settlements. Especially in the Third World where borders were imaginarily drawn blind to the patterns of cohesive social clusters, ethnic overlaps are frequently found.

We shall call this geographical overlap of ethnic groups into two or more states the ethnic affinity link. Living adjacent to each other may, however, be only a temporary event. Internal and overseas migration, triggered by ethnic conflict, may cause the transplantation of new non-contiguous ethnic affinity groups. Hence, the Irish have migrated heavily to Boston in the United States. Other notable cases include Sikh settlements in British Columbia, Canada and California; Palestinians have migrated to all parts of the Muslim Middle East; Tamils to Montreal and Toronto; Basques to Central America; Armenians to the United States, and so on. Hence, contiguous ethnic settlements quickly expand to non-contiguous areas, providing a wider arena to which ethnic strife spreads. Networks of communications keep these communities together, renewing and reinforcing the primordial ethnic struggles thousands of miles away, involving many more countries in the conflict.

Perhaps a more general tendency in the internationalization of a domestic ethnic conflict points to the intervention of unrelated non-ethnic actors pursuing their own political interests. We shall call this the political power link. An example will illustrate this type. In Guyana where Africans and East Indians have been involved in a protracted ethnic conflict, both the United States and the USSR entered the fray. Africans were organized under a social democratic party while the East Indians were represented by a Marxist–Leninist party. Given the location of Guyana within the Western hemisphere, Soviet support for the East Indian-based party and its ethnic supporters was calculated to breach American hegemony in the southern Caribbean and South America. Similarly, American support of the African-based party was intended to protect American security interests in the region. The Sri Lankan ethnic strife also illustrates the intervention of unrelated non-ethnic actors in the fray. There are numerous similar cases. It is noteworthy that in cases of the political power link, a domestic ethnic conflict can become transformed internationally into an ideological conflict. The Guyanese, Sri Lankan, and Arab–Israeli cases underscore this point. The original ethnic strife may become submerged under the power struggle of the foreign forces, but in the event it is nearly always made more complex, protracted, intense and intransigent. However, it is quite conceivable that external great power embroilment may set the stage for an imposed solution.

Another type of link in the internationalization of ethnic conflict refers to commercial and financial interests. This is the economic link. Ethnic strife can be both detrimental and attractive to the interests of multinationals as well as of states. When ethnic conflict disrupts vital mineral and fuel supply lines, such as the closure of the Suez Canal in the context of the Arab–Israeli war, international actors, especially the big powers, quickly become embroiled. From a different angle, ethnic strife often invites foreign interests to fish in these waters either to acquire advantageous access to resources or to sell arms. The former can be illustrated by the case of the West Irianese in Irian Jaya (New Guinea), allegedly offering concessions for natural resource extraction to Japanese investors in exchange for funds for the purchase of weapons badly needed to conduct guerrilla war against Indonesia. The latter case can be illustrated by reference to the supply of arms sales to the Arabs in the Arab–Israeli conflict; to the Tamils in the Tamil–Sinhalese conflict in Sri Lanka; to the Moros in the Philippines; to the Kurds in Turkey and Iran; and to the Irish in Northern Ireland. When external businesses enter an ethnic fray, they may restructure and perpetuate the conflict, which in turn looks to international sources for more support. Thus a cycle of internal and external stimuli and responses can create an ever larger conflict with dangerous world-wide implications.

Finally, the internationalization of domestic ethnic strife may occur through the conduit of a set of universally accepted values and ethical doctrines. This may be referred to as the moral or ethical link. The case of Biafra illustrates this. Here, a beleaguered Ibo population threatened with annihilation draws world attention and intervention to prevent human rights atrocities and possible genocide. Communal and ethnic conflicts tend to degenerate into ghastly acts of terrorism and state repression, producing widespread human rights abuses. This in turn draws the attention of a wide variety of monitoring groups including United Nations bodies, private organizations such as Amnesty International, and church groups. The international system has without exception of any of its numbers, accepted the Universal Declaration of Human Rights and its many amendments and additions as the standard of expectations in the treatment of the human person. Ethnic strife, as a variant of warfare, inevitably generates its share of victims. Where minorities are involved, as they are always in ethnic conflicts, special attention is drawn internationally to the conflict. This may be accompanied by various forms of support such as funds and international aid and political pressures.

In summary, this typology of domestic ethnic conflicts which have become internationalized emphasizes the mode of linkage between the internal and external environment. Every internationalized ethnic conflict can be covered by this typology. However, it is clear that a number of these conflicts may bear multiple links which make them more complex and intractable to resolve. Hence, the Arab–Israeli, the Sri Lankan and the Irish cases all bear multiple marks simultaneously spilling across contiguous borders, inviting external political and economic interests, and attracting human rights groups inquiring into the ethical dimensions of the strife. Some domestic ethnic strifes have stayed remarkably limited in their embroilment of external actors. These have included ethnic conflicts within the borders of the superpowers. The white–black conflict in the United States, while it provided an open theatre for an international audience, rarely involved outsiders. Similarly, the Soviet Union has closely guarded from external eyes, until recently, the ethnic conflicts among its diverse peoples. Apart from the fact that some ethnic conflicts have been confined to few foreign participants while others have exploded into regional wars, it must be pointed out that ethnic boundaries and groups have not been historically stable. Ethnic groups change and redefine themselves with old groups superseded by new formations. The implication of this fact is that regions which have been notable for their peace can quickly become consumed by emergent ethnic groups. This is a challenging area of research.

2. Ethnicity and the modern state

What are the features inherent in the contemporary state that engenders ethnic strife and, in particular, its spillage across national borders? Perhaps the most salient aspect of the contemporary state pertains to the preference for a democratic government. We live in an age when autocratic and kingly authoritarian states are condemned as anachronistic. The general orientation is that the state exists to serve its people and is accountable to the popular will for its actions. Leaders are legitimized by the electoral process. The democratic and not the autocratic state is the new norm.

Among other things, democratic systems are open and free; equally, they are accessible also to outside scrutiny. It is this elementary fact of contemporary life that makes it difficult for states to conceal complaints by ethnic minorities and thus easier for the matter to be investigated and widely ventilated. Apart from the universal value in favour of open, democratic governments that are sensitive to minority interests, the modern state is caught up in a comprehensive network of rapid journalistic systems which tend to sensationalize conflicts.

The modern state, with few exceptions, is multi-ethnic. Each has cleavages built around one or more primordial factors such as language, religion, region, race or tradition. Group consciousness tends to be built around these cleavages establishing an 'in' and 'out' group with the attendant set of stereotypes and prejudices. In an egalitarian democratic ethos embedded in the contemporary international order, even small slights develop into ethnic causes. While the Third World is replete with multi-ethnic cleavages, even in North American and European systems where dominant values have been long established, many 'residual' cleavages, minorities, and terminal communities exist in these states. The fact of incomplete integration and multi-ethnic formations fosters domestic communal disputes that often develop into open strife. The modern state constituently is prone to express subnational ethnic claims.

The modern state with its democratic, egalitarian, and multi-ethnic motifs exists in an international system that readily articulates and amplifies domestic strife. We have already discussed the role of comprehensive communications systems which are found in practically every state, projecting into and linking other states so as to create a veritable 'global village'. Mention has also been made of ethnic entrepreneurs and chauvinists, who receive immediate world-wide attention, coupled with the universal value preference for human rights, which draws particular focus on collective conflicts such as communal strife. The final factor that needs discussing is the fact of competing power blocs which have been created since World War II. States have been classified according to their allegiance or tilt in favour of the United States or the USSR. Until recently, the People's Republic of China was also a credible alternative bloc. The critical point, however, is that conflicting communal groups in unintegrated states may seek a separate relationship with one of the power blocs. The superpowers themselves fish fruitfully in these ethnically troubled waters for allies. In Guyana, for instance, one ethnic group has been aligned to the United States and the other to the USSR. Put differently, the conflicting ethnic elements in an internally fragmented state discover ready allies in a competitive bi-polar or multi-polar international order. An internally divided domestic system dovetails into an equally divided international system.

3. Facilitating factors

For domestic ethnic conflicts to spread across borders and embroil a wider set of direct and indirect participants, certain structural and organisational features must be present. Among these are:

1. the international dispersal and distribution of at least one of the ethnic groups in a conflict;
2. the strategic location of the strife-torn country in relation to international power rivalry;
3. the organizational and communications capability of the adversaries and their allies;
4. the ideological identification of any of the ethnic groups in conflict with one of the major international or regional powers; and
5. the presence of the international organizations which are sensitive to the mass atrocities that tend to occur in communal conflicts.

We shall develop each of these factors next.

Ethnic dispersal and distribution
It is self-evident that ethnic affines, wherever they are located, generally tend to become involved supportively in some way with the struggles of their community. In a number of well-known cases, as noted earlier, ethnic affines reside along contiguous state borders. Ethnic affines can also be found in far-off places because of migration or forced dispersal. Indeed, ethnic conflicts themselves tend to trigger migration to nearby and distant places alike, thus implanting new nuclei of support links, which in turn exacerbate the original conflict and cause even more migration to occur to many other countries, creating in the end an uncontrollable chain of ever-widening involvement of host communities and new interests in the conflict. Notable among such cases include Indians and Pakistanis; Sikhs and Hindus; Sri Lankan Tamils and Sinhalese; Irish Catholics and Protestants; Arabs and Jews. Networks of connections, subterranean and legal, dealing with legitimate aid and illegitimate trade in drugs and arms, are established, bringing greater resources and new non-ethnic interests, encompassing both govern-

mental and non-governmental actors in the fray. Hence the international dispersal and distribution factors can become critical links in sustaining a domestic ethnic conflict which originally was small and limited.

Strategic location
Clearly, the location of the country with an ethnic conflict can be very pertinent to the intervention of external actors. Turkey is an excellent example. Stategically located contiguous to the Soviet heartland, the Armenian and Kurdish minorities have been the subject of Russian penetration. Each of the superpowers has given close attention to the ethnic conflicts in Turkey deeming this area a vulnerable spot in their military posture. Similarly, the strategic location of Sri Lanka *vis-à-vis* Indian and American security interests has invited these powers into the dispute. The struggle between East Indians and Africans in Guyana, which is located within the traditional American sphere of influence, offered an opportunity to the Russians for a foothold on the South American continent. The case of South Africa is also germane; the country's strategic location has attracted inordinate superpower interest in the black–white struggle.

Location can also be significant if the strife-torn country in question is easily accessible to news reporters or close to a major metropolitan centre. Lebanon was easily accessible and it was itself a major metropolitan and cosmopolitan centre in the strategic Mediterranean; Northern Ireland is a case of easy access as well as closeness to major metropolitan centres; and places like Lagos, Nigeria, and Delhi, India are also relatively easily accessible from outside. However, places like New Zealand where renewed conflict between Maoris and whites could intensify; Irian Jaya on the Indonesian–Papua New Guinea border involving Asian–Melanesian confrontation; and Fiji located in the remote South Pacific, are all cases of important ethnic strifes which have received only minimal attention. Overall, the location of an ethnically-torn country has much bearing on the chances of the dispute becoming internationally entangled.

Ideological identification
In a number of cases of ethnic conflict, the parties or organizations which represent the ethnic groups may also espouse a strong left or right-wing ideological position. In the context of a world that had been bi-polarly divided between the capitalist and socialist camps, with high military and security stakes tied in, the ideological-ethnic groups may covertly or overtly identify with one of the superpowers. The Guyana

case, already discussed, illustrates this point. Other similar cases involve the PLO in the Arab–Israeli conflict as well as the pro-Western Jewish parties; the major political organizations associated with the blacks and whites in South Africa; certain groups involved in the Sri Lankan conflict; the Chinese and Malay groups in Malaysia, etc.

Ideological affinity linking a domestic group with an international power provides resources and allies. Where one of the ethnic groups is propertied and dominant, their ideological posture may be the convenient mechanism to involve one of the superpowers which may otherwise not be interested in the ethnic conflict *per se*. Ideology can be a false bridge linking internal and external interests. The 'falsity' factor refers to the fact that the ideology adopted by an ethnic organization may not be understood or practised by most of the group's members. However, ideology could also be quite a coherent structure that is supportive of the economically disadvantaged position of an ethnic group. This may apply to the Palestinians who are represented by the PLO. Overall, however, ideological projection of a group often bears little relation to grassroots beliefs of its members. Finally, the ideology of the leadership of an ethnic group may be deliberately crafted to conceal the racist or ethno-centric character of a group. It may also provide a more powerful and persuasive linkage to a wider network of friends apart from just ethnic sympathisers. Whatever the role of the ideological factor to the interests of the participants in an ethnic conflict, the result is the extension of the conflict to co-confessional ideological affines internationally. When this is fed into the cold war, the ideological factor can become a dangerous link indeed.

Organizational and communications capability

The internationalization of an ethnic conflict is often perceived as beneficial to at least one of the involved ethnic groups. Internationalization can confer visibility and therefore protection where a minority is about to face defeat, repression, or even extermination in a conflict. It can yield new sources of sympathy, material resources and organizational skill. Israeli Jews illustrate how the internationalization of the ethnic conflict can confer the upper hand in a propaganda war. Immense organizational skills and financial aid from the United States permit Israel to mount highly competent representation at the United Nations and other international bodies. It is only recently that the Arabs have been able to deploy a similar presence. The critical point is that certain ethnic groups, for historical, cultural and other reasons, are better equipped to express themselves internationally and effectively. The fact of comparative organizational endowment facilitates the efficacious entry of a dispute into the international arena. Weak groups can conduct an ethnic conflict in relative obscurity for a long time.

The presence of international and voluntary associations
In certain countries with ongoing ethnic conflicts, numerous international institutions and non-governmental voluntary associations may be present, serving as a conduit to communicate the strife to the external world. Among these associations are non-indigenous churches; aid and charitable organizations; branches of multinational corporations and their expatriate settlements; and various clubs, educational bodies and cultural groups. In some countries such as Nigeria, India, Sri Lanka, and Caribbean countries, because of their size and long colonial links, there are large densities of these associations. More than just a conduit of news, some of these associations may have a vested interest in an ethnic strife. For instance, the Presbyterian Church, originating from Scotland, had given particular attention to East Indians in Trinidad and Guyana. In the ethnic conflict between Indians and Africans, the international network of Presbyterian churches have offered sympathetic help to the plight of East Indians in the Caribbean. Similar church links exist between the Dutch Reformed Church in South Africa and that in the Netherlands.

Apart from links stemming from transnational cultural and religious associations, certain groups examine the issue of repression and human rights in particular. Among these are Amnesty International, as well as official United Nations monitoring groups. Aid donor countries themselves also assemble data on human rights violations and examine those given them by voluntary associations. Ethnic conflicts tend to produce inordinate numbers of atrocities by all parties to the conflict so that these facts quickly attract international attention through the internal network of voluntary associations. Reports by such high-profile groups as Amnesty International can cause donors to terminate aid to a country.

4. Consequences of the internationalization of ethnic conflict

The consequences of the internationalization of ethnic conflict vary considerably from case to case. Five patterns are discernible: (1) exacerbation; (2) prolongation; (3) moderation; (4) conciliation; and (5) supercession.

20   *Ralph R. Premdas*

Exacerbation

With the internationalization of an ethnic conflict, it may appear obvious that with the expanded scope comes greater complexity, intensity and hardening of the dispute. When new participants enter the fray, new irrelevant interests may compound the original problem. When new funds and friends are found overseas, more effort may be put into the fight, intensifying and spreading the struggle. As the conflict envelops more communities with greater intensity and issues added, more damage and destruction is experienced, greater passions are aroused, more deaths incurred and are to be avenged, and inevitably, the dispute hardens, erstwhile extraneous issues become significant, and the parties, losing perspective, becoming uncompromising.

The Arab–Israeli conflict is a clear example of the pattern. Huge sums of money have been raised by both sides to develop and purchase sophisticated weapons to fight three wars and a continuing protracted one. Casualties have risen on both sides; anguishing mass funerals are frequent; and more friends are engaged daily on all continents. The very fact of such visibility to the dispute puts national reputations on the line, rendering face-saving concessions and compromises difficult to find. With the United States and the USSR brought into the dispute, strategic and ideological interests of these participants have been enmeshed. The Arab–Israeli conflict has, therefore, suffered exacerbation in the form of intensification, greater complexity, hardening and enlargement as a result of its internationalization.

Other cases of exacerbation at some stage of an ethnic conflict include the Kurdish minorities who straddle several borders; Hindus and Muslims in the Indo-Pakistani conflict; Tamils and Sinhalese in Sri Lanka are other pertinent examples. Note should be taken that exacerbation may occur at a particular time in the life of a conflict. Exacerbation can occur internally also, but it appears that a qualitative change in the conflict occurs with its internationalization, involving new actors, extended territories, and greater resources and access to more sophisticated weaponry.

Continuation

It is difficult to evaluate the impact of internationalization on the continuance of a conflict. No ethnic conflict comes with a pre-set clock indicating its domestic longevity versus its lifespan when it becomes internationally implicated. Ethnic conflicts can continue sporadically and with various intensities over extended periods without any or much international entanglement. Internationalization can impact in either direction, for a longer or shorter duration. To involve international actors may well lead to immediate intensification of the struggle. But this could also serve as a positive precursor to a halt in hostilities because of the damage done, atrocities committed and immense costs incurred. The case involving the Ibos of eastern Nigeria is illustrative. While according to the government of Nigeria the international aid to the Ibos kept the conflict going, to others it was at least equally true that when ethnic participants developed a dependence on their non-ethnic adversaries for supplies, this offered the necessary leverage to the external sponsors to put pressure on their clients to terminate the conflict. Often, the ethnic groups in conflict lose perspective and rationality in the dispute so that external actors restore a measure of sanity to the dialogue. External intervention may well both prolong and intensify a domestic ethnic conflict, but in some instances, this may be a preliminary stage which then becomes a vital prerequisite for the solution of the problem. The paradoxical nature of this fact stresses the leverage conferred on rational external agents who may have an interest in seeing an end to the struggle. This argument may be applied to Western intervention in the South African ethnic conflict. While some people view the persistence of Western trade and investment as the fuel that keeps the fires of the conflict alight, others argue that such a policy tends to offer leverage to the West, causing South Africa to make concessions such as leaving Namibia. The argument that Western aid and trade prolong the conflict simply cannot be measured against a laboratory condition that separately tests how long the struggle will last without such support. Some argue that the partial withdrawal of Western trade, investment and aid has led to greater South African self-sufficiency and resolve which can only prolong and perpetuate the conflict. Nothing in this commentary must be taken to mean that the author knows whether Western aid, investment and trade can prolong or shorten the ethnic conflict in South Africa. The general point is that external intervention can prolong an ethnic conflict, but there is nothing predictable or inevitable about it.

Moderation
Internationalization of an ethnic conflict may have the general impact of focusing more eyes and ears on the dispute, bringing more reporters and television cameras to the scene of the struggle. Human rights organizations may also become greatly involved in the internationalization of the fray. One effect of all of this attention tends to be efforts to curb the level of atrocities and abuses. No party to the conflict wants to

have its image smeared, and would prefer to be viewed as right and reasonable. The very fact of restraint, even in attempts to conceal atrocities, is a small but positive contribution to resolving the dispute. For instance, in Fiji the conflict between Indians and Fijians could have easily degenerated into bloody civil war with the more lightly-armed Indians likely to receive the worst of it. However, the quick internationalization of the conflict restrained the Fijian military. Further, it forced the Fijian coup makers to limit ethnic violence lest the tourist industry on which the country depends for half of its foreign exchange be crippled. Moderation in the Fiji case also rebounded positively towards the two sides reaching agreements over harvesting the sugar-cane which is under Indian dominance.

Once moderation has been established, many more avenues towards conflict resolution are thrown open. It is posited here that although from time to time extremist acts of violence are deliberately committed to catch the eye of the world, by and large, such attention tends to encourage moderation. The opposite may also be true in some instances. When foreign television reporters were permitted to work freely in South Africa, there was a deliberate attempt by coercive forces to be moderate. Since the removal of the television cameras, more stringent rules were promulgated along with strong law enforcement.

Conciliation

The internationalization of an ethnic conflict may lead to third-party intervention and ultimately to conciliation. The case involving the Ibos in Nigeria is a typical example. Often conciliation occurs only where the intervening parties are powerful enough to impose a solution. The Sri Lankan case, however short-lived, illustrates this. In Cyprus, the inclusion of Greece and Turkey in the domestic ethnic strife at one point led to successful peace efforts involving Greece, Turkey and Britain. In the conflict between the Dutch and Sukarno in the post-World War II period, the intervention of the United States led to conciliation.

Conciliation as a mode of conflict resolution depends in part upon the parties to the dispute agreeing in principle to the role of a conciliator. The internationalization of an ethnic conflict can usher big-power interests into the dispute rendering a peaceful solution very difficult. Conciliation is more likely to succeed where the dispute occurs between groups within the same alliance or sphere of influence. For instance, the dispute between Turks and Greeks over Cyprus has been more susceptible to resolution by conciliation because both parties are within NATO. Conciliation is a definite possibility, but its frequency is not high.

)al powers enter a domestic ethnic dispute,
s and suppliers, the original issues in the
by the interests of the external contenders.
Lanka where Indian involvement led to
security interests ahead of the Tamil Tigers'
ng 'sold out' is often heard in this context.
nes to mind and their claim of being 'sold
anese of West Papua claim that they were

nderline is that external forces do not enter a
es. National self-interest is the governing
motivation. When ethnic contestants engage external allies, they risk
incurring a level of dependence that can be turned against them.

Multinationals can enter on one side of a domestic ethnic conflict with
a view to obtain concessions or access to valuable mineral resources. In
early colonial history, several companies interceded on behalf of one
tribe or the other, in an ongoing dispute so as to win access to local
resources. In Fiji, the entry of certain trading companies into tribal war
resulted in superior explosives and guns given to one group over
another. This turned the direction of the ongoing tribal war, giving
victory to one particular ethnic group. After the victory the company
became the main beneficiary.

What starts as an ethnic conflict can be transformed into another
animal as a consequence of external intervention. The entry of the
United States into Guyana's ethnic strife was conditional on the African
leader, Forbes Burnham, adopting initially a capitalist programme even
when his own ethnic group seemed to be situated to benefit from a
socialist strategy. The United States and the USSR intervening in
the South African ethnic strife gives the conflict, at one level, the
dimensions of an ideological dispute. White South Africans argue that
the black-based ANC is communist, thereby deflecting the issue of
apartheid.

Another consequence of external intervention in domestic ethnic
strife is the introduction of ideological beliefs into the fray. More
particularly, an external power may offer assistance only if an ethnic
group adopts a particular ideological stance. This can split an ethnic
movement into competing ideological parts, each seeking its own
external sponsor. The upshot is the lack of coherence and organization
in the position of an ethnic bloc, rendering the conflict more complex
and thus more difficult to resolve. The Tamil and Sinhalese groups

suffer from this ideological intervention factor which has made a nightmare out of the conflict. To solve the dispute at the level of ethnicity is itself sufficiently daunting, but when ideological faction-alism splinters the ranks of an ethnic grouping, then the chances of reaching a resolution recede greatly. External actors bring their own agenda and interests to a domestic dispute. They may make the prospect of reconciliation more difficult, but not necessarily. Transforming an irrational ethnic dispute into a power struggle between great powers may result in a temporary resolution of the problem in a forced accord for instance. However, the underlying issues would be left unattended, one day to be resurrected to haunt interethnic relations.

Conclusion

The ways in which ethnic conflict are expressed internationally are manifold. That these disputes are by themselves very intense and generally irrational can be witnessed in the cases of Northern Ireland, Sri Lanka and Lebanon. That they can explode into threats to inter-national peace and mankind's future can be demonstrated by the Middle Eastern Arab–Israeli conflict and the black–white South African struggle. Violent actions taken by Sikhs, Armenians, Tamils, Kurds and others on international airlines, in kidnappings, and other acts of terrorism point to our general vulnerability.

The chapter does not address the 'ethnicization' of non-ethnic domestic issues and conflicts. This is also a provocative area. For instance, poverty in the Third World has been translated internationally and ethnically as a North–South issue. The Third World poor are organized as if they belong to a new tribe called the 'South', with fingers accusingly pointed to the 'North', another tribe equipped with special imperialist claws. Many other non-ethnic issues are becoming ethnicized and politicized internationally. In some ways discrimination against women is called 'racial'; this can be expressed in new irrational solidarity movements against men collectively seen as 'an ethnic patriarchy'.

Soon every issue becomes ethnicized. Whatever the future of the international system, it is clear that these issues must be understood, contained locally and wherever possible interpreted not in symbolic ways but as pragmatic problems that can yield to compromise and practical solution.

suffer from this ideological intervention factor which has made a nightmare out of the conflict. To solve the dispute at the level of ethnicity is itself sufficiently daunting, but when ideological faction-alism splinters the ranks of an ethnic grouping, then the chances of reaching a resolution recede greatly. External actors bring their own agenda and interests to a domestic dispute. They may make the prospect of reconciliation more difficult, but not necessarily. Transforming an irrational ethnic dispute into a power struggle between great powers may result in a temporary resolution of the problem in a forced accord for instance. However, the underlying issues would be left unattended, one day to be resurrected to haunt interethnic relations.

Conclusion

The ways in which ethnic conflict are expressed internationally are manifold. That these disputes are by themselves very intense and generally irrational can be witnessed in the cases of Northern Ireland, Sri Lanka and Lebanon. That they can explode into threats to inter-national peace and mankind's future can be demonstrated by the Middle Eastern Arab–Israeli conflict and the black–white South African struggle. Violent actions taken by Sikhs, Armenians, Tamils, Kurds and others on international airlines, in kidnappings, and other acts of terrorism point to our general vulnerability.

The chapter does not address the 'ethnicization' of non-ethnic domestic issues and conflicts. This is also a provocative area. For instance, poverty in the Third World has been translated internationally and ethnically as a North–South issue. The Third World poor are organized as if they belong to a new tribe called the 'South', with fingers accusingly pointed to the 'North', another tribe equipped with special imperialist claws. Many other non-ethnic issues are becoming ethnicized and politicized internationally. In some ways discrimination against women is called 'racial'; this can be expressed in new irrational solidarity movements against men collectively seen as 'an ethnic patriarchy'.

Soon every issue becomes ethnicized. Whatever the future of the international system, it is clear that these issues must be understood, contained locally and wherever possible interpreted not in symbolic ways but as pragmatic problems that can yield to compromise and practical solution.

Supercession

When larger regional or global powers enter a domestic ethnic dispute, playing the role of sponsors and suppliers, the original issues in the conflict may be superseded by the interests of the external contenders. Such instances include Sri Lanka where Indian involvement led to priority assigned to Indian security interests ahead of the Tamil Tigers' interests. The charge of being 'sold out' is often heard in this context. The case of the Kurds comes to mind and their claim of being 'sold out' by the Shah. The Irianese of West Papua claim that they were 'sold out' by the Dutch.

The important point to underline is that external forces do not enter a fray for altruistic purposes. National self-interest is the governing motivation. When ethnic contestants engage external allies, they risk incurring a level of dependence that can be turned against them.

Multinationals can enter on one side of a domestic ethnic conflict with a view to obtain concessions or access to valuable mineral resources. In early colonial history, several companies interceded on behalf of one tribe or the other, in an ongoing dispute so as to win access to local resources. In Fiji, the entry of certain trading companies into tribal war resulted in superior explosives and guns given to one group over another. This turned the direction of the ongoing tribal war, giving victory to one particular ethnic group. After the victory the company became the main beneficiary.

What starts as an ethnic conflict can be transformed into another animal as a consequence of external intervention. The entry of the United States into Guyana's ethnic strife was conditional on the African leader, Forbes Burnham, adopting initially a capitalist programme even when his own ethnic group seemed to be situated to benefit from a socialist strategy. The United States and the USSR intervening in the South African ethnic strife gives the conflict, at one level, the dimensions of an ideological dispute. White South Africans argue that the black-based ANC is communist, thereby deflecting the issue of apartheid.

Another consequence of external intervention in domestic ethnic strife is the introduction of ideological beliefs into the fray. More particularly, an external power may offer assistance only if an ethnic group adopts a particular ideological stance. This can split an ethnic movement into competing ideological parts, each seeking its own external sponsor. The upshot is the lack of coherence and organization in the position of an ethnic bloc, rendering the conflict more complex and thus more difficult to resolve. The Tamil and Sinhalese groups

References

Anderson, B. (1985), *Imagined Communities*, London, Verso.

Enloe, Cynthia (1975), *Ethnic Soldiers*, London, Penguin.

Matthews, H.G. (1972), *Racial Dimensions of United Nations Behaviour*, Denver.

Mazrui, Ali (1969), *Post-Imperial Fragmentation: The Legacy of Racial and Ethnic Conflict*, Denver.

Premdas, Ralph R. (1973), *Party Politics and Racial Division in Guyana*, Denver.

—— (1989), 'Fiji: The Anatomy of a Revolution', *Pacifica*, January.

—— (1985), *Ethnic Conflict and Decentralisation*, Montreal Centre for Developing Area Studies, McGill University.

Shepherd, G.W. (1970), *The Study of Race in American Foreign Policy and International Relations*, Denver.

Sigler, J. (ed.) *International Handbook of Racial and Ethnic Relations*, Greenwood Press.

Suhrke, A. and L.G. Noble (eds) (1977), *Ethnic Conflict in International Relations*, New York, Praeger Publishers.

2 INDIA'S RELATIONS WITH ITS NEIGHBOURS: THE ETHNIC FACTOR

Partha S. Ghosh

The words 'neighbours' and 'ethnic' used in this chapter need some definition. In international relations the term neighbour connotes a nation contiguous to another, either by land or by territorial waters. India has nine neighbours, namely, Afghanistan (considering that Azad Kashmir belongs to India, at least in theory), Bangladesh, Bhutan, Burma, China, the Maldives, Nepal, Pakistan and Sri Lanka. Only five, namely, Bangladesh, Bhutan, Nepal, Pakistan and Sri Lanka are considered here. All of them belong to the South Asian Association for Regional Cooperation (SAARC). The SAARC framework automatically excludes Afghanistan, Burma and China. The exclusion of the Maldives, a SAARC member, was warranted by the fact that the ethnic factor is non-existent in its relations with India.

There is no universally acceptable definition of the concept of ethnicity. Like 'nation' and 'nationality', 'ethnic' and 'ethnicity' are also conceptual puzzles. Louis Snyder, the celebrated author of *The Meaning of Nationalism* confessed that he attempted 'to clarify the meaning of nationalism' and 'ended up with a definition of 208 pages'. Urmila Phadnis's recent study on ethnicity in South Asia[1] underlines the same hazards of definition:

> The explanatory inadequacy of the existing literature on the subject is to a great extent rooted in the ambiguities prevailing on the meaning and content of terms like ethnic, ethnicity and nation. The ambivalence has reflected fluidities and flexibilities in their usage over time and space. Consequently, it is not surprising that there has been a quest to clearly define these terms which has brought to the fore an ongoing definitional debate.

Drawing on the wisdom of a UNESCO team, INTERCOCTA (International Committee on Conceptual and Terminological Analysis), set up to resolve some documentational problems pertaining to various social science terms, 'ethnic' here would mean a subject 'defined so as to include problems of minority groups, nationalities and race relations, at both the intra-state and inter-state levels'. For obvious reasons, only the inter-state dimension of the issue would receive attention here.

South Asia presents a complex ethnic mosaic. All the states in the region, except the Maldives, are ethnically pluralistic. Of these states India is the most heterogeneous, and Bangladesh the least. In between are Pakistan, Sri Lanka, Nepal and Bhutan, in order of diversity.[2] India, situated at the centre and the most heterogeneous, is unique in having its co-ethnics in all the neighbouring states. No two of the other countries studied in this chapter have cross-national ethnic minorities sizeable enough to be of any consequence.

India–Bangladesh

The ethnic factor in India–Bangladesh relations has two principal manifestations: large-scale infiltration of poor Bangladeshis into India, particularly Assam, and the resulting threat to the political stability of the latter, and the issue of the Chakma insurgency in the Chittagong Hill Tracts (CHT) of Bangladesh and its impact on the Indian state of Tripura in particular and the north-east in general.

This influx of Bangladeshis had begun in 1974, a year of widespread food shortage in Bangladesh, and has continued unabated ever since. The 1981 census of India revealed that in the eight border districts of West Bengal, the population had grown over 30 per cent between 1971 and 1981, whereas in the rest of the border districts the reported growth rates were below 20 per cent. In a town in northern West Bengal, population had jumped from about 10,000 to 150,000.

The state most affected by these infiltrations was, however, Assam, where it was feared that the local population was or would be actually outnumbered by these foreigners. Some critical components of the 1981 census data on Assam were withheld so as to avoid aggravating an already inflammatory situation. Political turmoil could not be averted. The Assam 'anti-foreigners' protest which began in 1978 focused on the unabated infiltration of Bangladeshis. The agitators, at the forefront of whom were the Assamese students, demanded the physical ousting of all unauthorized settlers who came from East Pakistan (Bangladesh) after 1951. Though the agitation was eventually contained through the signing of the Assam accord (1985), Indian–Bangladeshi relations were strained as a result, and the problem has the potential to damage seriously those relations, depending upon the political situation in Assam.

The implementation of the Assam accord itself, however, could rake up the issue once again. The accord has provided for identification and deportation of Bangladeshi nationals who came to India after 25 March 1971. Mercifully, the process has hardly taken off, otherwise the deportation question would have to be addressed. The current Bodo agitation for autonomy has completely overshadowed the foreigners issue within Assam, at least for the time being.

The Bangladeshi government eventually conceded that emigration into India was taking place and that measures to discourage it needed to be adopted, but no Bangladeshi government has been willing to take these measures. This is too much to expect. The Mexican government for instance, does precious little to prevent its people from crossing over into the United States. It is the latter which has compulsive reasons to take steps to control the flow.

On the question of fencing the border, India and Bangladesh interpret their 1975 border agreement differently. Under the terms of the agreement no defensive structure could be built within 150 yards of the border. While Bangladesh interpreted a barbed wire fence as a defensive structure, India argued that the expression 'defensive structure' meant walls or bunkers which could impede the movement of military vehicles. India also argued that the agreement had provided for efforts to stop unauthorized immigration and smuggling and that the fence was supposed to help do both. The Bangladeshi government appears to have acquiesced to the Indian programme of fence construction when it was resumed on 18 March 1989 well within the Indian borders.

As for the Chakma insurgency, it may be noted that the problem is basically integrational, but since its locus is close to Indian soil it has spilled over into India. Successive Bangladeshi governments have failed to tackle the problem politically and have preferred instead a military solution. This has resulted in large-scale migration of tribespeople from the Chittagong Hill Tracts (CHT) into India, particularly into the state of Tripura. According to Indian sources, an estimated 60,000 refugees have taken shelter in India, which is not only an economic burden for the country but also complicates the ethnic politics of Tripura state. The perceived cross-connection between the extremist activities of the Tripura National Volunteers (TNV) and those of Shanti Vahini of the CHT vitiates relations between the two countries. India alleges that the TNV is aided and supported by the Bangladeshi government while the latter alleges that the Shanti Vahini operates under Indian aegis.

Lately, there have been some mixed indicators. To defuse the problem the Bangladeshi government has set up autonomous district councils in three CHT districts: Rangamati, Khagrachari and Bandarban. Apart from other powers conferred on them, these councils have the right to refuse permission to outsiders (meaning Bangladeshi non-tribespeople) to settle in these districts. This was one of the main demands of the Chakmas. Elections to the councils were held on 25 June 1989 in spite of Shanti Vahini threats to disrupt the polls. The main complaint of the Shanti Vahini was that the district councils plan kept out almost 90 per cent of the CHT from the purview of the councils, for the Kaptai dam area, Betbuniya earth satellite station, and the reserved forests all remained within the administrative jurisdiction of the Bangladeshi government. It is premature to predict how the whole experiment will fare. If it works, it will certainly encourage the Chakma refugees in India to return, which would reduce tensions between the two countries. But if it fails, it will further complicate the refugee problem with its resultant impact on Indian–Bangladeshi relations.

The ethnic factor in Indian–Bangladeshi relations has taken a new twist recently around the controversy over *Swadhin Bangabhumi* (Independent Bengali land) movement. Based entirely in West Bengal, it is organized by a small group of Hindu refugees from erstwhile East Pakistan and the present Bangladesh, who want to 'free' two and a half border districts for Bangladesh to resettle minorities (meaning Hindus) who were 'forced' to migrate to India. The only physical expression of this demand has so far been a few people gathering at the border and shouting slogans. The Bangladeshi government, however, attaches greater importance to the movement. On 24 May 1989 the Jatiya Sansad (Parliament) of Bangladesh spent over three hours discussing an adjournment motion on the '*Swadhin Bangabhumi* controversy' and contended that a conspiracy was being hatched in India 'to undo Bangladesh's territorial integrity'. Several ministers, including the then Prime Minister Moudud Ahmed, expressed concern at the development and hoped that India would curb the movement. The leader of the opposition, A.S.M. Abdur Rab, urged President Ershad to raise the 'Indian conspiracy against Bangladesh sovereignty' at international forums and at SAARC meetings. He also suggested compulsory military training for all citizens and raising the strength of the army. It appears that the motivation behind the *Bangabhumi* agitation in Bangladesh was to embarrass the Awami League, which had argued that ever since Bangladesh was declared an Islamic state in 1988 there had been migration of Hindus to India for they felt insecure.[3]

India–Bhutan

Although there is not much of an ethnic factor in Indo-Bhutanese relations, it may be hypothesized that if relations between the two countries ever deteriorate, India might choose to use the Nepalese and Tibetan minorities there to regain the initiative. The Nepalese are Hindu and ethnically different from the Drukpas, the majority community of Bhutan, while the Tibetan refugees, though ethnically akin to the Drukpas and of the same Buddhist religion, have a record of activities against the King of Bhutan and are deemed to have extra-territorial loyalty towards the Dalai Lama who lives in India. The Bhutan State Congress (defunct since the late 1950s) comprised primarily of alienated Nepalese who used to operate also from their bases on Indian soil.

The passage of the nationality law in 1959 gave them a new lease of life even though their activities were suppressed. The law had banned Nepalese immigration and restricted already settled Nepalese from moving north of a specified line. This and other socio-political discriminations led to the formation of the Bhutan National Congress under the leadership of B.B. Gurung. It operates from bases in Assam and West Bengal in India where there is already a large concentration of ethnic Nepalese. The main demand of the party is the abolition of the 1959 nationality law and for democratic rights for the Nepalese. Given the reality of India's support for the Nepalese elements in Sikkim politics *vis-à-vis* the Bhutia-Lepcha communities, which eventually led to the merger of the state into the Indian union, Bhutan has reason to worry about its political vulnerability. In a political competition between the Drukpas and the Nepalese, the latter may even paralyse the system from within. According to a survey carried out in the early 1980s, six out of twenty state functionaries were ethnic Nepalis.

The fact that the Bhutanese monarchy has to live in the shadow of a thriving Indian democracy is in itself not a happy situation for the royal house. Should Bhutan step out beyond India's perceived limits of tolerance of Bhutanese independence of action, especially in external affairs, New Delhi is certain to use the maximum pressure possible to restrict Bhutan to the acceptable bounds of activity. India could in that situation make use of the ethnic Nepalese and Tibetan refugees settled in Bhutan to the detriment of the Bhutanese royal house.

India–Nepal

The ethnic factor is one of the most important determinants of Indian–Nepalese relations. Actually it cuts both ways. There is a sizeable ethnic Indian population in Nepal while there is a sizeable number of ethnic Nepalese in India who form a significant minority in several north-eastern states (in Sikkim they are in the majority).

Politically Nepal comprises three regions: the Kathmandu Valley, the hills and the Terai. The Kathmandu Valley, is the most developed and the hills are the least developed. Racially (broadly speaking), the people of the Kathmandu Valley and the hills are Nepalese, while the substantial majority of the population in the Terai, which accounts for about 44 per cent of the total population of Nepal, are of Indian origin, generally from Bihar and the eastern Uttar Pradesh (UP), and speak Bhojpuri, Maithili and Awadhi. In 1980 there were an estimated 3,800,000 people of Indian origin in Nepal. According to 1981 census the population of Nepal was 16,020,651.[4]

The representation of the Indians in both the parliament (National Panchayat) and the bureaucracy is exceedingly small. They are also subjected to several discriminatory practices. For example, there is a system of weighting at the competitive examinations in favour of the ethnic Nepalese, which places the Terai Indians at a disadvantage: the weighting is as high as 10 per cent of the total marks. The Nepalese government's resettlement policies also affect them adversely. The Nepalese government has placed a ceiling of twenty-five bighas (about twenty acres) on family holdings of land. However, instead of distributing the surplus land in the Terai districts to the landless people of the area, the government has allotted the land to the people from the hills, many of whom are ex-servicemen. In the same way, the deforested areas in the Terai have also been allotted to people from the hills.

Since the greatest threat to the political stability of the Nepalese monarchy emanates from the democratic forces, the major breeding-ground of which is the Terai region, the ruling élites watch the people belonging to this region with suspicion. In this context the growth of population of the region has been a major issue in Nepalese politics. Indeed the population of the Terai has registered a significant growth over the years. While part of this growth is attributable to the normal demographic trend among the Indian Nepalese, it is also due to the migration of Nepalese hill tribespeople to the region. But the Nepalese government underplays the latter aspect and attributes the growth to the existence of the open border which allows Indians to enter Nepal without restriction. This attitude was reflected in the 1983 report of the Task Force on Migration of the Nepalese National Commission on Population, popularly known as the Gurung Report after its chairman, Harka Bahadur Gurung.

The Gurung Report provoked a major political controversy between India and Nepal. Although the report was not accepted by the Nepalese government officially, its implied endorsement of the recommendations was manifest. By making a clear case against the open border, the Gurung Report evidently highlighted the official concern about the 'anti-national' sentiments of the Indian Nepalese and their Indian connection.

Nepal's attitude towards Indian Nepalese has often been the cause of concern in India. The political leadership in India has often referred to 'insecurity' faced by the people of Indian origin in Nepal. In early 1984, such a reference by Indira Gandhi had actually caused considerable tension between the two countries. This had triggered off a heated discussion in the Nepalese press which was almost unanimous in projecting India as a bully, bent on interfering in the internal affairs of Nepal. It may be noted that since Bihar and UP wield considerable influence on Indian national politics and since the Terai people belong primarily to these two Indian states, the problems of Terai Indians receive undue attention in New Delhi.

Like the ethnic Indians in Nepal, there is a sizeable number of ethnic Nepalese in India. According to the 1971 census there were 1,419,875 ethnic Nepalese in India. The presence of these Nepalese Indians and their ever-growing political demands has been felt in an extensive area of the Himalayan foothills in the north-east, from Sikkim through northern West Bengal to Assam. Ethnic Nepalese are the most dominant political force in Sikkim, where they have wrested power from the traditionally powerful Lepcha-Bhutia communities.

Recently the Nepalese of the Darjeeling district of West Bengal under the banner of the Gurkha National Liberation Front (GNLF) not only disturbed the politics of West Bengal but also tended to provide irritants in the Indo-Nepalese relationship. The GNLF ritually burnt the 1950 Indo-Nepal treaty and argued that many of the problems faced by the Nepalese Indians actually emanated from it. The open border between the two countries blurred the Indianness of the Nepalese Indians — very often it was difficult to distinguish between them and the Nepalese emigrating to India. Some of the statements and activities of the GNLF became matters of serious concern for the Indian government. For example, Subhash Ghising, the leader of the GNLF, projected a military image by hinting ominously at the fact that there were 40,000 retired Gurkha soldiers in Darjeeling alone, whose services could be enlisted to press for a separate state of Gurkhaland within the Indian Union. It raised the spectre of another terrorist front in yet another strategically vulnerable part of India.

India's concern was heightened when the GNLF tried to internationalize the issue with Nepal as the nucleus. On 23 June 1986 Ghising wrote a letter to the King of Nepal, sixteen copies of which were endorsed to various governments and international agencies. The letter cited historical evidence in support of charges of gross injustice to the Nepalese of India.[5] Later, Ghising took the process of internationalizing his agitation a step further when he declared that the Indian government and the Gurkhas living in India 'should seriously study the proposal to declare Nepal as a Zone of Peace', a demand which the Nepalese government has been forcefully advocating and the Indian government has been consistently rejecting.

The Gurkhaland movement, however, has been contained through the expedience of an accord between the GNLF and the West Bengal government which has provided for reasonable autonomy for the Nepalese of Darjeeling. A Hill Council has been set up, elections have been held and unauthorized arms have been recovered through voluntary surrender. These are all positive indications. However, their political import for Indo-Nepalese relations cannot be underestimated. While one may only look at the possibility of Nepal influencing the Nepalese Indians, it must not be forgotten that democratization of ethnic Nepalese in India poses problems for the Nepalese monarchy as was so recently (1989–90) demonstrated. It would be naïve to think that India would ignore this advantageous factor in seeking to influence Nepalese politics to further its own interests.

India–Pakistan

In the case of Indo-Pakistani relations, the ethnic question has vital significance. The partition of the raj into two sovereign states was based on the principle that the subcontinental Muslims constituted a distinct nation separate from that of the majority Hindus, and that the Muslims needed a separate territorial entity to preserve and foster that identity. The partition and the horrifying massacres that accompanied it have left bitter memories in both countries and much of the pervasive tensions and the eruption of conflicts between the two can be attributed to this cleavage.

Pakistan's *raison d'être* was seriously eroded with East Pakistan's secession from the union in protest against what it called West Pakistani 'colonialism'. India took the maximum propaganda benefit from this, and turned it to her advantage by helping the secessionist forces to establish the state of Bangladesh. In terms of applied politics, India's secular ideology and Pakistan's Islamic ideology had confronted each other and the former had prevailed.

In the aftermath of the Bangladeshi crisis the ethnic factor in Indo-Pakistani relations did not wither away. Apart from the overall Hindu–Muslim dichotomy, several other irritants cropped up to keep the relationship on tenterhooks. It was expected that with the secession of Bangladesh the western wing of Pakistan would be more homogeneous and that it would be easy to complete the process of nation-building on the basis of an Islamic ideology. Soon, however, events showed that the West Pakistani unity had stemmed from a need to counterbalance the demographic reality of an overwhelming Bengali majority in East Pakistan, rather than from any compatibility amongst the various ethnic groups, namely, Baluchs, Pathans, Punjabis and Sindhis, which constituted the western part of the old Pakistan. The talk of West Pakistani domination which was once popularized in East Pakistan was now replaced with that of Punjabi domination of Pakistan, and on this point all the other ethnic groups closed ranks against the dominant majority. The physical proximity of India and the conflictual texture of its relationship with Pakistan enmeshed the whole question into one of India's alleged entanglements in Pakistan's ethnic problems. Against this background, statements such as Ataullah Mengal's tongue-in-cheek reference to possible Indian assistance in case Baluchistan went the way of Bangladesh was bound to be seen in a sinister light. During the Movement for the Restoration of Democracy (MRD) in the last years of the Zia regime, the latter accused India of complicity in the movement.

The ethnic dimension of Indo-Pakistani relations has lately taken a serious turn over the Punjabi and Kashmiri issues. The Indian state of Punjab has been in political turmoil for several years now. While the Sikhs in general are only asking for more autonomy within the Indian union, a small minority among them are fighting for secession and the establishment of an independent Sikh state of Khalistan. The situation has led to an unprecedented incidence of terrorism with complex international links, in which trafficking in guns and drugs form vital components. In the overall context the Pakistani connection in both issues has assumed crucial significance.

Indian authorities are convinced that Pakistan provides covert assistance to the terrorists to the extent of training them on Pakistani soil. The matter has been discussed in several Indo-Pakistani talks at various levels. While India argues that the Pakistani assistance is part of a well-calculated design to destabilize north India, the Pakistanis contend that gun-running and drug-trafficking through Pakistan are part of an international network beyond Pakistan's control. In 1989 there was, however, some easing of tension with both countries agreeing to patrol the border jointly to curb unauthorized trafficking in guns and drugs. How the experiment fares time alone will show. However, the Benazir Bhutto government found it difficult to cut the links between the Sikh terrorists on the one hand and the opposition *Islami Jamhoori Ittehad* (IJI) and the Inter Services Intelligence (ISI) on the other.

Disputes over Kashmir lie at the very core of the post-independence hostility between India and Pakistan. The two countries control parts of Kashmir. The Kashmiri issue is so intricately involved in the domestic politics of both India and Pakistan that it defies all efforts at treating it unemotionally. Kashmir has tremendous symbolic value for the nation-building strategies of the two countries. The inclusion of the Muslim majority state of Jammu and Kashmir into the Indian union symbolizes India's commitment to secularism as well as to its avowed theory that India is one nation. In the same vein, the loss of more than half of Kashmir including the Srinagar valley to India and its participation in the Indian political process as a full member of the Indian federation (Azad Kashmir is not a full member of the Pakistani federation) is the diametrical opposite of Pakistan's concept of nation-building based on Islamic ideology.

Of late, terrorism has grown exponentially in Kashmir, particularly in Srinagar and its neighbourhood. Various political organizations have surfaced which openly preach Islamic fundamentalism and urge accession to Pakistan. The Indian government and media believe that the activities of these groups are sponsored and encouraged by Pakistan and that there is an intricate and intimate link between the Sikh extremists, the Kashmir terrorists and the Afghan *mujahideen*. Pakistan of course refutes all these allegations, arguing that the Kashmiri disaffection has historical roots and unless the problem is solved by giving the Kashmiris the right of self-determination there cannot be any permanent solution to the problem. The latter demand is one which no Indian government can afford to consider, much less concede.

Pakistani involvement in the Punjabi and Kashmiri problems, or to be more precise, the Pakistani temptation to destabilize these states, must not, however, be considered merely in terms of drug and gun-trafficking or training-camps for Sikh and Kashmiri terrorists. It has to be viewed from a larger perspective. India's role in the dismemberment of Pakistan in 1971 still haunts the national memory of Pakistan, and if the latter ever has a similar opportunity, say in Punjab or Kashmir, it would have little hesitation in exploiting the disaffection to keep the secessionist forces active, and to pose a threat to India's stability. The Pakistani leadership always refers to the disaffection in the Punjab as a Sikh problem, and the Kashmir issue as one embracing the whole Kashmiri Muslim community. The object, of course, is to project them as separate 'nations'. Pushed to its logical conclusion such an assumption would have serious implications for the integrity of the Indian state.

India–Sri Lanka

The ethnic factor is most pronounced in the case of India's relations with Sri Lanka. The ethnic history of the island is such that not only does the dominant minority there claim its origin to India, a sizeable section of it looks upon the latter as its protector. India on its part tends to internalize the grievances of this minority partly to appease co-ethnics in the Indian state of Tamil Nadu and partly for geo-strategic considerations. As a result the Indo-Sri Lankan relationship is caught in a complex web of domestic and international politics from which both nations find it difficult to extricate themselves.

Three chapters of this present volume deal with this problem in considerable detail, and so my comments will be brief. In the light of withdrawal of the Indian Peace-Keeping Force (IPKF) from Sri Lanka (the process being completed in March 1990) it may be worthwhile to reflect upon some of the pertinent variables in the Indo-Sri Lankan relations in so far as they are concerned with the ethnic question. From the beginning of his tenure of office President Ranasinghe Premadasa committed himself to indigenize the ethnic conflict. This found expression in his insistence on an early and total withdrawal of the IPKF. In pursuance of this policy he established a dialogue with the most dominant Tamil militant group—the Liberation Tigers of the Tamil Eelam (LTTE). This strategy was intended to serve two purposes: to pave the way for Colombo to re-establish its political links with the Tamils; and to marginalize the Eelam People's Revolutionary Liberation Front (EPRLF) which was in power in the North-East Provincial Council. Colombo viewed the EPRLF as a proxy of the Indian government rather than a party with a genuine local base.

During the last months of Rajiv Gandhi's government, at a time when the question of withdrawal of the IPKF seemed to strain Indo-Sri Lankan relations, it appeared as though both governments were locked in a peculiar concern for the Tamils, each with a separate Tamil constituency to cater to: for India it was the EPRLF while for Sri Lanka it was the LTTE. The LTTE not only had an edge over the EPRLF in Sri Lankan Tamil politics, but its valiant resistance against the powerful IPKF for more than two years also enhanced its prestige among the Tamils even more. On the contrary, the EPRLF's (particularly its leader Varatharaja Perumal's) weakness became increasingly manifest through its tendency to look to New Delhi for getting things done by Colombo. Whether it was the question of dealing with the LTTE politically or that of devolution of power to the provincial council, Perumal's dependence on India was almost total. Understandably, Premadasa found it difficult to deal with such a man because it was not possible to work out a solution for Sri Lanka's ethnic crisis through him, a point which he expressed with great emphasis and clarity to a small group of Indian scholars (including myself) when he met them in Colombo on 4 August 1989.

With the establishment of the V.P. Singh government in New Delhi there were signs of a distinct improvement in Indo-Sri Lankan relations. There are at least two positive signs. In the first place the V.P. Singh government is keen on improving relations with Sri Lanka, a policy which the latter seems willing to reciprocate; and second, both the Indian and the Tamil Nadu government appear to be co-ordinating their stance in harmony with that of the Premadasa government. The denial of permission by the Tamil Nadu government to Sri Lankan Tamil refugees (allegedly EPRLF cadres) to settle on land in Tamil Nadu (leading them to take refuge in non-Tamil Orissa) is an indication of India's willingness to strengthen the hands of Premadasa in his dealings with the LTTE, especially after the latter had turned its guns on the Sri Lankan forces, quite unexpectedly in the second week of June 1990. Premadasa's attempt to persuade the LTTE to surrender its arms and join mainstream politics, as a legitimate political party, collapsed with this. Sri Lanka's ethnic politics and correspondingly her future relations with India would hinge on the outcome of this present conflict between the LTTE and the Sri Lankan forces.

Conclusion

For historical and geographical reasons the ethnic factor is one of the most crucial in India's relations with its neighbours. Since unlike other determinants it is the least prone to change, one must accept the reality that it will continue to be relevant for inter-state relations in South Asia in the foreseeable future. The fact is that India's size and location provides it with an in-built advantage *vis-à-vis* its neighbours. At the heart of the problem is an unfinished process of nation-building. Here again, unfortunately, the thrust is not uniform. The strategies followed by India on the one hand and the rest of South Asia on the other are not complementary to one another: they are actually contradictory. As a result, one's disadvantage becomes another's advantage.

Apart from India's size and its threatening nation-building strategy, the psychological fear of India's neighbours also emanates from the fact that the majority groups in these countries suffer from a minority complex. Since the minorities in these countries have a sizeable number of co-ethnics in neighbouring India this fear is not totally unfounded. Sri Lankan Tamils together with Tamil Nadu Tamils outnumber the Sinhalese, the Indian Nepalese of Terai together with their co-linguals in Bihar and UP outnumber the Nepalese of Nepal, and the Nepalese of Bhutan together with the Nepalese Indians outnumber the majority Drukpas. Pakistan and Bangladesh do not suffer from similar fear but the activities of Sindhis in India and those of Bengali Hindu refugees in West Bengal do sometimes worry them.

India's advantage is also structured on its multi-ethnicity. It not only provides some inbuilt balance, it also takes care of some logistical problems in dealing with ethnic turmoils. In this connection one may refer to the ethnic composition of the armed forces of the respective nations. For explainable reasons the Pakistani army or the Sri Lankan army is predominantly Punjabi or Sinhalese. In contrast to this, in the Indian army there is no predominance of any single ethnic group, notwithstanding the fact that the number of Sikhs is disproportionately high. The comparable advantages and disadvantages of the situation are obvious. An army intervention in Pakistan to quell an ethnic rebellion, say in Baluchistan or Sind, is bound to be interpreted in ethnic terms as Punjabi domination for the simple reason that the personnel happen to be Punjabi. Similarly, an army action in Sri Lanka's Tamil north is invariably seen as Sinhalese high-handedness simply because the men in uniform there happen to be Sinhalese. The Tamil critics overlook the fact that the same army is engaged in suppressing the Sinhala chauvinistic

JVP cadres in the south of the country. Had Pakistan or Sri Lanka been a multi-ethnic society like India the composition of its armed forces would have also been multi-ethnic which would not have created the type of suspicion among the minority ethnic groups, with which that one is familiar.[6]

In conclusion I should like to repeat what I have said in the concluding chapter of my book *Co-operation and Conflict in South Asia*:

A futurist vision of South Asia, given the persistence of the present 'insecurity' syndrome presents two diametrically opposite scenarios. The territorial enlargement of the Indian state reminiscent of the concept of *akhand Bharat* (undivided India), incorporating all the neighbours within the region. Or the further dismemberment of South Asian states, including India, on ethnic, religious and linguistic lines obliterating the present states from the political map of the world. A systematic evolution of regional consciousness alone can prevent the above situation from taking place.

Notes

1. Urmila Phadnis, *Ethnicity and Nation-Building in South Asia*, Sage, New Delhi, 1989.
2. The classification is based on broad political demographic considerations. Anthropological consideration would lead to a different classification, though probably the placement of India and Bangladesh would remain unaltered.
3. On 6 April 1989, the minorities of Bangladesh held a massive rally in Dhaka and demanded annulment of the constitutional amendment that made Islam the state religion of the country. Leaders of the Hindu, Buddhist and Christian communities described the eighth amendment to the constitution passed in 1988 as contradictory to Bangladesh's liberation movement. They demanded the restoration of the secular character of the nation. *The Hindu* (New Delhi), 7 April 1989.
4. It is difficult to find exact official statistics regarding Indian and Nepalese populations. Classifications on the basis of caste and religion blur the picture. For details, see Phadnis, *Ethnicity and Nation Building in South Asia*, op. cit.
5. For the complete text of the letter, see *The Hindu*, 24 December 1986.
6. In India, during Hindu–Muslim riots, Muslims do sometimes criticize the Hindu composition of the law enforcing machinery. It may be noted that these references are to the police forces which fall under the jurisdiction of state governments. So far as the army is concerned, no such allegation has ever been made, not even during the Operation Blue Star at the Golden Temple, Amritsar, in June 1984.

References

Bhattacharjea, Ajit K. (1982), 'Need to Resume No-War Dialogue', *Indian Express* (New Delhi), 15 March.

Biswas, Ashis K. (1982), 'The Unchecked Influx', *The Hindu* (Madras), 17 February.

Choucri, Nazli (1978), 'The Pervasiveness of Politics', *Populi* (New York), vol. 5, no. 3.

Connor, Walker (1973), 'The Politics of Ethnonationalism', *Journal of International Affairs* (New York), vol. 27.

Doordarshan (Indian TV) (1989), Telecast of Interview of Benazir Bhutto, former Prime Minister of Pakistan, on 22nd July. Interviewer: M.J. Akbar.

Embree, Ainslee T. (1973), 'Pluralism and National Integration: The Indian Experience', *Journal of International Affairs* (New York), vol. 27, no. 1.

Embassy of Pakistan in Washington (1987), *Pakistan Affairs* (Washington, DC), 1 March.

Ghosh, Partha S. (1989), *Cooperation and Conflict in South Asia*, New Delhi, Manohar.

—— (1989), 'International Terrorism', *Indian Journal of Social Science* (New Delhi), vol. 2, no. 4.

—— (1989), 'Evolving Indo-Pak Relations', *Defense and Diplomacy* (McLean, Va.), vol. 7, no. 5.

—— (1988), 'Indo-Pak Strategic Divide', *Defense and Diplomacy* (McLean, Va.), vol. 6, no. 10.

—— (1987), 'Terrorism and SAARC', *India Quarterly* (New Delhi), vol. 43, no. 2.

—— (1985), 'Ethnic and Religious Conflicts in South Asia', *Conflict Studies* (London), no. 178.

Hellmann-Rajanayagam, Dagmar (1988–9), 'The Tamil Militants — Before the Accord and After', *Pacific Affairs* (Vancouver), vol. 61, no. 4.

His Majesty's Government of Nepal, National Commission on Population, Task Force on Migration (1983), 'Internal and International Migration in Nepal: Summary and Recommendations', Kathmandu, August.

Kothari, Rajni (1972), 'Political Reconstruction of Bangladesh: Reflections on Building a New State in the Seventies', *Economic and Political Weekly* (Bombay), 29 April.

Lifschultz, Lawrence (1983), 'Independent Baluchistan: Ataullah Mengal's "Declaration of Independence" ', *Economic and Political Weekly* (Bombay), annual number, May.

Lokhandwalla, S.T. (1971), *India and Contemporary Islam: Proceedings of a Seminar*, Simla, Indian Institute of Advanced Studies.

Mandel, Robert (1980), 'Roots of the Modern Inter-State Border Dispute', *Journal of Conflict Resolution* (London), vol. 24, no. 3.

Mason, Philip (ed.) (1967), *India and Ceylon: Unity and Diversity: A Symposium*, London, Oxford University Press.

Muni, S.D. (1981), 'South Asia', in Mohammad Ayoob, (ed.), *Conflict and Intervention in the Third World*, London, Croom Helm.

North, Robert C. (1976), *The World That Could Be*, Stanford, University Alumni Association.

Phadnis, Urmila *et al*, (eds) (1986), *Domestic Conflicts in South Asia*, I, *Political Dimensions*, New Delhi, South Asian Publishers.

Riggs, Fred W. (1986), *Help for Social Scientists: A New Kind of Reference Process*, Paris, UNESCO.

Sinha, A.C. (1982), 'Bhutan: From Theocracy to an Emergent Nation-State', Ph.D. dissertation, Department of Sociology, North Eastern Hill University, Shillong.

Sen Gupta, Bhabani (1988), *South Asian Perspectives: Seven Nations in Conflict and Cooperation*, Delhi, B.R.

Snyder, Louis (1954), *The Meaning of Nationalism*, New Brunswick, N.J., Rutgers University Press.

—— (1983), 'Nationalism and the Flawed Concept of Ethnicity', *Canadian Review of Studies in Ethnicity*, vol. 10.

3 INTERNATIONALIZATION OF THE PUNJAB CRISIS: A PAKISTANI PERSPECTIVE

Rasul B. Rais

The Indian state of Punjab shares a long and porous border with Pakistan. In the context of the current crisis in the Punjab, and the rise of Sikh separatism as a major political issue, India has regularly expressed concern about Pakistani assistance, moral and material, to the Sikhs. This chapter seeks to explore these Indian charges, and to set them, as they should be, against the background of the Sikh problem in post-independence India.

I

The Pakistani connection?

New Delhi has frequently claimed that there is a link between the internal situation in Punjab and a 'foreign hand' or 'hands', and that the unrest there is projected as part of an international conspiracy to destabilize India. Pakistan has been singled out by the Indian leaders and media for its alleged involvement in Punjabi conflict. Indian sources claim that Pakistan has provided the Sikh secessionists with sanctuaries, arms, money, training and moral support; helped sustain the sense of alienation among the Sikhs; and encouraged and promoted their demand for a separate homeland.[1] Pakistan has allegedly connived at the flow of arms to Punjab and at the indoctrination of Sikh terrorists,[2] whatever that means, and has blunted India's fight against terrorism in Punjab.[3]

Academic analysis of the veracity of these charges is extremely difficult. Such accusations are difficult to prove, and indeed no substantial evidence of New Delhi's claims of a 'Pakistan connection' has been provided to date. If hard evidence of the involvement of foreign powers (in particular, Pakistan) was available, the Indian authorities would surely have used them.[4] The fact is that these charges lack 'consistency and conviction'.[5]

The core of this Indian contention is that since Delhi helped in the creation of Bangladesh, Pakistan was determined to pay India back in the same coin by fomenting trouble in Punjab. However, the Punjabi problem is not a creation of Pakistan.[6] It is rooted in the alienation of the Sikhs since the 1940s. Distrust of Pakistan has been used by the Indian government and by sections of the Indian press to make the Indian public believe that the deteriorating situation in the Punjab is a result of Pakistani manipulation. Adverse images cultivated at the societal level have been conveniently available and used to shift the focus away from the hard realities of domestic politics to the doorstep of the 'enemy'. It is important to note that Pakistan proposed to India in 1988 that they jointly condemn terrorism in Punjab and Sind, but the Indian government shied away from this suggestion.[7]

As for the supply of weapons and provision of training to Sikhs, a community with a long and flourishing martial tradition and thousands of ex-servicemen in the ranks of its militants does not need to look to Pakistan for weapons training and guerrilla tactics. In fact most of the weapons in the hands of Sikh militants were picked up by the people during the Indo-Pakistani wars of 1965 and 1971 and never accounted for.[8] As Lt.-Gen. (Retd) J.S. Aurora has pointed out: 'the impression that has been built up in the public mind of foreign governments deliberately arming the terrorists with a view of overthrowing the government is grossly overdone.'[9] Through contacts in the Indian army, militants found an easy means of obtaining arms within India. Some of the comments in the Indian press have been frank about the indigenous sources of arms supply to the militants. Commenting on the discovery of arms in the Golden Temple, the weekly *Sunday* wrote: 'It may be unpleasant to say so, but the fact is that most of the equipment that the terrorists had, come from the Indian armed forces.'[10]

Weapons have slipped through the Indo-Pakistani border into Punjab. With large-scale smuggling going on across the border and corruption in the border security forces, there has undoubtedly been some gun-running.[11] Checking the flow of weapons, though problematic, because of Punjab's porous border, could be achieved by sealing the border. The Indian government enacted a law to create a security belt along the Punjab border, but, for reasons not disclosed, it did not enforce it.[12] An accord with Pakistan on joint patrolling of the Punjab and Sind[13] border might help both the countries to control smuggling of weapons, among other things, into their trouble spots.

II

The Sikh problem in post-independence India

The problem of the Sikhs in India has been reviewed in detail in a number of books, monographs and articles.[14] What is attempted here is a brief summary of some events salient to understanding the political background to the Sikh problem, beginning with the early years of Indian independence.

At the time of partition of the raj, Sikh leaders supported a united India and never gave any serious thought to joining Pakistan or carving out their own independent state. In the communal frenzy that developed when the British decided to quit India, the Sikhs thought that they could secure, protect and foster their interests in a democratic, federal and secular India of the Congress. Pakistan had no attraction as the nationalism of the Muslim league was Islamic in character. Indeed the Sikhs feared religious persecution by the Muslims more than the unaccommodating attitude of the north Indian caste Hindu leadership. Even offers of complete autonomy, which the Sikh leaders could define for themselves, could not lure the Sikh ruler of Patiala state, for instance, to join Pakistan.[15]

In the post-colonial politics, the central aim of the Sikh community was to carve out a political unit in the Punjab, where they could have unrestricted opportunities of growth and development in preserving their language, culture and religion. This indeed is what was promised them by Jawahar Lal Nehru and his Congress party and Congress government.

The partition of Punjab between India and Pakistan which the Sikhs had demanded did not help the Sikhs gain political dominance.[16] Failing to gain acceptance of their claim for special communal representation for the Sikhs to the extent of half the seats in the Punjab legislature, the Akali leaders began to stress the need for the demarcation of a state within the Indian union, comprising the Sikh majority districts.[17] A second partition of the Punjab, based this time on language, was urged by the Sikhs during the first national election in 1952. This demand was rejected. Their position within Punjab became less secure when the state of Punjab was expanded in 1956 with the inclusion of the princely states of the Punjab.

From the late 1960s onwards the Akali demand for Punjabi *suba* reflected a consensus among all sections of the Sikh community for their own state within the Indian Union. Although the emphasis was on linguistic nationalism, the demand for Punjabi *suba* divided the Sikhs and Hindus along communal lines. Hindus of Punjabi origin opposed the creation of a Punjabi-speaking state, with a passion that led them to renounce their Punjabi language and culture.[18] This sowed the seeds of the current Hindu-Sikh antagonism in Punjab. It was after a prolonged and acrimonious agitation, that the Sikhs forced the centre to accede to their demand for a Punjabi *suba* in 1966.

However, the creation of Punjabi *suba* resulted in new problems, especially the integration of some Punjabi-speaking areas into Haryana and Rajasthan. It provoked, in fact, a new grievance, and led to a demand that these Punjabi-speaking areas should be restored to the Punjab.

Punjab has been under tremendous political and psychological stress since the adoption of the Anandpur Sahib resolution of 1973. The central themes of the resolution reflecting a new awareness among the post-independence generation of Sikhs emphasized three points in particular: the need to maintain consciousness of an independent entity of the Sikh Panth; to create an environment in which the national ethos of the Sikh Panth would find full expression; and for more powers to the states in general. The assertive demand of the Sikh leadership for a drastic redistribution of powers between the centre and the Punjab, leaving only foreign affairs, defence and communications with the centre, though radical in outlook, was not very different from similar demands made on other occasions by other Indian states. Stress on the national ethos of the Sikh Panth, however, was a manifestation of religious consciousness and the quest for a Sikh identity.

After Indira Gandhi returned to power in 1980 a confrontation began between the Akalis and the Congress government. Apart from the Anandpur Sahib resolution, other demands arose to keep the Punjab agitated. These included:

- the transfer of the city of Chandigarh to Punjab;
- acceptance of Punjab's sole right to the use of the waters of the Ravi and the Beas rivers;
- a greater share in electric power generated by the Bhakra Nangal dam; and
- a constitutional amendment to the Explanation II of Article 25, clause 2 of the Indian constitution, in terms of which Sikhism is defined as part of the Hindu religion.[19]

The Sikhs, including the prominent Akali leaders, deplored the indifference of the Congress government to this issue. They alleged that Congress with its majority in the Lok Sabha could have easily amended the constitution. But the fact is that this was not as easy as it seemed. Many prominent Congress leaders opposed the amendment for the reason that it could result in the acceptance of a Sikh personal law. The Sikhs, on the other hand, refuse to accept their classification as a part of the Hindu religion.

Since the creation of the state of Haryana, the question of Chandigarh has constantly fuelled tensions between it and the Punjab. This dispute is rooted in the distribution of territories by the Punjab Boundary Commission, whose report was published on 31 May 1960. The Akalis opposed the Commission's report as it ignored linguistic criteria for the distribution of territories. The allocation of Kharar Tehsil in particular, where Chandigarh city is allocated to Haryana, agitated the Sikh leaders. Immediately after the transfer in 1966, the Akalis started their political campaign, demanding the handing-over of Chandigarh to the Punjab. The political battle over Chandigarh intensified with rival agitations in Punjab and Haryana. The central government made an attempt to settle the dispute by announcing on 20 January 1970 that the capital project area of Chandigarh should go as a whole to the Punjab. To appease Haryana, the government decided to transfer parts of Fazilka and Abohar from Punjab and to help Haryana build its new capital it gave a grant of ten crores (millions) of Indian rupees.[20] Both states accepted the parts of the award favourable to them; both refused to surrender the territories under their *de facto* control.

A stalemate has persisted for more than two decades, hardening the attitudes of Punjab and Haryana. Akalis have fiercely opposed the complete transfer of Fazilka and Abohar to Haryana. These localities constitute approximately 350,000 acres of fertile land producing excellent cotton and fruit. The Punjab state has been unwilling to bargain away these revenue-generating areas, which have been parts of Punjab for centuries, and are not territorially contiguous to Haryana, for an exclusive right to the presently joint capital of Chandigarh.

The Sikh grievances remained unresolved through the mid and late 1970s. The question of independent Khalistan began for the first time to attract a wider constituency of disillusioned Sikhs. The Sikh identity and nationalism reinforced the movement for Khalsa rights and Khalistan. The Sikhs are, however, divided on the national question. There are moderates who would be satisfied with obtaining greater concessions for the Sikh community. The extremists, who seem to have gained political ascendancy for the time being, will accept nothing short of a sovereign state of Khalistan.

The Sikh extremism

Unresolved Sikh problems have over the decades produced two effects. First, the religious leaders among the Sikhs have acquired pre-eminence and have exercised considerable political influence over the events in Punjab. Traditionally Sikh priests have led the political battles along with the secular-minded Sikh leaders.[21] The role of religious leadership over the Punjab issue is in line with this. Another factor which helped the religious élite to capture a leadership position was the movement of Sikh revivalism in the 1980s. In this context Punjabi politics has become a heady mix of Sikh nationalism, territorial demands and a distinctive religious consciousness.

Second, the extremist Sikhs emerged a far stronger political force than the old centrist Akali Dal party. With the popularity and growth of Sikh radicalism, the moderates in the Akali Dal confronted a dilemma of their political survival. Opposition to extremism or even silence meant political isolation, and in some cases physical annihilation. Fearing political extinction, the moderate Akalis chose to compete with the radicalism of the fundamentalist Sikh leadership. While seeking to reach an agreement with the central government on a viable political solution, they have been unwilling, in the interests of their own political survival, to concede on vital points. Even this posturing has not helped the Akali Dal much in regaining the political initiative. The extremists such as the followers of Sant Gernail Singh Bhindranwale began to set the pace in Punjabi politics.[22]

The Akali hold on Punjabi politics has weakened for two reasons. First, as a religio-political organization, the Akalis have traditionally used religious slogans and platforms for their politics. Identification with the Sikh religion undoubtedly, gave political legitimacy to the Akalis. But failure or unwillingness to separate religion from politics, as many mainstream regional parties have done in India, eventually strengthened the religious constituency. Militants of this constituency have succeeded in capturing the religious pulpit which the Akalis had successfully used for decades.

Second, the central government was not only slow to make concessions that could strengthen the moderate Akalis against the rising power of the militants, but on occasions undermined their credibility by not honouring accords signed with them. Reneging on the Rajiv Gandhi–Longowal Accord, which committed New Delhi to transfer Chandigarh to Punjab is a case in point.[23] The Akalis appear discredited in the face of their failures to extract any significant concessions from the centre, despite the promises made to them.

Since operation 'Blue Star' in June 1984, the political scene in Punjab has undergone a major transformation. Press comments in India had long been suggesting a military action in Punjab to wipe out the 'handful of miscreants' who were seeking refuge in the Golden Temple. The supporters of military action argued that this was regrettable but inevitable because other less drastic measures such as imposition of President's rule, frequent curfews and motorized police patrols had failed to prevent terrorist attacks. Well-planned killings of prominent Hindu leaders gave a communal tilt to the political struggle of the Sikh militants. As their attacks became more frequent and indiscriminately targeted against Hindus, a sharp public reaction developed against the extremists, demanding a surgical use of force.

Whatever the rationale for a military option, its ferocity in implementation shocked the Sikh community all over the world. After the death of the principal Sikh militant leader, Sant Jarnail Singh Bhindranwale, the attack on the holy *Akal Takht* and indiscriminate killings of suspected extremists, the Sikhs vowed to intensify their struggle for their 'national rights'. The ensuing calls for a holy war, characteristic of the Sikh political style, and creation of a separate state of Khalistan have become common slogans among the Sikhs of Punjab.

The massacres which the Sikhs in Delhi and in other parts of India suffered[24] after the assassination of Prime Minister Indira Gandhi added fuel to the anger and humiliation which the Sikh community had experienced as a result of the military action against the Golden Temple. In times of coercion and insults, the Sikh community has activated itself by the sentiments of supreme sacrifice and martyrdom. On such occasions, their responses have been shaped more by political rhetoric than pragmatism. The holy scriptures, chronicles of war heroism and Punjabi folklore have all been sources of the Sikh political rhetoric. One can also see in the Sikh mystique a complex mix of religious implosion, emotion and the ethos of militancy.[25]

The contemporary militancy of the Sikhs is a manifestation of their traditional heroism and sense of religious obligation to fight against an unjust treatment. However, the problem with rhetorical posturing and use of symbolism is that quite often it not only escapes political realism but it also obscures political ends. This is, perhaps, currently the tragedy of Sikh militancy.

The movement for Khalistan, on which there is no consensus among the Sikh community, has gained some popularity as a reaction to the inept handling of the Punjabi issue by the Union government. The Khalistan slogan is an expression of anger, cynicism and estrangement of the Sikh community. Small but vocal groups of militants now argue that Sikh leaders had erred in agreeing to remain within the Indian union in India at the time of the partition of the raj.[26]

However, can the Sikh separatists carve out of India a country of their own? One has only to examine the geopolitical reality of the Sikh situation to understand the fertility of this quest. No state since World War II has suffered dismemberment except Pakistan in 1971. Two factors assisted the breakup of Pakistan. First, the peculiar geography of the state, with two units separated by the large Indian landmass; and second, the Indian military intervention. Compared with the difficult situation in which Pakistan found itself, Punjab is not only territorially contiguous to India but the majority of the people in Punjab, both Sikhs and Hindus, are opposed to the creation of Khalistan. Second, there is no threat of external military intervention in support of Khalistan. The Indian government has the freedom to tackle the secessionists in the manner it deems fit. Left to themselves, the Sikh militants cannot defeat the preponderant power of the Indian armed forces. What the militants need to ponder over is the fact that they confront geopolitical isolation. Enthusiastic supporters of Khalistan living abroad seem to lack a practical perspective on the issue.

Notes

1. Girilal Jain, 'Mainstay of Terrorists: Pak Border Has to be Sealed', *The Times of India*, New Delhi, 16 March 1988.
2. *Sunday*, 24 April 1988. See statements of Rajiv Gandhi, *Tribune*, 16 April 1988; Rajendra Sareen, 'Punjab, "Khalistan" and Pakistan', *Tribune*, 11 April 1988.
3. Jain, op. cit.
4. A.G. Noorani, 'A White Paper on Black Record', *The Illustrated Weekly of India*, Bombay, 22 January 1984. The opposition in India has persistently demanded that the government should come out with concrete evidence. *Times of India*, 20 April 1988.
5. Ghani Jafar, *The Sikh Volcano*, Lahore, Vanguard, 1987, p. 194.

6. Inder Malhotra, 'Punjab—The Pak Connection', *The Times of India*, 4 April 1988.
7. Bhabani Sen Gupta, 'How to remove the Pak Hand', *Hindustan Times*, 14 April 1988.
8. Lt.-Genl. (Retd) J.S. Aurora, 'Assault on the Golden Temple', in Amarjit Kaur *et al. The Punjab Story*, New Delhi, Roli Books International, 1984, p. 97.
9. Ibid.
10. Weekly *Sunday* of Calcutta quoted by Jafar, op. cit., p. 196; T.V.R. Shenoy, 'D-Day in Amritsar', *The Week*, Cochin, 17–23 June 1984.
11. 'Punjab: The Pak Factor' (Editorial), *The Tribune*, 4 April 1988.
12. 'Punjab's porous border' (Editorial), *Patriot*, New Delhi, 5 April 1988.
13. *The Statesman*, Delhi, 9 June 1989.
14. See Henry Hayes (ed.), *The Sikh Question in India, 1942–1984*, London, Helms Publishers, 1985; Rajiv A. Kapur, *Sikh Separatism: The Politics of Faith*, London, Allen & Unwin, 1986; and Kushwant Singh, *A History of the Sikhs*, 2 vols, Delhi, Oxford University Press, 1981.
15. On Quaid-i-Azam's offer to the Sikhs, see K.H. Khurshid, 'The Quaid-i-Azam and the Sikhs—A Prophecy Fulfilled', *Dawn*, Karachi, 10 July 1984.
16. Master Tara Singh quoted in Baldev Raj Nayar, *Minority Politics in Punjab*, Princeton, Princeton University Press, 1966, p. 37.
17. K.C. Gulati, *Akalis: Past and Present*, Delhi, Ashajanak Publications, 1974, p. 147. Quoted in Kushwant Singh, *History of the Sikhs*, vol. 2, op. cit., p. 296.
18. Gurbax Singh Dewan, 'Tangled Skein of Punjab Problem', *Patriot*, New Delhi, 21 March 1984.
19. Explanation of Article 25, clause 2 states: 'In sub-clause (b) of clause 2, the reference to Hindus shall be construed as including a reference to persons professing the Sikh, Jain or Buddhist religion, and reference to Hindu religious institutions shall be construed accordingly.' D.K. Singh, *The Constitution of India*, Lucknow, Eastern Book Company, 1982.
20. For the text of the award, see *The Hindu*, Madras, 29 November 1982.
21. Rajiv A. Kapur, *Sikh Separatism*, op. cit., pp. 2–3.
22. Ibid., pp. 249–50.
23. The Rajiv Gandhi–Longowal Accord promised among other things the transfer of Chandigarh to Punjab on 26 January 1986. For the text of the accord, see *Indian Express*, New Delhi, 25 July 1985.
24. Thousands of Sikhs were killed in almost every city of northern India, often with the connivance of the police and the ruling party. See *Far Eastern Economic Review*, 15 November 1984.
25. Darshan Singh Maini, 'The Political Style of the Sikhs', *Indian Express*, 27 March 1988.
26. Harsimran Singh of Dal Khalsa quoted in Standinder Singh, *Khalistan: An Academic Analysis*, New Delhi, Amar Prakashn, 1982, p. 135.

4 INTERNATIONALIZATION OF ETHNIC CONFLICT: THE PUNJAB CRISIS OF THE 1980s

Bhabani Sen Gupta

Increasing oneness of the world and decreasing distance among nations lend an international dimension to many issues that in other times were the exclusive concern of nation-states. The contradictions between national sovereignty, which is still the principal political ethos of modern states, and the growing irrelevance of national frontiers deny national governments the luxury of dealing with many 'internal problems' in the exclusiveness of sovereign isolation. The whole world looks at whatever happens anywhere in the world on a scale big enough to draw global attention. Globalization of information flows, satellite television, facsimile transmission and other means of telecommunication internationalize domestic crises and conflicts in the present time, trespassing on sovereign jurisdiction of governments. The irony is that most, if not all, national governments resent internationalization of domestic issues and zealously protect their sovereign rights to deal with them exclusively in accordance with their own laws and political wisdom or stupidities. At the same time, they need and solicit international help even to establish domestic jurisdiction over issues that assume international dimensions.

India is, after the Soviet Union, the world's largest multinational state. Since the late 1950s, India has been restructuring its internal political borders on the basis of statehood demands of ethnopolitical groups or nationalities. The process has been mainly orderly but attended at times by mass agitations and bloodshed. However, the creation of the linguistic states in late 1950 was accomplished within the exclusive jurisdiction of national sovereignty. No Tamil or Telugu or Maratha or Gujarati diaspora sought to 'internationalize' demands for the creation of Tamil Nadu, Andhra Pradesh, Maharashtra and Gujarat. The Nagas and the Mizos on India's north-east border carried out an armed insurgency against the Indian state for decades until the rebel leaders finally submitted to Indian sovereignty and their native lands were elevated to statehood within the Indian union. In the 1970s as many as six states were formed in the north-east meeting 'nationalist' demands of relatively small tribal groups. The entire process was accomplished without pressures of 'internationalization'.

The situation became entirely different when, in the 1980s, a segment of Sikhs in Punjab raised the demand of an 'independent Khalistan', independent of India, and the demand rapidly led to an armed conflict between Khalistanis and the Indian state. Indeed, the Sikh diaspora in the United States, Canada and the United Kingdom articulated the demand for a Sikh Homeland outside India several years before the demand was echoed by Sikh militants in Punjab.

The Sikh diaspora has grown through this century. As far back as 1907, Sikh immigrants to the United States founded the Khalsa Diwan Society which built a network of *gurudwaras* and educational institutions. At a later date Sikh immigrants founded the *Ghadr* (revolution) party in North America. It preceded the inauguration of the Communist party in India in 1920. In India, the Akali Dal had been active in nationalist political activity, at times projecting Sikh ethno-religious nationalism, at other times propagating the cause of Indian nationalism with a particular Sikh accent. Following the passage of the Gurudwara Prabandhak Committee Act of 1925, regulating the management of the powerful network of Sikh Gurudwaras, the Akali Dal emerged as the dominant Sikh political party although the community remained split into different sects and factions over the years. The Akali Dal have fought for a Sikh state in the Indian union ever since Indian independence and were not satisfied even when in 1966 they acquired the state of Punjab, in which the Sikh population of 52 per cent constituted a thin majority over the Hindus (48 per cent).

The Sikh diaspora has always been politically more radical than the Akali Dal with its leadership based on the support of peasants or farmers. The *Ghadr* party had few active supporters among the Akali Dal Sikhs. In the 1960s Sikh immigrants raised the slogan of an 'independent Punjab' much ahead of the Sikhs living in India. The Khalistan movement also originated in North America under the patronage of the Sikh *émigrés*, and only years later found a certain solid support from a section of Sikh youth. Between 1971 and 1978 a number of Sikh organizations abroad raised the slogan of Khalistan—a separate Sikh state. Among these were the National Council of Khalistan headed by Dr Jagjit Singh Chauhan in the United Kingdom; his activities later spread to West Germany, Canada and the United States. The Babbar Khalsa supported Khalistan from Canada. A third fragment of the diaspora was the Akhand Kirtani Jatha with units in the United Kingdom and Canada.

Dr Jagjit Singh Chauhan formed a National Council of Khalistan on

20 April 1980 with himself as president and Balbir Singh Sandhu as secretary-general. Three months later he proclaimed from London the formation of Khalistan; a similar announcement was made in India by Balbir Singh Sandhu. Chauhan went to the length of issuing Khalistani passports, postage stamps and currency notes. A White Paper on Punjab issued by the Indian government on 10 July 1984 said that Chauhan's 'intention was to exploit the sentiments of Sikh residents of Canada and West Germany who were facing difficulties with immigration authorities there'.[1]

Chauhan was intent on internationalizing the Khalistan movement. On 18 May 1983 he claimed, without clear evidence, that the United States was 'supporting' the Khalistan movement and that he expected Khalistan to come into being in four years. He advised two prominent Akali leaders in India, Sant Harcharan Singh Longowal and Bhindranwale, to constitute forthwith a fully-fledged government and parliament.

Chauhan had established contacts with a number of US Congressmen. Despite the Indian government's objections, he was able to obtain entry visas to the United States in 1982 and 1983. He also maintained contacts with neo-conservative American think-tanks like the Heritage Foundation. Chauhan and other Sikh immigrant supporters of Khalistan were helped by the perception of the American right wing that India was pro-Soviet. India's failure to condemn and oppose Soviet military intervention in Afghanistan and India's protests against the flow of high-technology American arms and weapons systems to Pakistan made the extreme right wing and even the moderate right wing in the United States quite hostile to India. Senators, Congressmen, intellectuals and activists belonging to right-wing groups were hospitable to Khalistanis like Jagjit Singh Chauhan.

The Indian government conducted vigorous diplomatic efforts to persuade the governments of the United States, Canada and Britain to restrict the entry into their respective territories of supporters of Khalistan. Delhi's efforts to classify Khalistanis as terrorists and their militancy as terrorism succeeded to some extent, for these foreign governments did co-operate with the Indian authorities to bring certain Khalistanis into the network of international terrorism, particularly after the hijacking of two Indian civil airliners and the destruction in flight of an Air India jetliner.

The Indian authorities also saw a foreign hand behind the Khalistani movement. They particularly accused Pakistan of rendering various kinds of assistance to Khalistanis, including training on Pakistani territory, arms supplies, media support and political backing. The Indian White Paper declared:

> Powerful forces are at work to undermine India's political and economic strength. A sensitive border state with a dynamic record of agricultural and industrial development would be an obvious target of subversion. In this context, the activities of groups based abroad acquire special significance. A section of foreign media is believed to be deliberately presenting totally distorted versions of the Punjab situation, which has the effect of encouraging and sustaining separatist activities.[2]

The White Paper added: 'The significant relationship between internal and external forces of subversion is a well-known fact of the contemporary international scene.'

The Indian White Paper identified a second Sikh body, the Babbar Khalsa, which was engaged in internationalizing the Khalistani issue. Set up in India in 1981, the Babbar Khalsa founded a branch in Canada three years later, with Talwinder Singh Parmar as Jathedar. 'It is trying to extend its activities to the USA, the UK, Holland and West Germany,' reported the White Paper. 'According to the Babbar Khalsa, Pakistan is the natural and cultural neighbour of the Sikhs, ready to assist their movement against the Government of India.' The Babbar Khalsa was said to be trying to model its movement on the Palestine Liberation Organization (PLO) and the 'national struggle of the Kurds.'

The Khalistani demand was embedded, though not explicitly, in what is known as the Anandpur Sahib resolution, named after the Gurudwara where it was adopted in October 1973. There are three versions of the resolution. What is significant for our purpose is that the Sikhs claimed that their nationhood had had the recognition of a host of countries including the United States, Britain, USSR and France, as well as 'China–Tibet', long before India became independent. The fact that this was a piece of historical fiction did not deter the new proponents of the Sikh nation in the least; they believed and they wanted others to believe that their demand had international legitimacy. It was not the historical legitimacy that disturbed the government of India headed by the late Mrs Indira Gandhi, but, since the early 1980s, the manner in which Khalistanis sought to internationalize their movement by hijacking or sabotaging Indian civil aircraft and by acquiring recognition as a 'terrorist' organization on the level of the PLO and other lesser-known organizations in Western Europe, Lebanon and Iran.

On 3 June 1984 the Indian government prohibited the entry of foreigners into Punjab and twelve days later ordered that British and Canadian passport-holders would also require visas to enter the state. Visas were introduced for nationals of other Commonwealth countries and Ireland as well.

Amnesty International played its own part in internationalizing the Khalistani issue. In its annual reports since 1985, Amnesty International began to draw international attention to arbitrary arrests, detention without trial and police atrocities in Punjab. We cite only one example of Amnesty International's reporting of police excesses and atrocities in Punjab. The annual report for 1989 stated:

> Several thousand critics and opponents of the government, including many prisoners of conscience, were held without charge or trial in preventive detention or under laws directed against 'terrorist' activity. There were widespread reports of torture and allegations that some prisoners had died in custody as a result of torture. Dozens of people were sentenced to death and at least four executions were carried out, in one case despite widespread doubts about the guilt of the convicted man. There were reports of extrajudicial killings by police, especially in areas where opposition groups resorted to violent actions.[3]

In the late 1980s, there was a perceptible decline in the political activities of the emigrant Sikhs in support of the Khalistani movement. Khalistani groups were discouraged by the authorities in the United States, Canada and Britain from conducting anti-India activities. However, Sikh communities are quite prosperous in certain parts of the United States, particularly California, and they were able to influence Congressmen relatively easily by contributing to their campaign funds. In June 1989 Khalistani lobbyists scored a success when one of their favourite Congressmen, Wally Hearger (Republican, California), moved a resolution in the House of Representatives proposing that the United States not only freeze its bilateral aid to India but also prevent international financial institutions like the World Bank from extending economic assistance to the Indian union until the Indian government stopped the violation of human rights in Punjab and abandoned its missile development programme.

US bilateral aid to India is a mere $25 million, but India's dependence on World Bank and IMF aid is considerable. The Hearger move was raised in the form of an amendment to the foreign aid bill. It was hotly debated on the floor of the House, and when put to vote was only narrowly defeated by 204 to 212, a margin of a mere eight votes. The

Washington correspondent of the *Indian Express* reported on 28 June 1989 that the Khalistani lobby was 'particularly active' in California where a large number of Sikhs lived in economic affluence.

The Hearger amendment, to be sure, had little chance of being passed into law even if it were adopted by the House of Representatives; it would not have passed through the Senate, and President Bush would certainly have vetoed it. However, the considerable support the amendment received from Congressmen startled most Indians. Congressmen were expressing their dissatisfaction with several aspects of India's domestic and foreign policies—India's Afghan policy; its rejection of the Nuclear Non-proliferation Treaty and its refusal to discuss nuclear restraint with Pakistan; its missile and space programmes; the trade friction with the United States; the sharp deterioration of its relations with Nepal and Sri Lanka; and human rights violations in Punjab.

One result of the Congressional pressure on India and of Amnesty International's reporting of police excesses in Punjab was that in 1989 the Indian government quietly lifted the ban on foreigners' entry into Punjab. Some US Congressmen as well as Delhi-based Western news reporters travelled to Punjab. This brought about a better relationship between India and Capitol Hill where the Indian government has always suffered from a lack of genuine friends.

Internationalization of the Punjab neither hurt the Indian government very much nor helped the Khalistan movement gain ground. The diaspora's effectiveness as supporters of the Khalistan movement was limited to just keeping the issue alive among emigrant Sikhs. The activities of these Sikhs made headlines in the Indian press and fed Indian fear and suspicion of the foreign hand. India has continued to blame Pakistan for aiding and abetting Sikh militants, though there was a sharp decline in Indian allegations after the December 1989 meeting in Islamabad between the then Prime Minister of India, Rajiv Gandhi, and the current Prime Minister of Pakistan, Ms Benazir Bhutto. In January 1990 Jagjit Singh Chauhan issued a statement from his home in southern England, saying that Prime Minster V.P. Singh should be given a chance to settle the Punjab problem through political negotiation.

Asian diasporas are nowhere as strong, politically and financially, as world Zionism. Nevertheless, diasporas now do present a significant role in the dissemination of propaganda and contributing substantial amounts of money to ethnopolitical struggles, whether the struggle is for a Khalistan or a Tamil Eelam.

Notes

1. *White Paper on the Punjab*, New Delhi, Government of India, 1984.
2. Ibid.
3. *Annual Report, 1989*, London, Amnesty International.

5 HARBOURING INSTABILITY: PAKISTAN AND THE DISPLACEMENT OF AFGHANS

Tom Rogers

Pakistan and the Afghan refugees

Well over five million Afghans have fled their country since the 1979 Soviet invasion. These refugees have settled in India (4,700) and Iran (560,000), but the majority (estimated at up to 3.5 million) have settled in Pakistan, with most of them living in 340 settlement camps along the Afghan–Pakistani border.

These refugees can be divided into five categories. First, a few refugees came from politically prominent and wealthy families with personal and business assets outside Afghanistan. Second, a small group arrived with the assets that they could bring with them such as trucks, cars and limited funds and has done relatively well in Pakistan, integrating into the new society and engaging successfully in commerce. Third are those refugees that came from the ranks of the well-educated and include professionals such as doctors, teachers and engineers. They have played an important role in the refugee society, providing services and contributing some element of stability to the camps. Fourth are those refugees who escaped with household goods and herds of sheep, cattle and yaks, but for the most part must be helped to maintain themselves. The fifth and largest group, constituting about 60 per cent of the refugees, are ordinary Afghans who arrived with nothing and are largely dependent on Pakistani and international efforts for subsistence.[1]

Since 1979 the international community has been mobilized to address the short-term needs of Afghan refugees and unilateral efforts have relieved some of the pressures of displacement. However, the potential political consequences for Pakistan—and indeed for other host countries—still remain unpredictable.

The region known as Pushtunistan (south-east Afghanistan and north-west Pakistan) has a long history of complex tribal and ethnic relations. Despite border disputes in 1961, the people of this region have flowed across borders relatively freely for generations. Afghan refugees fleeing famine settled in Pakistan in the early 1970s and the present migration is an extension of the historic movement of Afghans. The early migrations involved primarily peasant Afghans subject to the vagaries of natural calamity, while the present migration comprises a cross-section of rural poor and urban middle and upper classes. While many of the upper class have migrated on to the United States and Western Europe, a significant middle-class group have settled in Pakistan, giving the refugee population a political awareness hitherto unseen. It may well be for this reason that the Afghan state-in-exile has a highly politicized population, which was consolidated into a formidable resistance to the Soviet occupation and subsequent Najibullah government.

An equally important distinction between the present migration and previous migrations is the timespan involved. Whereas previous displacement had been temporary, the present situation tends to discourage repatriation. It is now ten years since Soviet troops invaded Afghanistan and the flow of refugees has swelled to an extent which not only distinguishes the present migration from the past but makes it comparable with the occupation of Palestine and its attendant complexities.

The United Nations High Commission for Refugees (UNHCR) has noted that to the credit of Pakistan, in the initial stages of the Afghan crisis the refugees were fed and sheltered by the local residents in extraordinary acts of charity and hospitality. They have suffered few of the problems that often plague great refugee migrations. There have been no epidemics, no serious cases of malnutrition, and relatively little friction with the local population.[2] But their numbers continued to increase.

Most of the two million Afghans that have crossed into Pakistan's North-West Frontier Province are Pathan, but increasingly Tadjiks and Uzbeks populated Peshawar as the Soviets and Afghan government expanded operations throughout Afghanistan. Notes the UNHCR:

> not only has Dari (Afghan–Persian) begun to flow as freely as Pashto in the bazaars, but the clothes, the facial features and customs representing the Afghans' varied ethnic background point to a gradual transformation in Peshawar's traditional Pathan character.[3]

Most refugees (75 per cent) live in Pakistan's North-West Frontier Province, the remainder primarily in Baluchistan (20 per cent) and Peshawar (4 per cent). The majority are Pathan tribesmen largely from the eastern regions of Afghanistan, but the number of refugees representing other ethnic groups has increased. According to some observers, Peshawar has become the largest Afghan enclave outside Kabul, while the refugee population has also grown in cities such as Islamabad, Quetta and Karachi.[4]

However, most of the refugees are concentrated in camps located in the border areas of the North-West Frontier and Baluchistan provinces. The influx forced thousands of Pakistani government workers and transportation vehicles to be diverted to refugee care. In 1982 the authorities began to move refugees into camps in Punjab province to alleviate the social, economic and ecological pressures caused by the increased population.

On 7 November 1984 President Zia noted that there were very few social problems between Afghan refugees and Pakistanis. On the question of the social costs due to the refugee influx, Zia said there was no limit to the contribution Pakistan was prepared to make:

> Because if there was a limit then we would have reached that point many years ago. Pakistan was created in the name of Islam, there was nothing here. Pakistan was carved out from the Indian sub-continent as a homeland for the Muslims so we feel that Pakistan must be the home of any Muslim anywhere in the world. If 3,000,000 refugees have come from Afghanistan we feel it is our moral religious and national duty to look after at least 3,000,000 if not all of the 15,000,000 Afghans if they want to come to Pakistan.[5]

However, Zia also noted that there has indeed been a price which Pakistan has sustained and sacrifices that it has had to make. The costs have been in terms of the pressures placed upon the Pakistani infrastructure of schools, hospitals, lands, water, employment, the economy and other dimensions of refugee asylum.

Afghan refugees are not only noteworthy for their numbers, but for the duration of their stay. While it can be assumed from previous experiences that they will seek repatriation, the longer they remain in Pakistan the greater the chances of their becoming a political force in that country. Increasingly the refugee population and the resistance movement it harbours have sought status in the United Nations and membership in the Islamic Conference Organization. The resistance has also sought diplomatic recognition from the United States and European as well as Muslim countries, and status as the sole legitimate representative of the Afghan people in any negotiations to resolve the crisis in Afghanistan. There have been increasing indications of political autonomy as the seven major resistance groups have attempted to consolidate the refugee population. Efforts have been made to establish legal structures for the resolution of disputes among Afghans in

Pakistan, and the elections in the refugee camps have been planned to reinforce the concept of a nation-in-exile.

Prolonged displacement could see the formation of an Afghan nation in Pakistan, placing a political burden on that country despite its best intentions and the efforts from the international community. Indeed, if one considers the case of Palestinians, it can be assumed that a long-term problem may be in the making in Pakistan. For over forty years efforts on behalf of Palestinians have been extensive, and while their short-term needs have been satisfied, the long-term problem of their displacement has remained central to Middle East disputes and instability in the region.

Pressure on the Pakistani economy

Although government officials have emphasized publicly how few problems exist between Afghan refugees and Pakistanis, privately it is felt that unless appropriate measures are taken, conflicts could result. The refugees' requirements for pastures for their herds of camels, goats, cattle and sheep have provoked disputes with the indigenous population over grazing rights. Afghan settlements have also placed greater pressures on available resources such as water and firewood.

When relief food is adequate or in excess, a different set of problems may occur. The price of food may decrease as relief goods find their way into the general economy. Such a deflation in prices can subvert local food producers, and some resentment has arisen where refugees have better living conditions than their hosts. In parts of Pakistan, refugees have shared relief food with destitute Pakistanis who descend upon refugee camps, hoping to take advantage of relief supplies.

Local economies can be disrupted when prices drop and reduce the cash income of near-subsistence farmers who rely on the sale of small surpluses. This has caused concern in certain regions in Pakistan and demands have been made for the government to stem the dispersion of refugees and control Afghans in camps and settlements.

Competition from a large refugee population for common property resources (CPRs) can be particularly damaging to the local poor, increasing tensions between host populations and refugees. The poorer rural people are, the less mobile they tend to be and the more they depend on local CPRs for their livelihood. The tension in Pakistan has been most acute over grazing lands, but has also been felt over available water and wildlife. In one area of Pakistan local people started to detain firewood collectors from the refugee settlements, while refugees resorted to gathering firewood under the cover of darkness.[6]

Competition over scarce employment has resulted in some of the first signs of friction between Afghans and Pakistanis as both place demands on a fragile developing economy. Refugees have been willing to work for lower wages than their Pakistani counterparts: for example, an Afghan construction worker will work for 25 per cent less than a Pakistani. Other refugee crises in other parts of the world have resulted in similar problems.

There are few options available to host communities or the poor within those communities. They have no resources such as food, medical aid, or the programmes of refugee relief-work agencies unless it is through a black market, or the generosity of refugees themselves. They do not have the services or the tools and materials that may be available to refugees, nor can hosts compete with refugee labour. These disruptions to the host society can result in resentment for the advantages accorded to refugees, and tensions created by a sense of injustice.

Compared with other countries of asylum, Pakistan allows the Afghans relative freedom of movement, so they are able to live and work where they wish and engage in radical politics. They live in camps rent-free, draw relief benefits and work to supplement their incomes. As refugees establish businesses, primarily in urban centres, Pakistanis have begun to resent the competition and Afghan domination in certain trades.

The world recession has also had an impact on the refugee population. Many Pakistanis who had gone abroad to work were forced to return to Pakistan when the construction boom in the Gulf ended. The return has placed a greater premium on jobs, resulting in competition between Pakistanis and Afghans. At this point it is hard to predict the impact this return will have on the relations between the two peoples but it can be said that the potential for friction has been heightened.

Ethnic barriers to assimilation

The economic and political problems of Afghan displacement have been compounded by cultural/ethnic behaviour which have caused problems for Pakistani authorities. For many Afghans the maintenance of tribal autonomy has meant relative distance from government, whether in Afghanistan or Pakistan. Historically these people have felt that when there was tension or pressure from authorities on one or the other side of the border, they could cross over to a safe haven. This manoeuvre, however, has been minimized by the continued occupation of Afghanistan, leaving many Afghans no alternative but to remain in Pakistan. Pakistan itself, however, is in the process of nation-building. Political legitimacy will depend on people's capacity to reconcile tribal and ethnic loyalties with national loyalty. If repatriation is unlikely, will Afghans be willing to assimilate into Pakistani society and will they submit to Pakistani law and nationalism? Political legitimacy, which is the goal of most developing countries, is complicated in the case of Pakistan by the Afghan nation-in-exile. The refugee crisis is a situation where there is a refugee nation attempting to establish its legitimacy within a country which is also attempting to establish political legitimacy and development.

Among the problems facing Pakistan is the ethnic quality of 'ghairat' which refugees have and which translates as bravery or zeal expressed in the pursuit of one's objectives of self-identity. It may well be this cultural characteristic that has imbued the Afghan resistance with the vigour which proved such a formidable obstacle to Soviet intervention. For Pathans, the dominant ethnic group among refugees, 'ghairat' is the ability to protect one's self, one's property and rights, extended to the family or group. The dilemmas here for Pakistan stem from the fact that 'ghairat' also defines a man's capacity to be self-determined and independent, despite the attempts of others to limit or circumscribe his activities. Thus Pathans define themselves by being self-determined, autonomous and capable of defending self, family, tradition, customs, property and home, living under rules outside the jurisdiction of national governments.

'Ghairat' is commonly expressed by maintaining distance from the state and its authority. This quality has been exercised in the mountainous regions of Afghanistan where government influence has traditionally been inhibited by rugged terrain. However, as Afghans are increasingly forced into Pakistan, an issue facing Islamabad is how to overcome tribal independence so as to avoid creating tensions. Indeed, future stability in Pakistan may be determined by Islamabad's ability to cope with an independent refugee Afghan population.

There have already been disputes between Pakistani officials and refugees where bureaucratic issues have come into conflict with tradition. Authorities have been denied entrance into refugee houses and arguments have occurred where Afghans felt the government had overstepped its bounds in the administration and control of refugee settlements. As the Afghan resistance continues to wage war against Kabul, Pakistan will continue to attempt to bring it under some form of administrative control. The outlines of a confrontation seem to exist between the national aspirations of Afghans and Pakistan.

The question of autonomy and sovereignty rights arose in 1984 when refugee camp authorities attempted to recount the camp population to stem the flow of illegal ration cards. From a bureaucratic point of view, the procedure was a reasonable response to an administrative problem. The authorities proceeded to inspect each individual family compound in order to count the number of family members. For refugees this was an unacceptable invasion of privacy, an intrusion of state into the restricted universe of domestic relations. Without repatriation and with continued confinement to Pakistan, such efforts to exercise autonomy and maintain cultural identity could affect Pakistan.

The strength and autonomy of Afghan customs have been evident since the refugees came to Pakistan. The arbitration of disputes is customarily adjudicated under traditional tribal systems involving elders and tribal law specialists. Many disputes among Afghans are turned over to mullahs or to provincial judicial committees set up by the various resistance parties. This system seems to indicate that geographical dislocation has not necessarily caused cultural dislocation. Part of the Afghan nation continues to exist within Pakistan, constituting a nation within a nation.

The relationship between Afghans and Pakistanis has varied between different regions of refugee settlement. Most notably in Baluchistan, Afghans have been received relatively well. This has been due largely to the cultural similarities that make it easier for Afghans and Baluchis to identify with one another. On both sides of the border in Baluchistan refugees live in surroundings which are culturally similar. Indeed, assimilation has progressed more rapidly in Baluchistan than in the North-West Frontier and in Peshawar, and some observers feel that it could be in Baluchistan that separatist sentiment might be fuelled by refugees. Moreover, it is in Baluchistan that the Soviets have threatened to support local separatist sentiments if Islamabad does not reconsider its policy to harbour the Afghan resistance.

Accusations against Pakistan

Pakistani stability and sovereignty have been severely tested by the Soviets and Afghan government. In attempting to check the Afghan resistance based in Pakistan, the Soviet Union and Afghanistan have violated Pakistan territory and airspace on more than 600 occasions since 1979. In the process, refugee camps in Pakistan have been bombed, resulting in the death of civilian Pakistanis as well as Afghans. Kabul's grievances against Pakistan are as follows:

1. Pakistan has provided sanctuary to Afghan rebels and has thus become an accomplice to Western anti-Kabul schemes.
2. It allows training facilities for counter-revolutionaries in camps set up on its soil where American and Chinese experts train rebels in guerrilla warfare.
3. By permitting the flow of weapons to these insurgents it has become a conduit for arms supplies.
4. Pakistan is therefore waging an undeclared war against the government in Kabul.[7]

Perhaps the greatest threat to Pakistan is that the Afghan insurgency has drawn it into the South Asian conflict. It has also compromised Islamabad's ability to act autonomously. Kabul has identified Pakistan as a collaborator in a Western strategy against the Afghan government and has emphasized Pakistan's role in harbouring the Afghan resistance. Moscow also openly accused Pakistan of complicity in Mujahideen attacks on Afghan government troops. As Pakistan became increasingly an integral actor in the South Asian conflict, Islamabad was subject to external influences necessary to aid Pakistan in manoeuvering through the Afghan crisis.

Destabilizing factors

Throughout Pakistan the attitude toward refugees has varied. In Punjab the reaction to Afghans has differed from that in the North-West Frontier Province and Baluchistan. Punjabis have encouraged the government to isolate Afghans in the North-West Frontier and not permit them to migrate to other provinces. This seems to be a dangerous analogy to the Palestinian problem. Both scenarios indicate a homeless people, isolated in settlements, unable to return to their homelands yet unable to assimilate. In both the Middle East and Pakistan a highly politicised refugee population represents a volatile political force created by virtue of its isolation from its homeland and tensions with ethnic factions in the host country. For their part the Punjabis are in a position analogous to that of Jordanians, Lebanese and Syrians. In all these cases from the Middle East to the Punjab, the indigenous nationals fear the settlement of refugees and the economic, political and social instability displaced persons can bring to their regions. Despite the relative freedom of movement for Afghans in Pakistan, there is nevertheless attendant social, political and economic isolation.

The problems that can arise when refugee populations are not assimilated into host societies have been long recognized. Historically, when chances of voluntary repatriation have been limited or when assimilation has been incomplete, the refugee problem has tended to reverberate at the national level. The Afghans in Pakistan, the Khmers along the Thai border and the Miskitu Indians in Honduras all provide examples of ways in which unintegrated refugees can cause difficulties between the government of the country of origin and the government of the country of asylum. In all of these cases, refugees have become militarily active in conducting operations against the government of the country of origin.

The situation in Pakistan is not unusual; it conforms to present and historic scenarios that attest to the destabilizing nature of great refugee populations in developing areas and the complications they can create for entire countries. A large influx of migrants poses a particularly serious problem for developing countries without strong political institutions. In most of these countries the mechanisms and resources for assimilation are not sufficiently advanced. This has been the case in countries of Africa, Central America and the Middle East, and it is also the case in Pakistan. The requisite institutions for assimilation do not exist or, indeed, the affected countries may resist assimilation for political reasons. Where the Palestinians are concerned, other Arab countries have hesitated to assimilate refugees in the belief that the question of Israel's existence would in time be ameliorated, or because of a legitimate concern for the political instability that could be created by a Palestinian nation of refugees. Such concern has resulted in enclaves of refugees festering with political tensions.

Rather than assimilation, nearly three million Palestinians have been displaced or isolated in settlements which have themselves been the target of political and military reprisals. Perhaps the greatest lesson to be learned from the occupation of Palestine is that people without a homeland do not cease to be a nation, and the resultant nation-within-a-nation can create the political pressures that lead to instability. Because the similarities between the Palestinian and Afghan cases are so striking, it may be possible by studying the former to see into the future of the latter.

Afghan resistance and Pakistan's security

Since the pro-Soviet regime first took power in Afghanistan in April 1978, the opposition parties have been divided along ethnic, tribal, political and personal lines on the means of subverting the government in Kabul. Even though they have a common commitment to fight the regime, they have found it difficult to forge a common front. Indeed, along with waging a resistance war against the Soviet-backed regime, the various factions of the Afghan resistance have often warred against one another.

The leading political parties have their headquarters in Peshawar. The groups advocating the establishment of an Islamic state are known collectively as the Alliance and consist of seven dominant parties. The three most important are Jamiat-i Islami Afghanistan (the Islamic Society of Afghanistan); Hizb-i Islami Afghanistan (the Afghanistan Islamic Party); and a breakaway group using the same name as the latter. Whereas Jamiat-i Islami derives support primarily from the Tadjiks and Uzbeks in north-eastern Afghanistan, the other two groups are mainly Pushtun in character, although they are also able to appeal across ethnic lines to northern peoples.

The Jamiat-i Islami and Hizb-i Islami groups can be traced back to the period of King Zahir Shah, whose monarchy was overthrown in 1973. They oppose a return to a monarchical government, blaming the King for the introduction of communists into the political system in the first place.

The second group of parties known as Unity was formed after the struggle against the Afghan Communist regime began in 1978 and is more moderate and pro-monarchist. The three main parties are Harakat-i Inquilab-i Islami Afghanistan (the Movement for the Islamic Revolution of Afghanistan); Payman-e Ettehad-Islam (the National Islamic Front); and Jabha-ye Azadire Afghanistan (the National Liberation Front of Afghanistan). Their leadership comprises primarily the heads of important families noted for their religious authority and their support is predominantly drawn from the Pushtun areas of eastern and southern Afghanistan. To this group of six parties should be added the fundamentalist Islamic Alliance.

All these parties are Sunni and constitute the principal parties operating in Peshawar although there are dozens of other smaller Mujahideen organizations. Little is known about the Shiite groups based in Iran, the most important of which are held to be An-Nasr (Victory) and the Afghan Islamic Revolution Freedom Front.[8]

In April 1982 external pressures (primarily American and Saudi) forced the seven leading parties in Peshawar to consolidate and attempt to achieve some kind of political consensus and co-operation. In July 1983 former King Zahir Shah called on all parties to set aside their differences and establish a united front to confront the regime in Kabul and to exhibit unity in international fora. The most successful effort along these lines took place in May 1985 when the seven leading resistance movements formed a new coalition— the Islamic Unity of Afghan Mujahideen. The coalition planned to create a defence council and a rotating chairmanship to co-ordinate guerrilla activities inside Afghanistan and to conduct a more vigorous campaign for recognition abroad.

In the past there have been over a hundred different resistance factions in Peshawar. Despite its apparent disorganization, however, the resistance was a constant source of trouble for the Soviet Union, which was forced to retreat from Afghanistan in the winter and spring of 1989. The resistance has also been a formidable obstacle to the Kabul government which has been unable to consolidate its influence over rebel or refugee Afghans or in most of the countryside.

The resistance has successfully used classic guerrilla tactics by employing hit-and-run manoeuvres. They used rocket attacks against Soviet installations in and around Kabul, so that even in the capital the Soviet hold was limited to the city centre. According to one leading American military analyst, Soviet forces generally '[dealt] very poorly with ambushes', preferring to permit the guerrillas to take 'the vehicles they have disabled and to move the rest of the convoy to safety', after which Soviet troops would bomb and shell local villages in frustrated efforts to root out the insurgents.[9]

Soviet firepower was compromised as helicopter losses mounted. Initially it appeared that the Soviet M1-24 'Hind' helicopter would demoralize and eventually defeat the resistance. These gunships, capable of carrying a dozen fully-equipped soldiers, have such overwhelming firepower that in the early stages of the war there appeared to be little the rebels could do to offset such an advantage.

However, with sound guerrilla tactics and growing availability of shoulder-held surface-to-air missiles like the American Stinger and captured Soviet SAM-7s, some balance in firepower was achieved. Pakistan has experienced throughout the Afghan crisis pressure to support the insurgent movement, and to act as a conduit for *matériel*. The result was President Zia's inability to act as a neutral actor, and the consequent threat of having Pakistan drawn further into the Afghan conflict. Indeed, it is possible that had Pakistan not aided Afghan insurgency, it could have remained apart from the Afghan fray, limited the incentive for Soviet and Afghan government forces to operate right up to and even sometimes within its borders, and reduced the numbers and flow of refugees. Support for the rebels, however, has become a policy with which Islamabad is reconciled but which has been costly and threatening. In March of 1985 Zia visited Moscow to attend the funeral of Konstantin Chernenko. At that time the Soviet leadership warned that if Pakistan did not rethink its policy and cut off aid to Afghan rebels, Moscow would encourage the disgruntled Baluch minority to rebel.[10]

In May 1985 some of the heaviest fighting in Afghanistan took place in the province of Paktika adjacent to the Pakistani border, and in and around the city of Khowst. On 10 April 1986 Soviet and Afghan government troops captured and destroyed one of the resistance's largest bases in the border city of Ahawar and there was heavy fighting in Nangarher Province near the strategic Khyber Pass leading to Peshawar.[11] Throughout the crisis and up to the present, the 1,200-mile border Pakistan shares with Afghanistan has become increasingly vulnerable to Afghan government incursions.

In 1985 there were over 200 Afghan or Soviet violations of Pakistan's territory or airspace involving bombing or artillery fire. These incidents, which increased in 1986 and by 1987 numbered over 600, have aggravated political tensions in Pakistan.

In late February 1987, a bomb explosion outside the office of an Afghan guerrilla group killed ten and injured sixty-two people. Pakistanis crowded the streets near the explosion, shouting anti-Afghan slogans and throwing debris at the wrecked Afghan office. Eventually the riot evolved into a gun battle between Pakistanis and Afghans resulting in four dead and numerous injured. Resentment also resulted in raids on refugee camps throughout the North-West Frontier Province. Rampages by Pakistanis in Peshawar resulted in the burning and looting of shops, homes and cars, followed by bombings against Afghans in which dozens were killed.[12]

On 26 February Afghan warplanes bombed two Pakistani villages and the refugee camps of Matasanga and Khardand in the North-West Frontier Province, killing thirty-five and wounding over two hundred. The limit of Pakistan's tolerance for Afghan refugees was indicated in January 1986 when a demonstration against the Afghan presence in Pakistan took place after a series of bomb explosions attributed to pro-Soviet Afghans.

Pakistan has also been subject to Afghan subversion. Infiltrators have been apprehended by Pakistani authorities and incidents of bombing within Pakistan have been attributed to Afghan communists.

In late March 1987, during a Pakistani national holiday, Afghan air raids occurred in which eighty-five people were killed and over a hundred wounded. The raids were directed against guerrilla camps but were also intended to convey Kabul's disapproval of Islamabad's policy of harbouring rebels.

Soviet threats

The Soviet Union also increased pressure on Pakistan to stop support for the Afghan resistance. On 23 December 1983 Ambassador Smirnov, the Soviet representative in Pakistan, threatened Islamabad with 'combined Soviet–Afghan action' if the 'terrorists' pursued their 'meddling' in Afghanistan from Pakistani territory. Following these and other threats, on 2 February 1984 Smirnov warned the Pakistani government about the Afghan resistance movement and advised them on future policy:

> We are close neighbours; both of our countries are interested in peace and stability in the region. To achieve these goals, it is important not only to assess the present situation correctly, but also to see everything in perspective, to practice political realism, to be guided by genuine national interests and not by the interests of those forces who try to block the development of these relations, because it contradicts their strategic military plans in the area.[13]

Smirnov's advice amounted to warning Pakistan to cut its relations with the United States and change its policy on Afghanistan or face the consequences.

Pressure on Pakistan was also evident in March 1986, when at a meeting between Gorbachev and President Zia, the Soviet leader used unusually harsh language in criticizing Pakistan's policies. A TASS report of the meeting charged that Pakistan was supporting aggression against a Soviet ally and that the CIA was maintaining a number of bases and camps to train and equip Afghan insurgents within Pakistan. Since most of the weapons used by Afghan rebels passed through Pakistan, the Soviet Union was prepared to increase its attacks inside Pakistan and along its borders.[14]

As attacks against Pakistan increased, American officials became concerned about the psychological effect such pressure might have on Pakistan, for fear that if the Soviets managed to make life sufficiently difficult, Bhutto's opposition might have the mandate it needed to destabilize the government. While there had been general agreement on government support for Afghan rebels, a significant number of members of the National Assembly had criticized the government's policies. Domestic factions, together with the pressure of ethnic minorities, principally in Baluchistan, have combined to lobby the government. At the same time, Bhutto was not free to formulate policies independent of the American, Chinese, Saudi and other influences. Unwittingly the pressure applied by Pakistan's allies could contribute to instability in the country.

The trends developing in Pakistan are important for a number of reasons. Although Pakistan has been praised internationally for its treatment of refugees, very real tension appears to be developing. The government has acted to minimize the impact of the resistance domestically by isolating activist refugees, while at the same time continuing to support the rebel movement against the Kabul government. This action has been one of the most delicate balancing acts Islamabad has had to perform. To avoid retribution from the Soviet Union or Afghanistan, Pakistan must cope with the refugee crisis without provoking resentment from or against refugees. The resulting pressure is considerable, for it comes not only from Kabul and the Soviet Union, but from allies as well.

Political consequences

When the Soviet Union invaded Afghanistan, Pakistan became a front-line state commanding international attention. As such its stability became central to Western strategy and there has been an international response to provide economic support for a beleaguered Islamabad. Assistance has come from agencies such as the International Monetary Fund, the World Bank and the Consortium for Pakistan, as well as the United States, Japan and countries of Western Europe and the Middle East. In December 1980 the IMF approved a loan of $1.7 billion, which included relief funds for Afghan refugees. In addition, Pakistan's major creditors have agreed to reschedule its debts and stimulate trade between Pakistan and the United States, Japan and the European Community. As an Islamic bastion in the face of Soviet hegemony, Islamabad has also received considerable aid from Saudi Arabia (which has matched American aid nearly dollar for dollar) as well as from other Muslim states.[15]

Some analysts characterized the Soviet invasion of Afghanistan as a windfall for the Zia government which had become increasingly significant in the Gulf region. As a key actor in the area, Pakistan has been the beneficiary of generous attention. However, unless efforts are made to repatriate Afghans, these measures could collapse under the weight of a long-term refugee presence.

Being in a strategically significant part of the world, Pakistan will be the object of Soviet and American attention as the superpowers attempt to influence events in South Asia. So far Pakistan's foreign policy has been conducted with skill by both the Zia and Bhutto governments. It has maintained its relative independence from undue foreign influence and its non-aligned status is intact. Unrest due to domestic factions, however, has been festering throughout the 1980s and the Afghan crisis which thrust Pakistan onto the global stage has further threatened its stability.

The new Kabul regime has had a significant impact on the domestic affairs of Pakistan by attempting to foment rebellion among the Baluchis. As part of their strategy Kabul has extended aid to the Baluchi separatists, even recognizing Baluchistan as a separate nation.

Baluchistan, as an ethnic region spanning both sides of the Afghan–Pakistani border, was originally split by the British to demarcate the boundary between India, Afghanistan and Iran. Since the independence of Pakistan, there have been significant Baluchi political movements seeking the unification and independence of Baluchistan. The Marxist coup in Kabul has helped these movements, giving them assistance and attempting to imbue them with an element of legitimacy.

To cope with this target of Afghan attention, Islamabad has given priority to developing the economy of Baluchistan, thereby hoping to counter the attractiveness of Afghan overtures. One of the greatest dangers to both Iran and Pakistan is the possibility of a significant movement demanding the independence of Baluchistan, which might inspire other minorities to seek autonomy.

The Afghan nation-in-exile

Evidence of Afghan nationalism among refugees and within the resistance is increasingly open. Although the alliance has been split over approaches to the Soviet Union and the Kabul government, they represent a bona fide nation-in-exile with nationalist sentiments and seeking repatriation.

The Reagan administration, which met the leaders of the Afghan Alliance in June 1986, hinted that under the right conditions it would grant diplomatic recognition to the Alliance. Those conditions include the establishment of a capital in Afghanistan, an administrative apparatus similar to other governments, popular support from a majority of Afghans and the necessity for the resistance movement to consolidate itself sufficiently to present a united front. While these demands were first made by the Reagan administration, they have not been revised under the Bush presidency. Under such conditions the United States would support the rebels' demands that negotiations over the withdrawal of Soviet forces from Afghanistan would be between the 'warring factions' — that is, the Afghan rebels and the Soviet Union.[16] In so far as the conditions were not met, the Geneva Accords were negotiated by Islamabad and Kabul with Moscow and Washington as observers.

The efforts of the Afghan resistance to achieve diplomatic status is similar to the efforts of the Palestinian Liberation Organization's campaign to achieve legitimacy. The PLO has received recognition in many quarters as the sole representative of the Palestinian people, empowered to conduct negotiations on their behalf. This recognition has earned the PLO diplomatic status in nearly all Muslim countries and in important non-Muslim countries of the Third World as well as international bodies, and consultative status at the United Nations. These achievements have helped the Palestinian movement to become accepted as 'a nation without a state', attempting to regain sovereignty. The political legitimacy of the PLO has also given a dynamism to the Palestinian community which has contributed to political tensions in the Middle East. The implications for Pakistan are important, for they indicate that nations in exile can seek political legitimacy and can threaten regional stability. The American position is a delicate one. Washington would like to see the Alliance gain a degree of legitimacy, but not sufficiently to destabilize Pakistan.

Conclusion

The Afghan refugee problem still has the potential to threaten Pakistan's stability in several ways. Having a common border with Afghanistan has made it a haven for the rebel movement. As such, the war conducted by Kabul against the resistance has been carried to the border of Pakistan and increasingly within the country itself.

In attempting to combat the resistance, the Soviets threatened to exacerbate secessionist sentiments among ethnic separatists in Pakistan. This threat has been directed largely at the sensitive and unstable region of Baluchistan, already a source of separatist problems in the past.

While they are themselves the victims of the Soviet invasion of their country, Afghan refugees constitute a potentially destabilizing nation within Pakistan. Historically great refugee movements have been destabilizing to countries and regions, and at times have formed new nations. In considering the Palestinian diaspora it is possible to see parallels with the Afghan refugee migration. It is likely that the nearly four million displaced Afghans in Pakistan will cling to their ethnic and cultural character and increasingly assert themselves as a powerful political force. With international recognition as the legitimate Afghan nation, this state-in-exile could have serious destabilizing consequences for Pakistan and the Gulf region.

Notes

1. Alvin Rubinstein, 'Afghanistan at War', *Current History*, March 1986, vol. 85, p. 117.
2. Ekber Menemencioglu, 'Self-Reliance as a Short-Term Solution', *Refugees*, no. 16, April 1985, a publication of the United Nations High Commission for Refugees.
3. Edward Girardet, 'Urban Refugees in Peshawar', *Refugees*, no. 27, March 1986.
4. For an analysis of the refugee population in Pakistan, see *The State of Population in Pakistan*, published by the Pakistan National Institute of Population Studies, Islamabad, 1988, p. 238.
5. Zia ul Haq interview with the United Nations High Commission for Refugees, 7 November 1984.
6. Hanna Christensen, 'Sustaining Afghan Refugees in Pakistan: Report on the Food Situation and Related Aspects', Report No. 83.3, United Nations Research Institute for Social Development, Geneva.
7. Ali Mahrunnisa, 'Soviet–Pakistan Ties Since the Afghan Crisis', *Asian Survey*, vol. 23, no. 9, September 1983.

8. Alvin Rubinstein, op. cit.
9. Marvin Zonis, 'Middle East Responses', *Orbis*, Winter 1987, vol. 30, no. 4, p. 609.
10. William J. Holstein, Mark D'Anastasio and Boyd France, 'Gorbachev Raises the Ante in Afghanistan: Threatens Pakistan to Cut Aid to Afghan Rebels', *Business Week*, 20 May 1985.
11. Craig M. Karp, 'The War in Afghanistan', *Foreign Affairs*, Summer 1986.
12. Associated Press, 19 February 1987.
13. Marvin Zonis, op. cit.
14. Donald Zagoria, 'The USSR and Asia in 1985', *Asian Survey*, vol. 26, no. 1, 1986.
15. William Richter, 'Pakistan: a New "Front-Line State"?' *Current History*, May 1982.
16. Richard Holloran, 'Official Says Afghan Rebels May be Recognized by US', *New York Times*, 18 June 1986, p. 8.

6 INDO-SRI LANKAN RELATIONS, 1975–89: A STUDY IN THE INTERNATIONALIZATION OF ETHNIC CONFLICT

K.M. de Silva

I

Introduction

From the mid-1970s Indo-Sri Lankan relations were to be dominated by Indian responses to Sri Lanka's ethnic conflicts, Sinhalese versus Tamils. The mid and late 1970s mark the beginning of the second phase in the post-independence violence in the island. The first phase was in the mid and late 1950s. At that time India had treated it as a matter of Sri Lanka's domestic politics and therefore not for diplomatic or political intervention. It was the heyday of India's perception of itself as the conscience of the Third World, and Nehru acted with a restraint in regard to domestic turmoil among India's smaller neighbours (with the possible exception of Nepal) which his daughter and successor did not show.

In the 1970s the situation had changed. After the intervention in East Pakistan and the creation of Bangladesh India was in a more self-confident mood. The débâcle of 1962, when China had inflicted a humiliating defeat on India had long been forgotten. India's neighbours would have to learn to live with the fact that Indira Gandhi was not the heiress of her revered namesake, but of the great British imperialist expansionists Dalhousie and Curzon.

The other factor which influenced the relationship between the two countries was the Tamil Nadu connection and its impact on the Sri Lankan situation. Within the Indian union, Madras, or Tamil Nadu as it became later, was one of the main centres of separatist tendencies in India.[1] The rise of the Dravida Kazhagam (DK) and later the Dravida Munnetra Kazhagam (DMK) in the early 1950s reflected the same powerful force of linguistic nationalism that had transformed the politics of Sri Lanka in the same period.

The DK and the DMK were even more conscious of the rights of Tamils in South Asia than the Congress-dominated state governments of Madras had been, but acted with much less restraint in demonstrating their concern about these, so much so that the increasingly turbulent politics of Sri Lanka's Jaffna peninsula (the main concentration of the Tamil population in the island) in the early 1970s began to be treated as an integral part of the internal politics of Tamil Nadu. Tamil politics in South Asia thus had a regional rather than a purely local impact. The DMK, effectively checked from pursuing its separatist goals in India, took vicarious pleasure in giving encouragement and support to separatist tendencies among the Tamils of Sri Lanka.

There was an unmistakable intensification of separatist agitation from 1974 to 1975 as well as an increase in terrorist activity, of which the shooting by Velupillai Prabhakaran, now leader of the Liberation Tigers of Tamil Eelam (LTTE) in 1975, of Alfred Durayappa, the Mayor of Jaffna (the administrative capital of the northern province) was the most significant incident.[2] The security forces found the search for actual and potential troublemakers a frustrating experience as the local population would not voluntarily help in apprehending these young men; besides, when there was the slightest chance of capture, they moved across the Palk straits to Tamil Nadu which served them as a refuge, and as a bridgehead for raids into the Jaffna peninsula.

It was at this point — the passage between Jaffna and the Tamil Nadu coast — that smugglers entered the picture both as transport agents for fugitives, and as sources of ready money. Also the safe houses established on both sides of the Palk straits for the traditional smuggling trade were now put to other uses as havens for men on the run, and for storing arms in support of the separatist cause. Very soon the more politically conscious smugglers and the terrorist groups had joined forces. Each needed and used the other. There was the inevitable metamorphosis of the smuggler into 'guerrilla' and 'freedom fighter', and indeed some of the most dynamic and powerful leaders in recent times thrown up by this blending of clandestine trading activity and militant and violent political agitation were prominent smugglers.

The Tamil Nadu factor and its impact on the relations between India and Sri Lanka have been analysed in some detail in Shelton U. Kodikara's chapter in this present volume. Suffice to say here that the Tamil Nadu factor forms an important facet of India's complex role in the ethnic conflicts of Sri Lanka in the 1980s. As we shall see, India has had three roles in this conflict: participant, mediator and combatant. The role of participant is inextricably linked to the Tamil Nadu factor, but not to that alone. Seldom has a constituent unit (a province or state) of one country influenced the relationship between it and a neighbouring country with the same intensity and to the same extent that Tamil Nadu did and continues to do in the case of India's relations with Sri Lanka. Indeed the India-Tamil Nadu-Sri Lanka relationship is unique in international affairs. India's own role is a more complex one than merely reacting to the issues of domestic politics in Tamil Nadu. Tamil Nadu provided Sri Lankan Tamil separatist activists with sanctuaries, training and bases. Not only did the central government connive in this, but it also tolerated the provision of training facilities, and the existence of camps and bases in other parts of the country. These began under Indira Gandhi, and in the early 1980s, well before the riots of July 1983, in Sri Lanka.

After July 1983 India began its role as mediator, not that India under Indira Gandhi was an impartial arbiter in the island's ethnic conflicts. Under her son and successor, Rajiv Gandhi, there was greater concern about impartiality but even then India did not entirely abandon her self-appointed role as the guardian of the interests of Sri Lanka's Tamil minority.

India's third role in this conflict, came in 1987-9, that of combatant. That too is unique in the history of mediation in regional conflict: never before has a mediator taken on the role of combatant, and the presumed guardian of an ethnic minority's interests fought a bitter war against sections of that minority, and in a neighbouring state at that.

II

India as participant and mediator: Indira Gandhi and Sri Lanka, 1980-4

The return of Indira Gandhi to power at the general election of 1980 marked a decisive change in the relations between Sri Lanka and India, away from the cordiality between the two neighbours under Moraji Desai and the Janatha government. Her decision in 1978 to stand for election at a by-election to the Lok Sabha from the Andhra Pradesh constituency of Medak, and to return to Parliament from there was deeply significant. When the general election came she preferred to remain in her new constituency rather than return to her old seat in Uttar Pradesh. The southern states, in particular Andhra Pradesh and Karnataka, had rallied to her in 1977 when the old strongholds of the Hindi heartland had deserted her party. Now, by standing for Parliament through a southern constituency she underlined Congress I's reliance on its southern bastions. She was more sensitive than ever before to the concerns and interests of the south, and more particularly of Tamil Nadu.

Once she returned to power, she found herself at odds with President J.R. Jayewardene and his government on their outlook, attitudes and policies on regional and world affairs. There was, first of all, the Afghan issue on which the two governments adopted diametrically opposed policies: Sri Lanka, like most other South Asian states strongly condemned the Soviet invasion. India was out of step with the rest of South Asia on this issue. There was also Sri Lanka's futile attempt to secure membership of the Association of South East Asian Nations (ASEAN). This was regarded as proof of the Sri Lanka government's general pro-Western attitudes, of which latter, further evidence was presumably provided in the expanded facilities granted to the United States for its Voice of America (VOA) relaying station in the island, and also in the choice of a consortium consisting of Oroleum (Pvt) Ltd, Singapore, Oil Tanking, West Germany, and Tradinaft, Switzerland, to restore to commercial use a complex of oil-tank farms in the vicinity of the strategically important port of Trincomalee. Then came the Falklands war where Sri Lanka alone of Third World countries backed Britain rather than Argentina.

Sri Lanka, for its part, found the new Indian government less than helpful with regard to Tamil separatist groups operating from Tamil Nadu. After the riots of 1977 a period of quiet and slow improvement in relations between the government and the principal Tamil party, the Tamil United Liberation Front (TULF), had seen the passage of the District Development Councils bill in August 1980 and the establishment of a second tier of government in the island. This was a major political achievement, considering that two previous attempts (in 1958 and 1968) had failed in the face of extra-parliamentary agitation and internal bickering within the then ruling party or coalition.[3] There were, nevertheless, occasional outbursts of ethnic violence (in 1981 for instance) and an ongoing conflict between security forces located in Jaffna and Tamil separatist activists and terrorists. As in the past the latter were using safe houses, if not 'bases' in Tamil Nadu.

Given this background the Indian government's response to the anti-Tamil riots of July 1983 was predictable: it took the form of expressions of official concern, and pressure on the Sri Lanka government on behalf of the island's Tamil minority. With the Sri Lankan government greatly, if temporarily, weakened politically at home, and more so internationally, Indira Gandhi stepped up the pressure and put India on the way to its role as the mediator in Sri Lanka's ethnic conflict, and with it became heir (or heiress) to all the ills from which mediators are prone to suffer, especially where the mediator is also a participant.

First of all, India was demonstrating her right to a say in the settlement of a potentially (and actually) destabilizing domestic conflict in a neighbouring state.[4] Second, because one of the parties to the conflict had linguistic, cultural and religious ties with a neighbouring state of the Indian union, the conflict itself had a regional rather than a purely local one. Third, with general elections due in 1984 and her electoral base eroding in many parts of India, including some of her strongholds in southern India, Indira Gandhi was anxious to mollify Tamil Nadu and to retain if not consolidate her, and the Congress I party's base there.

Thus in July 1983 Mrs Gandhi did what Moraji Desai refused to do in August 1977 in the aftermath of the Sri Lankan riots of that year: she sent a Cabinet minister, Narasimha Rao, the Foreign Minister, to Colombo on 27 July 1983 while Colombo was still in flames as it were, to review the situation there. Later on, with the consent of a chastened Sri Lanka government, she appointed a mediator, G. Parathasarathy, an experienced diplomat. The objective at this stage was to seek to alter the strategies of the participants—the Sri Lanka government and the various Tamil groups, in particular the TULF—and to encourage a settlement of the conflict under Indian auspices.

In retrospect it appears that the choice of G. Parathasarathy as mediator was an unfortunate one. He was chosen because of his long experience and the confidence that Indira Gandhi had in his judgment. But he was a South Indian Tamil, and while this won him the confidence of the TULF and other Tamil groups—not to mention the Tamil Nadu government and opposition—he put himself in the position of seeming to be the advocate of TULF policies, and therefore became increasingly suspect to both the Sri Lankan government and its senior officials, who had to deal with him in Sri Lanka and India, as being too partisan.

In Tamil Nadu there were demands for Indian 'intervention' (a euphemism for invasion) and the strong possibility of 'volunteers' moving in across the Palk straits from Tamil Nadu. The parallel quoted was Bangladesh and the Indian intervention in 1971. Over 35,000 Tamil refugees crossed the seas to Tamil Nadu in the aftermath of the riots. Their numbers increased, in time, to about 125,000.

There was also a significant change in the basis of India's declared interest, during times of ethnic tension, in the affairs of Sri Lanka. Generally, on previous occasions the main concern had been with the 'stateless' Indians resident in the island, and with Indian citizens here, both categories being largely plantation workers. This, by any standard of assessment, was a legitimate interest, although the presence in the island of plantation workers with Indian citizenship was due to a concession made to the Ceylon Workers Congress (CWC), the main political party cum trade union of the plantation workers—with the knowledge and approval of the Indian government—by the United National Party (UNP) governments (of 1965–70 and 1977–89), whereby they were permitted to remain in the island for the duration of their working lives. (Under Mrs Bandaranaike's government such persons were required to leave the island once their status changed from stateless to Indian citizens). In the late 1970s and early 1980s Indian interest in the affairs of Sri Lanka extended to all Tamils, and not merely to Indian citizens or 'stateless' persons of Indian extraction.

The riots of 1983 had given the TULF the opportunity to revive the debate on the devolution of power, and with Parathasarathy's approval they formally withdrew their support for the District Development Councils, claiming that these were inadequate in meeting the needs of the Tamil minority as they perceived it in the changed situation. Their main aim now as in 1957 was the creation of a large regional unit encompassing the northern and eastern provinces in which the Tamils would be a dominant if not overwhelming majority.

President Jayewardene visited India in November 1983 on a fence-mending trip, for which the opportunity was provided by the Commonwealth Heads of Government meeting held in New Delhi. He found that Mrs Gandhi had absorbed Parathasarathy's views on Sri Lankan affairs, especially the proposition that the unit of devolution should be much larger than a district, and the powers transferred much wider than under the system introduced in 1981. Under tremendous pressure from India, Jayewardene tentatively accepted a set of proposals embodied in a document which came to be known as 'Annexure C', setting out the framework of a settlement with the TULF and other Tamil groups. A key feature in this was a merger of the northern and eastern provinces into a single Tamil ethno-region.

On his return to Sri Lanka, Jayewardene called a conference—the All Party Conference (APC)—to discuss this, among other proposals. These discussions began in January 1984. The UNP's election manifesto for the general election of 1977 made reference to such a conference to seek a resolution of the island's ethnic conflicts, but once in office it had preferred bilateral negotiations between itself and the TULF. Now the scope of the participation at the conference was widened to include representatives of the *sangha* (the Buddhist order), generally hard-line opponents of all schemes of devolution. The SLFP refused to participate in the discussions of the APC.

At the APC a consensus was reached on the crucially important issue of the devolution of power to regional bodies, and much progress had been achieved in regard to other matters including language policy. By the end of the year, however, this consensus evaporated when a legislative framework based on it was published. The TULF rejected the proposals as inadequate (partly because the unit of devolution remained the district, and not a province). The government thereupon withdrew its own support for these proposals in December 1984, relieved no doubt to jettison a scheme which appeared to have so little support in the country.

In the meantime that hardy perennial in Indo-Sri Lankan discord over the last five decades — the political status of Indians resident and working in Sri Lanka — was well on the way to amicable settlement in the post-1977 period through the operation of the democratic political process in Sri Lanka.[5] One of the more fruitful results of the APC of 1984 was the decision that 94,000 stateless persons — Indian plantation workers — be granted Sri Lankan citizenship. This recommendation was accepted in principle by the government. Legislation for this purpose was ready in 1986/7 and approved by Parliament (through the *Grant of Citizenship to Stateless Persons Act of No. 39 of 1988*). With its adoption, plantation workers of Indian extraction fell into two clear categories: Sri Lankan citizens, and those with Indian citizenship but resident in the island for the duration of their working lives.

These discussions on the mechanics of devolution took place against the backdrop of an increasing frequency of guerrilla attacks and terrorist incidents in the north of the island, and the extension of these into the eastern seaboard. The guerrilla forces were now much larger, much better trained, (the training was largely in India) and much better equipped than they were before. The training and equipping of guerrilla forces in India and with the active support of Tamil Nadu had begun in the early 1980s, well before the riots of July 1983, but there is no mistaking the intensification of these processes as a result of the violence inflicted on the Tamils in July 1983. Tamil Nadu had always been a ready haven for these guerrilla forces, but now the support they received was strengthened immeasurably, as was the extent of the protection they enjoyed. Their morale was stronger, and their motivation keener after these riots than before, and by the end of 1983 they demonstrated a greater willingness to take risks, and greater resourcefulness and daring in their attacks on the security forces and on carefully chosen targets.

Till about the end of 1985 they were in many ways better equipped than the small security services stationed in the north of the island.

The first reports on these training-camps and 'bases' located in India appeared in Western newspapers in April 1984, at much the same time that comprehensive coverage of the camps and bases appeared in a prestigious Indian journal, *India Today*.[6] And if more solid evidence was required of the use of Indian soil by Sri Lankan guerrillas and terrorists, this was forthcoming when a section of the Madras International Airport was accidentally blown up on 2 August 1984 by bombs due for transfer to Sri Lanka for the destruction of aircraft of the Sri Lankan national airline at Colombo's International Airport: the explosion killed over two dozen Sri Lankan passengers in the transit lounge of the Madras airport on this occasion. The identity of the perpetrators of this terrorist outrage was soon known to Madras police.[7] Some of them were arrested and brought to trial. The Indian government generally refused to acknowledge the existence of training-camps and facilities for Sri Lankan Tamil guerrillas and terrorist groups on Indian soil. Instead it sought to divert attention from Sri Lankan charges and protests about these with countercharges of human rights violations in Sri Lanka, attributing these quite explicitly to the lack of discipline among the Sri Lankan security forces. In so doing they met an embarrassing fact with a half truth.

The fact is that Sri Lankan Tamil guerrillas and terrorists operated in Tamil Nadu with a freedom and publicity for which the only parallel is the PLO and its various factions in the Arab world. Quite apart from the public support they enjoy in such large measure in Tamil Nadu, they engage in fund-raising drives at public meetings in other parts of India as well, in particular Bombay city.[8] This double standard on separatism and terrorism— to crush separatism ruthlessly when it is seen to pose a palpable threat to the Indian polity as was done in 1984 in the Punjab through Operation Blue Star, to protest vigorously at the tolerance accorded to Indian extremists and terrorist groups operating in the Western world (the Sikhs in Britain, Canada and the United States for instance), and yet to feign ignorance of the existence of training-camps and 'bases' for Tamil guerrillas and terrorist groups on Indian soil was one of the great stumbling-blocks to cordial relations between India and Sri Lanka during this period and on to 1987 or later.

India's policy in regard to the internationalization of Sri Lanka's ethnic conflict was a two-pronged affair. While discussions and negotiations with the Sri Lankan government on a settlement of differences between the government and the Tamil minority were proceeding, with India in her role of mediator, India was using its formidable diplomatic resources through its High Commissions and embassies in the West—in Ottawa, London, and Washington, in particular—to accuse the Sri Lankan government and its armed forces of violations of human rights in attacks on Tamil civilians, in the course of or in the wake of security operations in the north and east of the island. At the United Nations Organization Indian delegates—generally a Tamil Nadu politician (a Tamil Nadu minister in 1983)—would raise the Sri Lankan issue in the course of debates there.[9] The situation was even more favourable to this diplomatic offensive at the United Nations Office in Geneva, and the sessions of the Human Rights Commission where the Indian representative would either raise the Sri Lankan issue on his own, or more often back countries such as Argentina (smarting under Sri Lanka's support of Britain in the Falklands war) and Norway in raising the issue officially. Since some of the Western nations—the United States and Great Britain—were represented on the Commission by non-governmental organizations, and there was in addition the conspicuous presence of Human Rights groups, Sri Lanka was under much greater pressure in Geneva than in New York.[10]

In the meantime the TULF leadership were living in self-imposed exile in Madras as guests of the Tamil Nadu government. This was quite apart from more radical Tamil activists who also lived in Madras and conducted their clandestine operations and political campaigns through Madras and India, linking up with well-funded diaspora groups living in the West. These latter groups sought and received political support from Indian embassies and High Commissions, in Washington for instance, and Ottawa, not to mention London.

Then again, while persistently ignoring the provision of training facilities to Tamil activists in Tamil Nadu (and elsewhere in India) and the transfer of weapons from India to Jaffna, the Indian government under Indira Gandhi used pressure on Western powers to prevent the sale of sophisticated weaponry to the Sri Lankan forces. Sri Lanka purchased weapons from Pakistan and the People's Republic of China; Pakistan also provided much of the training, and in addition Sri Lanka turned to Israel for assistance in training its forces.

III

From mediation to intervention: Rajiv Gandhi, November 1984 to June 1987

Rajiv Gandhi's early moves gave confidence to the Sri Lankan government and encouraged hopes that unlike his mother he would be an impartial mediator. The fading away of G. Parathasarathy, Mrs Gandhi's *eminence grise* in Sri Lankan affairs was a bonus. In his place there was Romesh Bhandari, India's Foreign Secretary, who proved to be distinctly more acceptable to the Sri Lankan political leadership and officials.

In this improved atmosphere there were direct talks in New Delhi in June 1985 between President Jayewardene and Prime Minister Rajiv Gandhi. These resulted in a major breakthrough when the Sri Lankan government agreed to begin negotiations with Tamil separatist groups in addition to the TULF, something they had hitherto refused to do on the grounds that this would give these armed separatist groups a legitimacy they were not entitled to have. As a result of the Indian mediation, talks began in Bhutan in July and August 1985 with H.W. Jayewardene (the President's brother), an eminent lawyer, leading the Sri Lankan delegation.[11] While these talks did not yield any positive results immediately, the momentum was kept up, first of all by extending beyond October the cease-fire agreement negotiated prior to the dicussions (a cease-fire of three months' duration).

This was followed by a second set of discussions between the Sri Lankan government and the Tamil leadership, once again through Indian mediation. These talks were more fruitful. The new agenda for ethnic reconciliation which emerged was, in essence, an expansion of an original working paper prepared for the Thimpu and the post-Thimpu discussions in New Delhi between H.W. Jayewardene and Indian government representatives in July and August 1985. The crucial issue continued to be devolution. In the new agenda the unit of devolution was to be a province and no longer a district; in addition the powers devolved to these units were wider than they had been earlier.

Meanwhile sporadic regular outbursts of ethnic violence, especially in the north and east of the island, and clashes between the security forces and Tamil guerrillas and terrorist groups disturbed the peace of the country. Greatly improved relations between the two countries did not extend to any serious efforts to prevent the use of Indian territory by guerrillas and terrorists for attacks on a friendly neighbour, much less to close down the facilities and camps. Rajiv Gandhi, so much less dependent on the southern Indian political base than his mother, and intent on taking a more even-handed approach than she did to the problems posed by Sri Lanka's ethnic conflicts, found his options more limited than he would have liked them to be. And the constraint lay in the ethnic politics of Tamil Nadu. The Tamil guerrillas and terrorist groups continued to have training facilities and bases there.

In addition, there was internecine fighting among the Tamil separatist groups, in the course of which the LTTE won a bloody victory over its main rivals in the last week of April 1986 in Jaffna.[12] The LTTE was also helped by a decision of the Sri Lankan government, taken in mid-1985 as part of an understanding that was reached with India, that its forces in the north of the island would be kept within their barracks or camps. In a serious tactical error the Sri Lankan army stopped their regular patrols of the streets of Jaffna. Taking immediate advantage of this the LTTE mined all roads leading out of the army camps, and proceeded thereafter to build barricades across them. The next step was to convert makeshift barricades into concrete bunkers. As a result the army in Jaffna fort could only be supplied by air. The armed Tamil separatist groups now had effective control over the Jaffna peninsula.

The guerrillas and terrorists seldom directed their attacks against the security forces in open confrontations. When they did so the attacks were generally repulsed. So they chose softer and easier targets—unarmed Sinhalese peasants in the remoter areas of the north-central and eastern regions. The most serious of such attacks occurred on 14 May 1985. A heavily-armed group of terrorists made a surprise raid on Anuradhapura, killing nearly 150 civilians. Attacks on civilians became more frequent thereafter. A new pattern became evident in these attacks in 1986. Large numbers of Sinhalese peasants were shot or hacked to death in the east of the island during the relaxed atmosphere of religious festivals in May and June.

By this time the Tamil separatist groups had become a formidable guerrilla force, much stronger than their Indian mentors had believed they would ever be. The Sri Lanka government for its part was compelled to divert an increasing proportion of its annual budget to the expansion and equipping of its armed forces. There was also an escalation of military action against these Tamil separatist groups in the north and east.[13] The Sri Lankan armed forces were now better equipped and better trained than before. Much of the training was done in Pakistan, while small groups of Israelis and British mercenaries honed the skills of special counter-terrorist units in the army and police.

As clashes between the security forces and the Tamil separatist activists became more frequent and casualties increased, India's mediatory role gave way to a return to the Indira Gandhi policy of a diplomatic offensive against Sri Lanka; thus a propaganda blitz was conducted through its embassies and High Commissions abroad, accusing the government of human rights violations. Sri Lankan and Indian diplomats clashed at the United Nations in New York and Geneva, all parts of a policy of 'moral' sanctions aimed at persuading Sri Lanka to return to the bargaining table.[14] The Indian embassy in Washington and the High Commissions in Ottawa and London in the meantime continued to be centres of support for Tamil separatist groups operating in those countries. Indian newspapers, led by *The Hindu*, gave their support to this Indian government-inspired campaign.[15] At a different level, the Sri Lankan government found traditional Western arms suppliers reluctant to supply arms to Sri Lankan forces, and most of the Western powers were unwilling also to provide training facilities on any large scale for them. All of them were anxious not to give offence to India.

In the meantime the mediatory role was renewed with the visit of P. Chidambaram, the youthful union state minister for personnel, who arrived in the island with a delegation of officials in May 1986.[16] Chidambaram was an aspirant to political leadership in Tamil Nadu on behalf of Congress I. In choosing him to replace Romesh Bhandari as head of the Indian negotiating team, India was perhaps signalling a tougher stand in the negotiating process. Assisting Chidambaram at the New Delhi end was another Indian with distinct pro-Tamil sympathies, A.P. Venkateswaran, India's new Foreign Secretary.

The discussions Chidambaram conducted while in Colombo sought to build upon the foundation provided in the H.W. Jayewardene— Bhandari proposals of July–August 1985. They went beyond these to the extent that as far as the provincial structure envisaged in those earlier proposals was concerned, the model was now, quite explicitly, the states of the Indian union, but with powers that fell short of those in India because of the constraints imposed by Sri Lanka's constitutionally-entrenched unitary structure, which was to remain undisturbed. Nevertheless, a radical reconstruction of Sri Lanka's political and administrative system was the aim. These proposals were published by the Sri Lankan government on 9 July 1986. The TULF and the Tamil separatist groups continued to press for the creation of a single regional unit, encompassing the northern and eastern provinces as a Tamil ethno-region, but this was unacceptable to the Sri Lankan government as well as to the main opposition party, the Sri Lanka Freedom Party (SLFP). The LTTE remained firmly committed to a separate Tamil state.

President Jayewardene summoned a second conference, this time of political parties only (PPC), to discuss the proposals that emerged from Chidambaram's initiative. The *sangha* representatives were not invited on this occasion. The conference began its sessions in June 1986. The SLFP refused to participate in its deliberations. However, all the other parties, including the traditional Left, not represented in Parliament, participated in the conference. These deliberations continued for the next three months, and in general endorsed the proposals submitted for discussion. In many instances the discussions helped to clarify issues, and to identify potential points of difficulty and ambiguity.

By the time President Jayewardene and Prime Minister Rajiv Gandhi met next, at the South Asia Association for Regional Co-operation (SAARC), in Bangalore in November 1986, so much progress had been made that the Indian government for the first time imposed restrictions on Sri Lankan Tamil activists operating from Indian territory. The initiatives of the Indian government in this regard were nullified by the Tamil Nadu government's unconcealed reluctance to co-operate in these moves. But Velupillai Prabhakaran of the LTTE, the most prominent of the Tamil separatist leaders, thought it prudent to move across the Palk straits to the Jaffna peninsula and continue to fight from there.

Throughout the second half of 1986 Indian mediators made a sustained effort to break the deadlock over the creation of a Tamil ethno-region in the north and east of the island. They recommended the division of the eastern province into three units, one Muslim, one Tamil and one Sinhalese, with the Tamil unit being linked to the northern province by a narrow land corridor. When this proposal won no support, least of all among the Tamils, the Indian negotiators proposed the excision of the Sinhalese parliamentary electorate of Amparai from the Batticaloa district of the eastern province so that the Tamil ethnic component in the province would reach a level of near-parity with the other ethnic groups there. This formed part of the 19 December 1986 formula, which the Indian government proposed as the basis for further negotiations between the Sri Lankan government and the Tamils.[17] The LTTE, however, rejected this formula as totally unacceptable.

Prabhakaran's return to the island marked the beginning of a more activist and violent phase in the ongoing conflict between the Tamil separatist groups spearheaded by the LTTE, and the Sri Lankan forces. In early 1987 the LTTE was believed to be on the verge of making a unilateral declaration of independence in the north of the island. Treating this as a gravely provocative move, the government sent troop reinforcements into the eastern and northern provinces with instructions to clear these areas of the LTTE and other separatist groups. Contrary to expectations, the LTTE did not put up much of a fight. The LTTE's retreat was anything but orderly. They fled to the Jaffna peninsula.

The Indian government, apparently much perturbed by this turn of events, urged the Sri Lankan government to abandon these military moves and to continue with a search for a political solution. In response, the Sri Lankan government offered the Tamils a cease-fire for the duration of the national holidays in April. The LTTE spurned this offer and responded with the Good Friday bus massacre where 130 people were killed by machine-gun fire on the road from Trincomalee to Colombo, and they followed it up with a bomb explosion in Colombo's main bus station in which over a hundred people were killed.

Faced with the prospect of a serious erosion of political support as a result of these outrages, the government decided to make an attempt to regain control of the Jaffna peninsula. 'Operation Liberation', which began on 26 May 1987 in the Vadamarachchi division on the north-eastern part of the peninsula, was directed at preventing the hitherto easy movement of men and *matériel* from Tamil Nadu. By the end of May Sri Lankan forces had gained control of this area. The LTTE, the most formidable Tamil separatist group, had suffered a major setback, and in a region they had dominated for a long time. It was this demonstration of the LTTE's failure as a fighting force that triggered off the chain of events that resulted eventually in Indian military intervention in Sri Lanka's ethnic conflict.

At this point India moved swiftly to prevent the capture of Jaffna by the Sri Lankan forces. The first move came from Tamil Nadu with a well-publicized monetary grant of US$3.2 million to the LTTE and its allies. The Indian government, for its part, announced that it was sending shipments of food and petroleum products to Jaffna, which, it claimed, was facing a severe shortage of these items through a blockade by the Sri Lankan forces. Despite the refusal of the Sri Lankan government to accept this offer, or concede the need for it, a first shipment in a flotilla of about twenty Indian fishing-vessels was dispatched on 3 June 1987 but was turned back by the Sri Lankan navy. When this happened, the Indian air force in a blatant violation of international law and of the Sri Lankan airspace dropped food and medical supplies in Jaffna on the following day. All these actions constituted an unmistakable demonstration of Indian support for the Tamil separatist movement in Sri Lanka. The Indian supply of food to Jaffna continued over the next few weeks by sea with the formal but clearly reluctant agreement of the Sri Lankan government. The result was that by the end of June, Indo-Sri Lankan relations were mired in mutual recrimination and deep suspicion. And the island's ethnic conflict seemed headed for prolonged and debilitating deadlock. However, the LTTE had been saved from humiliation by the intervention of India.

IV

The intermediary as combatant: India in Sri Lanka, July 1987 to 1990

The tensions and dramas of the early days of June were followed by weeks of mutual recrimination between the two countries. On the diplomatic scene stalemate and immobility replaced the frenetic activity of May and early June. Yet in the first two weeks of July an exchange of political signals set the two governments on the road to serious negotiations to break the deadlock. The initiative came from India with the offer to underwrite the implementation of a political programme that would ensure the end of the current ethnic conflict in the island. In return the Sri Lankan government was urged to consent formally to implement that substance of the agreements reached on devolution and related subjects in the negotiations which had taken place between 1985 and 1987. There was a second proviso: the Sri Lankan authorities were asked to agree to a link between the northern and eastern provinces, the large Tamil ethno-region on which the Tamil political activists had set their hearts. This was the final step in the adoption of the devolution package which the TULF as well as the armed separatist groups had demanded since 1983, and which the Sri Lankan government and the SLFP had refused to consider, much less to accept. A loophole was left to make the offer more palatable to the government: the link would be a temporary one, and its fate would eventually be decided by a referendum to be held in the eastern province. Even so, there was no mistaking the enormity of the political risks inherent in its acceptance by the government. Once this was agreed upon, the negotiations proceeded beyond the devolution issue to foreign policy matters related this time to India's security consensus and interests.

The news that an accord was about to be signed leaked out despite all the efforts of the negotiating teams to keep the discussions as confidential as possible. The opposition parties and the JVP sensed much more accurately than the government the public mood of hostility to an agreement with India so soon after the humiliation inflicted on Sri Lanka in early June. The accord ignited massive protests in the country in the last week of July. The opposition was partly a reflection of an innate hostility to Indian pressure, partly a rejection of the more controversial features of the accord such as the link between the northern and eastern provinces, but much more because of the antipathy if not antagonism to Rajiv Gandhi for his violation of Sri Lankan air space, which had occurred just six weeks earlier.

President Jayewardene decided to brave the hostility of the opposition forces, and went ahead with preparations for the signing of this controversial and fateful accord. On 29 July Rajiv Gandhi arrived in Colombo to sign it on behalf of India.[18]

The main points of the accord were:

- a complete cessation of hostilities, and the surrender of all weapons held by the Tamil separatist activists, within seventy-two hours of the implementation of the accord;
- the provision of Indian military assistance to help with its implementation (more than 7,000 Indian troops were drafted in August);
- the establishment of a system of provincial councils in the island, based on the island's nine provincial units;
- the joining together of the northern and eastern provinces into one administrative unit with an elected provincial council there (to be elected within three months);
- the holding of a referendum in the eastern province to determine whether the mixed population of Tamils, Sinhalese and Muslims there would support its merger with the northern province into a single Tamil-dominated province;
- a general amnesty for all Tamil separatist activists in custody, imprisoned or facing charges, after the general surrender of arms;
- the repatriation of about 100,000 Tamil refugees in India to Sri Lanka;
- the resumption of the repatriation of Indian citizens from Sri Lanka, under the terms of agreements reached between the governments of Sri Lanka and India in 1964 and 1974;
- the prevention of the use of Indian territory by Tamil militants for military or propaganda purposes; the prevention of the military use

of Sri Lankan ports, Trincomalee in particular, by any country in a manner prejudicial to Indian interests; and
• a provision that Tamil and English have equal status with Sinhala as official languages.

Although the Cabinet eventually approved the signing of the accord, the divisions among Cabinet members on this issue could not be concealed. Lalith Athulathmudali, as Minister of National Security, was the most consistent critic. Prime Minister R. Premadasa was scarcely less hostile. Much of the opposition was based on personal antagonism to Rajiv Gandhi; some of it reflected a sense of despair at the political risks incurred by the government; and some of it stemmed from the foreign policy implications, and especially its infringement of Sri Lanka's sovereignty, beginning with the use and entry of Indian troops to supervise and enforce the cease-fire. The Sri Lankan government opted for an Indian army presence for this purpose for two reasons: the need for speedy implementation of the accord within two weeks or a month; and because such an Indian contingent would be more acceptable to the Tamils, who would more readily surrender their arms to them rather than to the Sri Lankan security forces, with whom they had been in conflict for so long, or to a Commonwealth/UN peace-keeping force. Another point of division related to the following clause in Annexure I of the agreement:

5. The Prime Minister of India and the President of Sri Lanka agree that a joint Indo-Sri Lanka observer group consisting of qualified representatives of the Government of India and the Government of Sri Lanka should monitor the cessation of hostilities from 31 July 1987.

The general feeling was that an international observer group, or even a Commonwealth group would be better than an Indian contingent. It appeared that India had strong objections to such groups in this instance, and India had its way.

As for Indian security concerns set out in the annexure to the accord, Sri Lanka, for its part, would not, at any cost, want to be involved in any military use of ports—particularly Trincomalee—by other nations, especially any military use directed against India. The attempt to restrict if not ban the employment by Sri Lanka of foreign military and intelligence personnel directly concerned Sri Lanka's own interests and was seen as a constraint on its choices in security. The references related to an Israeli presence in Sri Lanka, and to British mercenary groups engaged in training Sri Lankan forces. The resort to these had been forced upon Sri Lanka by Indian pressure on Great Britain and other countries likely to be of assistance to Sri Lanka to desist from establishing training facilities for Sri Lankan forces in the island. The Indian offer to provide training facilities and military supplies for Sri Lankan security forces was regarded as one-sided when the threat to Sri Lankan security was, and still is, seen to come from India alone.

The signing of the accord led to violent protests and widespread civil unrest among the Sinhalese majority in and around Colombo and in the south-west of the country. These demonstrations had the support of the SLFP, of sections of the *sangha*, and of a revived Janatha Vimukthi Peramuna (JVP). Rajiv Gandhi himself narrowly escaped serious injury, if not death itself, when an enraged sailor swung his rifle butt at him at the guard of honour ceremony prior to the Indian Prime Minister's departure from Colombo.

Although many risks were expected in any progress towards the stabilization of the accord (given the opposition of the SLFP, the Prime Minister and of several other members of the Cabinet), the early indications seemed encouraging. Sri Lankan security forces in the northern and eastern provinces returned to their barracks and the paramilitary forces there were disarmed as part of the Sri Lankan government's obligations under the accord. The LTTE began a symbolic handing-over of arms. However, it is in the nature of things that peace accords seldom work according to the wishes of those who negotiate them. The early signs of progress proved to be deceptive.

If a swift pacification of the north and east was envisaged by the Indian and the Sri Lankan governments, they were quickly disillusioned. The Indian Peace-Keeping Force (IPKF) entered Sri Lanka under the assumption that they would be welcomed in the Tamil areas of the north and the east as liberators and that the separatist forces would quickly and willingly surrender their arms to them. What happened was that its presence was very soon resented by the Tigers, who decided to defy them. They began with attacks on their Tamil rivals, of whom nearly 150 were killed. The massacre of about two hundred Sinhalese in the eastern province shortly thereafter (in September) led to a toughening of the Indian attitude.

Urgent discussions between President Jayewardene and Prime Minister Gandhi brought into force part of the hidden agenda of the peace accord, that Indian troops would eventually be used against the LTTE. With practically world-wide condemnation of the LTTE, and severe criticism of India for its failure to maintain the peace, the Indian government at last decided to disarm the LTTE, and to make an effort to destroy it as a political force.

Accordingly the IPKF now moved in to disarm the LTTE, and when faced with resistance from the latter, launched a major attack on the LTTE strongholds in the Jaffna town and peninsula in the second week of October. Despite stiff opposition from the LTTE, which necessitated the deployment of thousands of reinforcements, the LTTE's hold on the peninsula was eventually broken.[19] Both the Indian army and the LTTE suffered heavy casualties, but those who suffered most were the people of Jaffna and the Jaffna peninsula as the Indian army set about its business of defeating the LTTE with a heavy-handed professionalism.

The Indian Peace-Keeping Force (IPKF) proved to be a propaganda disaster for India.[20] Its presence in the island and in such large numbers was a self-defeating exercise. Its size, variously estimated at between 75,000 and 100,000 at its peak, was larger than the *whole* British element of the Indian army in the days of the raj,[21] more than half the size of the Soviet army in Afghanistan in the 1980s. Besides, it was all located within an area of about 10,000 square kilometres. The Indian policy seemed to be one of saturating an area by throwing in enormous numbers of troops into action, and seeking to submerge the LTTE that way. This was only partially successful, however. Despite the size of the army, it was not able to eliminate the LTTE. It thus opened itself to the charge that it was *either* inefficient and incapable of carrying out the task, *or* that it was not intended to eliminate the LTTE. Either way it eventually eroded India's credibility as an impartial peace-keeper.

The LTTE, defeated but not decisively so, continued to oppose the IPKF and the accord from their jungle hideouts in the northern province to which they had retreated. The IPKF's presence became the catalyst for confusion and violence in some of the Sinhalese areas, especially in the southern province, which presented the Sri Lankan government with a challenge of very serious proportions to its authority. Apart from acts of sabotage, the violence that ensued resulted in the death of hundreds of Sinhalese, in particular supporters of the government, at the hands of the JVP which unleashed its second major insurrection against a Sri Lankan government in less than twenty years. In the scale of violence and the number of deaths, this rebellion was far more destructive than that of 1971.

There was thus an ultimate irony: the Indian government, which intervened to prevent the destruction of the LTTE by the Sri Lankan army earlier in the year, was doing it on its own; the Indian government which objected to the Sri Lankan army taking Jaffna city, used the

Indian Peace-Keeping Force (IPKF) to storm the city and in that process inflicted much heavier casualties and far greater hardships on the people of the Jaffna peninsula than anything done so far by the Sri Lankan security forces. The Indian government, which accused the Sri Lankan forces of violations of human rights in their confrontations with Tamil separatist groups, now found itself facing similar charges, and with even greater frequency.

The opprobrium attached to the Indo-Sri Lankan accord was focused on its architects within the government, and especially President Jayewardene. The JVP, the most vocal, violent and consistent critics of the accord, called for his assassination through posters and inflammatory speeches. The slogan 'kill JR' was scrawled on walls in all parts of the country, and painted in white across public highways. On 18 August 1987 the JVP very nearly succeeded in assassinating him within the parliamentary complex. One District Minister was killed on that occasion, and several Cabinet Ministers and MPs seriously injured. Earlier, one MP had been killed by the JVP in the violence that broke out in the wake of the signing of the accord on 31 July 1987.

Over the next fifteen months the JVP assassinated one Cabinet Minister and one District Minister, as well as the Chairman and Secretary of the UNP. Several MPs narrowly escaped death at the hands of the JVP. It is estimated that over a thousand UNP cadres were killed during this period. The object of this violence, in the early stages, was to prevent the implementation of the legislative programme envisaged in the Indo-Sri Lankan accord. That this programme was implemented at all was due in the main to the political skills and personal courage of President Jayewardene. When Parliament debated the 13th amendment to the constitution, which made provision for the establishment of a system of provincial councils— by far the most controversial part of this programme—the security precautions taken within and outside Parliament were unparalleled in the history of the country's national legislature.

These councils were constituted in the teeth of opposition from the SLFP and the JVP. Elections were conducted to all these councils— including the council of the north-east province— between April and November 1988. The campaign was conducted by President Jayewardene with a few of his Cabinet colleagues while influential sections of the government stood conspicuously aloof. The elections to the seven councils in the Sinhalese areas were boycotted by the SLFP and JVP and the latter mounted a sustained campaign of violence against the candidates and their key supporters. The election of the council of the north-east province took place in November under the auspices of the IPKF.[22] The LTTE boycotted it, and the JVP's campaign in the Sinhalese areas of that province was totally effective.

The UNP won a majority in seven of the provinces; and the newly created left-of-centre coalition, the United Socialist Alliance, emerged as the main opposition. A left-wing coalition, the Eelam People's Revolutionary Liberation Front (EPRLF) won control of the north-east provincial council, in an election marred by systematic vote-rigging for which the IPKF was generally believed to have been responsible.[23]

The last quarter of 1988 were months of turmoil and instability as the JVP made a concerted bid to bring the government down through hartals, strikes, systematic acts of sabotage, the closure of schools and universities, and prison riots, quite apart from the assassination of prominent politicians and the killing of hundreds of supporters of the government. In October, in an attempt to arrest the escalating violence, the government invoked emergency regulations, imposed strict curfews in troubled areas, and deployed armed riot police and the army. The JVP campaign of destabilization reached its peak in the first two weeks of November. Strong measures taken by President Jayewardene kept the JVP at bay.

In September 1988 he had announced that he would not seek a third term in office, and on 9 October he handed over the leadership of the party to Ranasinghe Premadasa, whose selection as the UNP candidate for the forthcoming Presidential election was secured without opposition. The SLFP chose Mrs Sirimavo Bandaranaike as its candidate for the presidential election, and she obtained the support of a group of smaller parties in a coalition—the Democratic People's Alliance. However, attempts to bring in the JVP and the LTTE failed, as did all efforts to secure nomination of a single opposition candidate. The Sri Lanka Mahajana Pakshaya (SLMP), part of the United Socialist Alliance, put up a candidate of its own.

The election took place on 19 December in an environment of phenomenal violence directed by the JVP and was boycotted by both the LTTE and JVP. Only around 55 per cent of the electorate voted, a very sharp drop from earlier elections. Ranasinghe Premadasa gained 50.4 per cent of the votes for a narrow victory. The SLFP and the SLMP secured 44 per cent and 4.6 per cent of the vote respectively.

The new president was sworn in on 2 January 1989 and appointed an interim cabinet. In a conciliatory gesture to the JVP and LTTE alike, the new president decided to repeal the state of emergency which had been in force since May 1983. JVP activists taken into custody on a variety of charges were released. Premadasa invited all groups to take part in the electoral process for the forthcoming parliamentary elections. The JVP, however, intensified its bloody disruption of the campaigning for the general election, and the general election itself. The parliamentary election of 15 February, the first under proportional representation, saw the UNP securing 125 scats in the 225-member Parliament, while the SLFP who obtained 30 per cent of the votes won 66 seats. The total poll was only 64 per cent.

President Premadasa was under intense pressure from the beginning of his tenure of office, primarily from the JVP; a shared antipathy to the presence of the IPKF on Sri Lankan soil did little to reduce the JVP's opposition to the new government, and new President. Premadasa for his part was publicly committed to securing the withdrawal of the IPKF, and treated this as the most important political challenge he faced.

In a surprising move in May the LTTE responded to a call for talks with the government. The group at whom this invitation had been directed, the JVP, however, rejected it and continued its campaign of violence and terror. The JVP focused its attention on the IPKF's continued presence in the island and began an anti-India agitation. To keep the initiative in his own hands President Premadasa made a public demand, on 1 June, that the IPKF be withdrawn from the island by 31 July. This only served to strain relations between the two countries and between himself and Rajiv Gandhi. The upshot was that the departure of the IPKF, which the Indian government had planned to complete by the end of 1989, in time for the elections in India scheduled for late 1989 and early 1990, was eventually delayed by two to three months. In the first few months of 1989, five battalions of the IPKF left the island. However, this process came to a halt between 1 June and 29 July.

All this did little to check the JVP's campaign of violence. Indeed it reached a climax in June and July when a JVP front organization compelled bus workers in the state service to come out on strike. This strike was unique in the annals of industrial action in Sri Lanka in that the workers were compelled at gun-point to stop work. Over a hundred bus workers who sought to defy the strike call were killed by the JVP. The government conceded all the 'demands' the JVP front organization made on behalf of the strikers. The JVP followed this with a closure of all hospitals, including private hospitals, a brutal assertion of their power with a callous disregard of humanitarian considerations, again something unique in the annals of terrorist activity in any part of the world.

Under pressure from the security forces, the state of emergency was reimposed on 20 June 1989. The government parliamentary party resolved to reimpose the emergency, and President Premadasa implemented that decision. Within a month the security forces, under the leadership and direction provided by Ranjan Wijeratne, Foreign Minister, and State Minister for Defence, began to face up successfully to the challenge of the JVP. In the meantime, as a result of the relatively successful two-month round of direct negotiations between the government and the LTTE, the latter announced that it would transform its temporary cease-fire agreement with the Sri Lankan army into a permanent cessation of hostilities. The government for its part announced that it would henceforth collaborate with the LTTE to secure the withdrawal of the IPKF from Sri Lanka. The IPKF for its part, responded with a renewed offensive against the LTTE.

In August the government was teetering on the brink of collapse under attacks from the JVP. In a bid to widen his base of political support, Premadasa convened an all-party conference (APC) to discuss the country's multi-faceted political crisis. When the APC met for the first time under Premadasa's leadership some 70 delegates from 21 'parties' including the LTTE and the more moderate Tamil groups, participated. The JVP stayed conspicuously and truculently aloof. The first sessions of the APC co-incided with an announcement that the governments of Sri Lanka and India, following four months of acrimonious dispute and negotiation would sign an agreement in Colombo. This was signed on 18 September. India committed itself to make 'all efforts' to withdraw all its troops by the end of 1989; the IPKF was to declare an immediate unilateral cease-fire against the LTTE. In return, the Sri Lankan government agreed to establish a peace committee for the north-east province in an effort to reconcile the various Tamil groups and to incorporate members of the LTTE into the peaceful administration of the province. A co-ordinating committee for the withdrawal of the IPKF was established in mid-October. The IPKF began the final phase of its departure on 18 October. The LTTE had been saved from annihilation for a second time — on this occasion by the Sri Lankan government.

Over the next two months the whole political scene in the country was transformed. Between September 1989 and the end of January 1990 the Sri Lankan security forces effectively destroyed the JVP as a political force. Every member — save one individual — of the JVP's politbureau, including its leader Rohana Wijeweera, was killed, as were most members of the district-level leadership. The anti-JVP campaign, successful though it was, also revealed a curious lack of leadership in the top echelons of the government. Unlike in 1971 when Mrs Bandaranaike and senior Cabinet Ministers of her coalition government gave a clear political leadership to the forces who crushed the JVP on that occasion, in 1989–90 only Ranjan Wijeratne did so. Indeed the credit for the political direction of the successful anti-JVP campaign must go to him.

In the meantime the withdrawal of the IPKF continued apace. It was completed at the end of March 1990 under the new Indian government. The change of government in India did not lead to the hastening of the process of withdrawal, nor did it lead, immediately, to any real improvement in relations between India and Sri Lanka.

The departure of the IPKF left a vacuum in the north and east of the island, which the LTTE filled with the acquiescence of the government. The LTTE's morale was high: its leadership was intact, and it was better armed than at any time since 1987. It proceeded to stake a claim to a monopoly of power in the north and east of the island. During 1989 and 1990, even as it continued its negotiations with the government, the LTTE began rendering all their Tamil opponents in the north and east ineffective. Several prominent Tamil leaders were killed by the LTTE. This included TULF leaders Appapillai Amirthalingam, and M. Yogeswaram (former TULF MP for Jaffna city), killed in Colombo on 18 July 1989, and later on the leader of the People's Liberation Organization of Tamil Eelam (PLOTE), Uma Maheswaran, an arch-rival of LTTE leader Velupillai Prabhakaran. In April 1990 a prominent eastern province Tamil MP, Samuel Tambimuttu and his wife were shot and killed in the heart of Colombo's exclusive residential area, the Cinnamon Gardens by LTTE activists.

The LTTE made no attempt to lay down arms even on a symbolic basis. Neither the Sri Lankan police, nor the Sri Lankan army were permitted to operate freely in the north and east. The government had virtually conceded the LTTE demand that their forces should take over from the IPKF.

Thus a fragile peace was maintained while talks continued between the government and the LTTE till early June 1990 when quite unexpectedly the LTTE attacked the police in the Batticaloa and Trincomalee districts. Attempts to establish a cease-fire broke down, and the Sri Lankan security forces began a counter-attack. Why the LTTE should have chosen this moment to attack is a mystery. It is clear, however, that they had made elaborate plans to consolidate their position by building bunkers and mining all the roads in the north and east. They confronted Sri Lankan security forces who were not merely better trained and much larger numerically than they had been in 1987, but whose morale was high after its successful anti-JVP campaign. The fighting was severe, but by the end of July 1990 the Sri Lankan forces had established control over most parts of the north-eastern province outside the densely populated Jaffna peninsula.

The LTTE maintained its reputation for ruthlessness by its brutal massacre of nearly six hundred unarmed Sinhalese and Muslim policemen who had surrendered to them on or around 11 June. Then in the evening of 19 June, a LTTE execution squad operating in Tamil Nadu, raided a block of apartments in which the leadership of the EPRLF lived as refugees in Madras, and killed thirteen of them. Among the victims was Gnanasangari Yogasangari, MP for the Jaffna district, and K. Pathmanabha, Secretary General of the EPRLF. The victims were unarmed. The LTTE carried AK-47 assault rifles. The killing of unarmed Sinhalese peasants in the east and the border regions of the north-central province has continued apace. Scores have been killed. Then in a particularly brutal attack they killed nearly 200 Muslims during their Friday prayer evening at Kattankudy, a suburb of Batticaloa, on 3 August. They repeated it ten days later (Sunday, 12 August) by the massacre of a hundred Muslims at Eravur, near Batticaloa.

The battle for the LTTE strongholds in the Jaffna peninsula is likely to be a long and arduous one.

V

Conclusion: A conflict of illusions: Sri Lankan and Indian

It is still too early to pass judgement on the Indo-Sri Lankan Accord, but it seems that many of its shortcomings are the inevitable result of the conflicting illusions on which it was based. For the Indian government, the first illusion was that the enormous popularity that Indians enjoyed in Jaffna in June 1987 in the aftermath of the distribution of food there could be the basis of extracting support for a compromise settlement which called for sacrifices from all parties. The second illusion was that clients would inevitably do the bidding of their mentor, even when they were called upon to do many things they found unacceptable and unpalatable. The IPKF soon found that popularity and gratitude are the most ephemeral of political commodities; and that intruding foreign armies are hailed as liberators, only to be denounced, within a very short time, as arrogant and bumbling invaders.

The third of the illusions was one that the Sri Lankan government shared with its Indian counterpart, at least to the extent of a naïve belief that the Indian intervention would not only underwrite a complex and controversial settlement, but also impose it speedily on the Tamil separatists. The fundamental assumption on which the Sri Lankan government consented to accept the accord was that the separatist groups were clients of India, and would do as they were told by their Indian mentors.

The most unreal part of the accord lay in the speed with which some of the most complex issues were to have been settled: a cease-fire in forty-eight hours; the completion of the demilitarization process—the handing-over of arms by the Tamil separatist forces—within seventy-two hours; and, just as unreal, the completion of the political process involved in the introduction of the devolution package incorporated in the accord, within about six months. The devolution package would inevitably involve detailed and controversial legislation, thereafter a difficult process of institution-building, and of course the hard campaigning at elections in an atmosphere of violence.

For the Tamils, in general, especially the Tamils in the north of the island, the illusion was that the Indian forces would be infinitely better as protectors of the civil population, and as guardians of law and order, than the Sri Lankan police and armed services. They had few objections, if any at all, to India underwriting a compromise settlement. When battles broke out between the IPKF and the LTTE, and the civilian population of Jaffna was caught in the cross fire and suffered heavy casualties, quite apart from the privations imposed on them in the temporary relocation centres to which they were sent, the disenchantment was all the greater because illusions were being shattered. The IPKF, substantially larger than the Sri Lankan forces in Jaffna ever were, was more heavy handed in their treatment of the people than their Sri Lankan counterparts.

The various Tamil separatist groups, funded, protected and nurtured by Tamil Nadu, and infiltrated by Indian agents paid for by the Research and Analysis Wing (RAW), India's counterpart of the CIA, had their own illusions. They welcomed the departure of the Sri Lankan police and security forces to their barracks and looked forward to political contests for the provincial councils and Parliament. The TULF looked forward to playing a political role under the new system. The LTTE alone had no illusions. They had prevailed over their Tamil rivals despite all the efforts of RAW to prevent their success, and they were intent on playing their own game, and dancing to their own tunes.

There was yet another illusion. India generally assumed a tone of smug superiority in regard to Sri Lanka's ethnic conflict. Indian spokesmen convinced themselves and sought to convince the world that there was a 'qualitative difference' between the treatment of minorities in India and Sri Lanka; that, for instance, the Sikhs had less to complain about and fight against than the Tamils of Sri Lanka.[24] Thus Indian politicians—and some Indian journalists—sought to justify Indian intervention in Sri Lankan affairs, as mediator, and later on as combatant, on the specious grounds of a special quality of harshness in the Sinhalese treatment of the Tamils. There was, in fact, no great difference in the treatment of and attitude to minorities in India and Sri Lanka. However, if there is a single lesson to be drawn from the history of India's mediation and interventionist role in Sri Lanka's ethnic conflict, it is that most outside powers have less to offer by way of example in their own political system and political experience than they think they have. To be drawn into an ethnic conflict in a neighbouring state is the worst folly for a regional power no less than for a superpower, as Israel and Syria have learned or still are learning in the Lebanon, and India has learned in Sri Lanka.

India has paid an enormous price for this intervention. The IPKF itself has cost India something like Sri Lankan Rs.50 billion, and while it may be argued that a great deal of this money would have been spent on this force even if it remained in India, still the extra cost involved in maintaining troops in a foreign country would have been very considerable. Besides, at least 1,000 Indian soldiers have lost their lives in this exercise and more than double this number were injured, some severely so, and many maimed by the landmines and anti-personnel mines in the laying of which the LTTE has shown an expertise for which their Indian training should be given some of the credit. There is also that great intangible—the loss of prestige and the sense of failure, in short a propaganda disaster all the more unpalatable because of the moral high ground that India took in this exercise in *real politik*. At the time the IPKF entered Sri Lanka, only the Sinhalese were suspicious of it, and were opposed to it. At the end of two years even the Tamils are opposed to it, all except political groups associated with the EPRLF. The gains were few.

Through these experiences one bitter lesson emerges: it is often easier to end an international conflict than a civil conflict, especially where the latter is essentially an ethnic one. It is difficult to fashion an outcome that is intermediate between victory or defeat for one of the combatants. Yet conflict resolution requires an outcome that has something for everyone. Parties to the conflict cannot be expected to give up their claims without receiving some compensation, and this implies a willingness to compromise on some at least of the underlying issues. The LTTE, like the JVP, has never shown any readiness to compromise. Then again, because civil violence is often less well organized than international war, conflict resolution is much more difficult, since even a small number of unsatisfied participants can make it impossible to end the quarrelling.[25] All these are lessons that emerged from the Sri Lanka conflict, and the Indian involvement.

Outside intervention in a civil conflict can take many forms. First of all, the intervenor could begin by giving aid to one or other of the participants, or cut off such aid. This assistance may be to encourage the continuation of the struggle, to compel or persuade one or other of the participants to alter its strategy, or even to encourage a settlement. Second, the intervenor may try to resolve the conflict itself by acting as a mediator, applying sanctions to one, some or all parties, or underwriting a settlement. Third, the intervenor may become the common enemy which unites the warring factions against it.[26] The Indian intervention in the Sri Lankan conflict has the unique distinction of taking all these forms.

Notes

1. On the politics of linguistic nationalism in India, see Marguerite R. Barnett, *The Politics of Cultural Nationalism in South India*, Princeton, NJ, 1976. Robert Hardgrave, Jr, *The Dravidian Movement* (Bombay, 1965). Eugene F. Irschick, *Politics and Social Conflict in South India: The Non-Brahman Movement and Tamil Separatists, 1916–1929* (University of California Press, Berkeley and Los Angeles, 1969; and *Tamil Revivalism in the 1930's*, Madras, 1986.
2. The journal *India Today* published an adulatory essay on Prabhakaran in its issue of 30 June 1986. In an interview he gave to this journal he claimed that he 'shot and killed the former mayor of Jaffna, Alfred Duraiappah [sic]' Durayappa was a member of the SLFP, the core of the then governing coalition, and the hostility to him flowed for them.
3. For discussion of this theme, see K.M. de Silva 'Decentralization and Regionalism in the Management of Sri Lanka's Ethnic Conflict', *International Journal of Group Tensions*, 14 (4) 1989, pp. 317–38.
4. See Mrs Gandhi's speech to the Lok Sabha, 12 August 1983 for a cogent restatement of this view. The text of the speech was published in *The Times of India*, 13 August 1983.
5. For a brief review of the problems relating to the voting rights of immigrant Indians in Sri Lanka, see K.M. de Silva *Managing Ethnic Tensions in Multi-*

Ethnic Societies: Sri Lanka 1880–1985, Lanham, Md 1985, pp. 105–10.
6. See *India Today*, 31 March 1984 pp. 84–94, see particularly the essay in investigative reporting entitled 'Sri Lanka Rebels: An Ominous Presence in Tamil Nadu', also *The Sunday Times* (London), 1 April 1984, and Reuter reports on these bases published in Sri Lanka in the *Sun* of 23 May 1984, and the *Island* of 25 May 1984. See also the London-based journal *South: the Third World Magazine*, March 1985, pp. 14–15. See also *Time International*, 3 April 1989, pp. 10–11, for a later account.
7. The Inspector General of Police in Madras, Mr Mohandas, announced on 11 August that five persons, including two Sri Lankan Tamil activists had been arrested on charges of involvement in this incident; and he divulged the fact that the bombs had been assembled in a house in a Madras suburb. *The Hindu*, 12 August 1984.
8. There is a large Tamil population in Bombay and its suburbs, and this has been the source of support to the Tamil cause. One of the key figures in this was an underworld boss, Mudaliyar, a Tamil. Sri Lankan Tamils are now very prominent in Bombay's underworld, and especially its drug trade. See the Indian journal *Sunday*, 31 July–6 August 1988, which carried an article entitled 'Sri Lankan Tamils in Bombay's Underworld'.
9. One of the Indian delegates to the UN General Assembly was S. Ramachandran, a Minister of the Tamil Nadu State government. On 21 October 1983 he addressed the special Political Committee and raised the question of Sri Lankan refugees in Tamil Nadu. See the official publication issued by the Indian Mission to the United Nations, *Indian News*, 21 October 1983.

Ramachandran's speech was on Agenda Item 74: International co-operation to Avert New Flows of Refugees.

On 27 September 1984, Mr Mirdha, an Indian delegate made much the same points in a statement on behalf of his country at a general debate at the 39th session of the UN General Assembly.
10. Official records of the UN Geneva office show that in 1983, 1984 and 1985 Indian delegates raised the issue of human rights violations in Sri Lanka at meetings of the Commission on Human Rights, and the Sub-commission on Prevention of Discrimination and Protection of Minorities. Of particular interest in this regard is the speech of M.C. Bandhare, a member of the Subcommission on Prevention of Discrimination and Protection of Minorities in Geneva, 21 August 1984.
11. This document entitled 'Draft Framework of Terms of Accord and Understanding', dated 30 August 1985, was initialled on behalf of the Sri Lankan government by H.W. Jayewardene, and on behalf of the Indian government by an Indian official.
12. For three days beginning 29 April 1986 the LTTE turned their guns on their TELO rivals and crushed them remorsely. The TELO leader Sri Sabaratnam was among those killed. For an account of what happened on that occasion, see *The Hindu*, 13 May 1986, an article entitled 'The Wounds in the People's Psyche are Deeper'.
13. For an assessment of the military situation in Sri Lanka at this time, see Colonel Edgar O'Ballance, 'Sri Lanka and its Tamil Problem', in *Armed Forces*, vol. 5 (12), December 1986, pp. 542–3. *Armed Forces* is published by

Ian Allan Ltd. in conjunction with the Royal United Services, Institute for Defence Studies.

14. See the statement made by Dr G.S. Dhillon, Leader of the Indian delegation to the 42nd Session of the Commission on Human Rights, under Agenda item 12, on 5 March 1986. This brief statement was in response to a very comprehensive one made by Dr H.W. Jayewardene leading the Sri Lanka delegation on 4 March 1986, setting out in detail the negotiations conducted between the two governments, and also details of attacks by Tamil separatist groups on civilians, and clashes between the Sri Lankan security forces and Tamil separatist groups.

15. And not only Indian newspapers. Indian officials in New Delhi were talking to Western journalists based in New Delhi. See, for example, an article 'India shows Impatience with Sri Lanka Talks', by Steven R. Weisman, *New York Times*, 27 December 1985.

16. See the article 'Sri Lanka — Ominous Portents', in *India Today*, 31 May 1986.

17. Personal knowledge. I was 'conscripted' at very short notice as a member of the Sri Lankan delegation at these talks in Colombo on 18 December 1986.

18. On the background to the Indo-Sri Lankan Accord, see Bruce Matthews, 'Sri Lanka: An End to the Violence?', *Current Affairs* (Sydney), November 1988, pp. 11–17; R. Premdas and S.W.R. de A. Samarasinghe, 'Sri Lanka's Ethnic Conflict — The Indo-Lanka Peace Accord', *Asian Survey*, 28 (6), June 1988.

19. The tactical errors of the IPKF are discussed in Bruce Matthews, 'Sri Lanka: An end to the Violence?', op. cit., pp. 15–16; see also Steven Weisman, 'Sri Lanka: A Nation Disintegrates', in the *New York Times* Sunday Magazine, 13 December 1987

20. Less than a month after the accord was signed the criticism began. The most critical and surprising — considering the source — was an article in *The Guardian* (London) Third World Review. 'India the Big Bully'. It proceeded to describe the accords as 'The Infamous Contract that is Sri Lanka's Munich'. *The Guardian*, 21 August 1987. In its issue of 13 August 1987 the *Far Eastern Economic Review* described the accord as 'Rajiv's Gunboat Peace'.

21. I owe this point to Professor Arnslie Embree of the Southern Asian Institute, Columbia University, New York.

22. See M.S.S. Pandian's article 'The Election That was Not', in *The Economic and Political Weekly*, 3 December 1988, where he points out that the election was rigged by the IPKF.

23. Thanks to the LTTE enforced boycott, no election was possible in the four districts of the northern province, but the IPKF succeeded in securing the election of the EPRLF state uncontested there. In the eastern province there was an election of sorts in which the IPKF served, more or less, as election agents of the EPRLF.

24. See, for instance, the statement by the Representative of India, 4 March 1985 (right of reply) at the Commission on Human Rights, Geneva 1985: 'the situation in Sri Lanka is, in fact, qualitatively different from that prevailing in the Punjab, where all communities, including Sikhs enjoy full political, economic and cultural rights'.

25. I owe some of the points here to Professor Roy Licklider of the Deparment of Political Science, Rutgers University, New Jersey, and his unpublished paper 'Civil Violence and Conflict Resolution: A Framework for Analysis', from which these are derived.
26. Ibid.

7 INTERNATIONALIZATION OF SRI LANKA'S ETHNIC CONFLICT: THE TAMIL NADU FACTOR

Shelton U. Kodikara

Recent ethnic conflict between Sinhalese and Tamils in Sri Lanka has spread into the international system, to the extent that it has not only evoked international concern among 'state-actors' such as India, the United States, and Western donors of aid to Sri Lanka, but it has also created new links or revived old ones with cross-boundary Tamil ethnic groups in Tamil Nadu, and with other 'non-state' actors such as expatriate Tamil and Sinhala groups world-wide, the UN Human Rights Commission, and with non-governmental organizations (NGOs) concerned with minority and human rights.

Recent ethnic conflict between Sinhalese and Tamils has been sparked off by the demand for a separate Tamil state (Eelam), first articulated in 1976, which grew into a formidable threat to the unity and territorial integrity of Sri Lanka, and which became an issue in international politics after July 1983, when a Sinhala backlash against the mine-blasting of thirteen Sinhala soldiers in Jaffna took on the dimensions of a punitive wave of anti-Tamil violence throughout the island.

The basic questions at issue in the ethnic crisis in Sri Lanka were language, citizenship for immigrant Tamil plantation workers, rights to land, employment, and admission to universities. Some of these issues had lost their sharpness over the years due to government accommodation. But the Tamil militant leadership and terrorist cadres have grimly held on to the demand for a separate 'Tamil homeland' comprising the island's northern and eastern provinces, a demand made in the context of the Sri Lankan government's own offer of provincial devolution of power, and India's support for regional autonomy for the Tamils of Sri Lanka in contradistinction to accommodation of their demand for a separate state.

The proximity of Tamil Nadu, with its population of fifty-five million Tamils, and Tamil Nadu's own language problems and secessionist ideals make the 'homeland' theory a dreaded prospect for most of the Sinhalese. For India, too, it complicates issues of internal politics. Moreover, the Indian interest in the Sri Lankan problem, and its involvement in attempts to find political solutions to it, culminating in the controversial Indo-Sri Lankan Agreement of July 1987, have elicited the interest of extra-regional powers, principally the United States, in Sri Lanka's current situation, because Sri Lanka's strategic location in the Indian Ocean and the future of its strategic harbour at Trincomalee have become matters of international concern.

Role of Tamil Nadu

Tamil Nadu's role in Sri Lanka's ethnic crisis has always been of crucial importance. Tamil Nadu political parties and governments have a long history of support for the various causes espoused by the Tamils of Sri Lanka, and this was the case even before 1967, when state power was a monopoly of the Congress party. Before the idea of a separate state was adopted by Sri Lankan Tamils, Tamil Nadu's interest in the island's politics was centred essentially on three issues. First was the repatriation of Indian nationals with expired residence visas under Sri Lanka's citizenship laws, or of stateless persons of Indian origin opting for Indian nationality under Indo-Lankan citizenship agreements, which caused problems of resettlement and rehabilitation for the state government. The funding for rehabilitation and resettlement programmes came from the Indian union government, but Tamil Nadu never took kindly to the repatriation process. Second, the termination of the centuries-old tradition of free travel which had existed between Sri Lanka and mainland India by the institution of immigration rules and visa restrictions touched upon sensitive economic interests in Tamil Nadu. Third, Tamil agitation against the imposition of Sinhala as the only official language in 1956 found a responsive chord in Tamil Nadu, where, from the early 1960s, opposition Tamil politicians were themselves mounting a campaign against the constitutional provision which required Hindi to be the official language of India with effect from 1965.

The anti-Hindi agitation was spearheaded by the Dravida Munnetra Kazhagam (DMK), founded by C.N. Annadurai, and this agitation was marked by public burning of copies of the Indian Constitution, and a movement against the Brahmin ascendancy in the political establishment of Madras. Separatist tendencies were incipient in the DMK protest and, in fact, the DMK's forerunner, the Dravida Kazhagam, had been openly secessionist in its political programme. The anti-Hindi agitation in Tamil Nadu was temporarily halted by timely action taken by Pandit Nehru to permit the continuance of English as an associate link language in India indefinitely after 1965. But the fact that language still lingers as a divisive force in Tamil Nadu is demonstrated by the resuscitation of the anti-Hindi movement in November 1986, led by the DMK leader M. Karunanidhi, then in opposition but now Chief Minister of Tamil Nadu, who personally, with party activists, organized the burning of the provision in the Indian Constitution which said: 'The official language of the [Indian] Union shall be Hindi in Devanagari script.' In the context of the Sinhala–Tamil crisis in Sri Lanka, the timing of the new anti-Hindi agitation was especially significant. The agitation was marked by riots involving the burning of buses by Tamil students, the arrest of Karunanidhi himself with over three thousand DMK activists, and 'shoot-on-sight' orders given to the Madras police.[1]

Nehru's effort to scotch separatism in India was more effective. The Sixteenth Amendment to the constitution, enacted in 1963, declared that the advocacy by word or deed of anything against the sovereignty or territorial integrity of India would be deemed a penal offence not protected by the fundamental rights provisions, and all candidates for membership of Parliament or the state legislature, union and state ministers, Members of Parliament and state legislatures, judges of the Supreme Court and the Comptroller and Auditor-General of India were required to take an oath to uphold the sovereignty and integrity of India.

The support extended by Tamil parties in Tamil Nadu to Tamil causes in Sri Lanka must be understood in the light of the transnational ethno-linguistic affinities which have long subsisted between the Tamils of India and the Tamils of Sri Lanka. Since 1967 political power in Tamil Nadu has alternated between the DMK, led by Karunanidhi, and the All-India Anna Dravida Munnetra Kazhagam (AIADMK), a break-away group led by the former Chief Minister of Tamil Nadu, M.G. Ramachandran. Both were ardent supporters of the Tamil cause in Sri Lanka. Ramachandran, as Chief Minister of Tamil Nadu, was inolved in the peace parleys which were undertaken between the governments of India and Sri Lanka, especially in the role of mediator between Indian negotiators and leaders of militant groups sojourning in Tamil Nadu, and the leader of the largest and most powerful of these groups, Prabhakaran of the Liberation Tigers of Tamil Eelam (LTTE), was known to be close to him. Nevertheless, Ramachandran could not but toe the Indian government line that the unity and integrity of Sri Lanka were inviolable, and in November 1986 the Tamil Nadu police, probably with the foreknowledge of the union government, undertook a clinically smooth and effective operation to divest militant groups located in Tamil Nadu of their arms and ammunition, subjecting the leadership of these groups (including Prabhakaran) to interrogation, fingerprinting and photographing, following upon incidents between Sri Lankan militants and Tamil Nadu civilians, which led in one case to the shooting of a Tamil Nadu Harijan.

The fact that the confiscated arms included not only Soviet-made AK-47s, mortars and grenades but even SAM missiles, valued at Sri Lankan Rs 800,000,000, demonstrated the extent of the penetration of Tamil Nadu state by Sri Lankan Tamil extremists.

The ambivalence of the official Indian position as regards the Sri Lankan Tamil militants, however, is also highlighted by the fact that the telecommunication equipment with which contact with activist militant cadres in Sri Lanka was maintained from South India, though confiscated by the Tamil Nadu police in another operation, was subsequently restored when Prabhakaran undertook a fast unto death.

As an opposition politician in Tamil Nadu, Karunanidhi has been more active in his advocacy of Tamil militancy, constantly indulging his flair for the theatrical in his support of Sri Lankan Tamils. Though not an overt supporter of Tamil Eelam, Karunanidhi has been an advocate of Indian military intervention in support of Sri Lankan Eelamists, and in the aftermath of the July 1983 events in Sri Lanka the DMK was instrumental in organizing and sending to the UN Secretary-General a mammoth petition, estimated to have contained more than a million signatures, protesting at what Karunanidhi has called the genocide perpetrated on Sri Lankan Tamils. In 1986 Karunanidhi also concerned himself with bringing about unity between the six main militant groups mounting guerrilla operations in Sri Lanka from Tamil Nadu soil. The Eelam National Liberation Front (ENLF), which resulted from his initiative, did not include under its umbrella all the militant groups: besides the LTTE, it comprised the Eelam Peoples Revolutionary Liberation Front (EPRLF), the Tamil Eelam Liberation Organization (TELO), the Tamil Eelam Liberation Army (TELA) and the Eelam Revolutionary Organization of Students (EROS), but not the important Peoples Liberation Organisation of Tamil Eelam (PLOTE) led by Uma Maheswaran, whose personal feud with Prabhakaran had once resulted in a shoot-out on the streets of Madras. However, the ENLF, too, proved to be short-lived. To Karunanidhi's great disappointment, the LTTE embarked on a strategy of attempting to eliminate some of the other militant groups. Sri Sabaratnam, leader of TELO, and his core support-group were eliminated in Jaffna by LTTE cadres in March 1986; and the factional struggle between LTTE and EPRLF is part of the politics of militancy in Sri Lanka's northern region.

The LTTE and its leader Prabhakaran had emerged as the most

powerful single militant force in Tamil Nadu prior to 1987, and remains so in Sri Lanka. Prabhakaran's access to and support from Chief Minister Ramachandran was itself a factor which distanced him from Karunanidhi, who openly deplored the killing of Sabaratnam, presumably one of his own protégés. What all this portended, however, was that the ethnic problem of Sri Lanka had long since become an important issue in the internal politics of Tamil Nadu itself, and that the major Tamil Nadu political parties, DMK as well as AIADMK, were vying with each other to appear more ardent in their championship of the cause of Sri Lankan Tamils. As the Sri Lankan Foreign Minister told the UN Secretary-General, Tamil Nadu political parties were 'hitching their wagons to the Tamil problem in Sri Lanka', and attempting to outdo each other for acceptance in their own state as patrons of the Tamils of Sri Lanka.

In July 1984 two Tamil Nadu leaders, Eva Sezhiyan, President of the Tamil Nadu Janata Party, and V. Goplaswamy, DMK MP, met US Deputy Assistant Secretary of State Howard B. Schaeffer and expressed concern over 'continuing problems of Tamils in Sri Lanka', urging the US government to use its influence to safeguard basic rights of ethnic minorities in the island. These Tamil Nadu politicians were visiting the United States in connection with a Tamil International Conference held in Nanuet, New York, and were airing the standard Tamil view that Tamil terrorism was the outcome of repressive actions of the Sri Lankan armed services, rather than *vice versa*. The Deputy Assistant Secretary merely reiterated the American commitment to a political solution of Sri Lanka's ethnic problem.[2]

Commencing 29 April 1985, the DMK stepped up its agitation on the Sri Lankan issue, organizing state-wide demonstrations in Tamil Nadu, which called upon the government of India to intervene on behalf of Sri Lankan Tamils and support their demand for Eelam. The DMK agitation in April–May 1985 led to the arrest of more than eighteen thousand members of DMK cadres, including Karunanidhi himself. As a countermeasure the AIADMK was itself constrained to organize a protest march from Rameswaran to Madras, which too was abandoned due to the intervention of the union government. Though the government party in Tamil Nadu, the AIADMK had earlier organized a state-wide *bandh* (strike) in support of Sri Lankan Tamils, and initiated the debates in the Madras Legislative Assembly and Council on Sri Lanka's ethnic problem. From the point of view of the government of India, what was ominous was Karunanidhi's warning that the 'continued indifference' of the government of India to the situation in

Sri Lanka would force the DMK to revive its earlier demand for a separate state for Tamil Nadu.[3]

It was in the context of this sustained pressure from India's south that the government of India itself, after the events of July 1983, involved itself in negotiations with the government of Sri Lanka with a view to bringing about a political solution of Sri Lanka's ethnic problem, and extended its mediatory efforts towards this end. From Sri Lanka's point of view, the crux of the matter was that Sri Lankan Tamil guerrilla groups were arming and training themselves, and operating against the Sri Lankan government, its armed services and even against civilians from bases located in Tamil Nadu. Though quite unequivocal in its support of Sri Lanka's unity and integrity, India repeatedly denied the existence of training-camps of Sri Lankan militants on Indian soil, though the force of its denial was greatly diminished by the blatant existence and continued sojourn of large numbers of well-armed Tamil militant and terrorist groups, whose leadership was directing operations in Sri Lanka from their haven on south Indian soil. The government of India chose to treat these groups as refugees, but it was certainly infringing the norms if not the rules of international conduct by its tolerance, and even tacit support, of activities directed against a friendly neighbouring country, and its failure to heed repeated Sri Lankan government charges that some of the militant groups operating from Tamil Nadu were not only proclaiming their commitment to a separate state but even attempting the subversion of the democratic process in the island.

In giving sanctuary to terrorist cadres from Sri Lanka, India was brazenly infringing the specific UN Resolution which declared that 'no State shall organize against, foment, finance, incite or tolerate subversive, terrorist or armed activities directed towards the violent overthrow of the regime of another State, or interfere in civil strife in another State'.[4] India did become aware, belatedly, of the real significance of Tamil militancy as a factor in India's own internal politics. The shooting incident on 1 November 1986, when a Tamil Nadu civilian was killed, involved the EPRLF. More ominous for India was the association of TELO cadres in the anti-Hindi agitation in Tamil Nadu during the same month, and the arrest and detention of twenty TELO members in connection with bomb explosions which had been set off in Madurai in the course of this agitation. The TELO Secretary-General in Madras reportedly went on a 'fast-unto-death' in protest at the arrests, and expressed TELO's willingness to 'get out of Tamil Nadu within a few days time' if the Tamil Nadu government wanted it to do so.

Before the signing of the Indo-Lankan Accord in July 1987, each militant group in Tamil Nadu had some connections with some Tamil Nadu political party, as well as sources of local support. The government of India's insistence on treating known terrorists as refugees, and its ambivalence on the question of extradition, was enmeshed in this context of Tamil Nadu politics.

Things changed in Tamil Nadu after the signing of the 1987 Accord, but not completely. One of India's obligations under the terms of the Accord was to bring about a cessation of hostilities between Tamil guerrillas and Sri Lankan security forces, and to ensure the surrender of all arms held by militant groups. India has not been able to meet either of these obligations. Sri Lankan security forces did withdraw from the war with the guerrillas, and all Tamil militant groups did make a show initially of surrendering their arms. However, from October 1987 the LTTE became embroiled in a new guerrilla war with Indian 'peace-keeping' troops sent to Sri Lanka. This meant that LTTE cadres were now *personae non gratae* in Tamil Nadu, but it did not mean that they had lost all sources of support and sympathy in the state. The other militant groups accepted the Peace Accord and under India's tutelage renounced *Eelam*, but this may have been only tactical. None of these groups surrendered all its arms.

The tortuous course which Tamil politics has taken in recent times in Sri Lanka appears to indicate that matters are reverting to the pre-Accord situation. This is happening in a context of rapidly changing Sri Lankan politics. For one thing, the EPRLF became the governing party in the newly constituted North-East Provincial Council and converted itself willingly into an Indian surrogate, existing under the protection of India. For another, the LTTE and the Sri Lankan government patched up their differences in early 1989, declared a cease-fire with each other, and have held a series of talks on the subject of power-sharing in the north-east region, which apparently involves the calling of fresh elections to the North-East PC, which is seen by the EPRLF as a threat to its own present hegemony in this region. A further dimension of Tamil politics is that the Sri Lankan President R. Premadasa's call to India to withdraw its troops from the island by 29 July 1989, is strongly supported, and was in fact partly prompted, by the LTTE, while all other Tamil militant groups are opposed to it.

In Tamil Nadu itself, Sri Lankan Tamil militant groups are raising their voices again. Most of them have offices in Madras, which were never permanently closed in consequence of the signing of the Peace Accord. Secretary-General Padmanabha of the EPRLF operates from

Madras and issues statements from this vantage-point, while his colleague Varatharaja Perumal functions as Chief Minister of the north-east province from Trincomalee. TELO, the group favoured by DMK leader M. Karunanidhi, who made a spectacular comeback to power in Tamil Nadu in January 1989, are showing signs of activism in Madras again, and all indications are that Indian intelligence is once again indulging in cloak-and-dagger tactics, using Sri Lankan Tamil militant groups to pursue its own interests in Sri Lanka.

As for the new Chief Minister of Tamil Nadu, he has adopted a low profile so far. He enjoys a comfortable majority in the Tamil Nadu legislature; all other political parties in the state were soundly defeated at the January elections. Sri Lanka is not now a hot issue in Tamil Nadu, and Karunanidhi can afford to take a philosophical view. Asked whether he would provide financial aid to the Tamil Tigers (LTTE) as his predecessor M.G. Ramachandran did, he replied: 'Money cannot buy peace, only more arms and bloodshed. A solution can come only through negotiation.'[5]

Notes

1. See *The Ceylon Daily News*, 11 December 1986.
2. For Report on Sri Lanka presented by Howard Schaeffer, Deputy Assistant Secretary (South Asia) to the US Congress, see *Lanka Guardian*, vol. 7, 15 August 1984.
3. *The Island*, 6 April 1985.
4. Declaration on Principles of International Law concerning Friendly Relations and Co-operation among States in accordance with the Charter of the United Nations. *Official Records of the Gen. Ass., Twenty-fifth session, Supplement 18*, (A/8018), 24 October 1970.
5. *India Today*, 15 February 1989, p. 19.

8 INDO-SRI LANKAN RELATIONS AND SRI LANKA'S ETHNIC CONFLICT

S.D. Muni

Theoretical paradigms and analytical constructs provided by social anthropologists as well as political sociologists to understand and unravel the intricacies of the phenomenon of ethnic conflicts have proved to be generally inadequate. This is mainly because such constructs and paradigms are based upon what may be termed an introvert approach, i.e. evolution, intensification and possible resolution of ethnic conflicts is taken to be an internal process *alone* of the society in which such a conflict flares up. This is only partially so, not only because the world has shrunk and it is not possible to keep conflicts confined to or insulated in their respective locations, but internal social processes, particularly in Third World societies, are not autonomous. The external links — tangible or otherwise — play an increasingly significant role in these internal processes. Thus conflicts, which represent a particularly volatile and turbulent social process, have invariably an external dimension both as an input into the process, and as an overspill from it. This external dimension has neither been adequately accounted for, nor systematically conceptualized in the available literature on the phenomenon of ethnic conflicts.[1]

The roots of Sri Lanka's ethnic conflict

The roots of the present crisis in Sri Lanka may be traced to the bane of communalism in the evolution of the island's electoral politics since its independence. On the whole, the Tamils and the Sinhalese co-existed peacefully during the pre-independence history of Sri Lanka. The tensions started soon after independence, when in 1948–9 the United National Party (UNP) government disenfranchised the Tamil estate workers, not because they were Tamils, but because they voted *en bloc* for the UNP's opponents, the left-wing parties. Land colonization measures of post-independence governments encouraged settlement of Sinhalese in the Tamil-dominated eastern province and transformed its demographic and electoral composition.

The year 1951 was a major landmark in the evolving ethnic situation in the island when S.W.R.D. Bandaranaike broke away from the UNP to establish a new party, the Sri Lanka Freedom Party (SLFP). The main ideological and electoral bases of this new party were the Sinhala language and Buddhist religion. The SLFP won the general election of 1956 by mobilizing Sinhala votes on these sectarian issues, but only at the cost of deepening the ethnic cleavage. Sri Lanka witnessed its first ethnic riots between the Sinhalese and the Tamils in 1956.[2] Since then there has been no looking back on the communalization of ethnic politics, wherein the compulsions of competitive mobilization of Sinhala votes by the two major contenders for domestic power in Sri Lanka, the UNP and the SLFP, have led the successive governments to pursue anti-Tamil policies, thus vitiating communal harmony and understanding. Persistent emphasis on such policies gradually alienated the Tamils of the island so much that even the moderate Tamil organization, the Tamil United Liberation Front (TULF), otherwise committed to a peaceful and negotiated solution of the ethnic problem, contested the 1977 parliamentary elections and secured a majority of the Tamil vote on the basis of fighting for a separate Tamil state (Eelam). The UNP which was set to wrest power from the SLFP conceded in its election manifesto of 1977 that:

> There are numerous problems confronting the Tamil speaking people. The lack of solutions to their problems has made the Tamil speaking people support even a movement for the creation of a separate state. In the interest of national integration and unity so necessary for the economic development of the whole country, the party feels such problems should be solved without loss of time. The party when it comes to power, will take all possible steps to remedy their grievances in such fields as (1) education; (2) colonization; (3) use of Tamil language; and (4) employment in public and semi-public corporations.

After the elections which gave the UNP an unprecedented victory, the growing predominance of Sinhala chauvinism in the party was an important factor behind its changing stance on the ethnic issues. Two other mutually reinforcing factors — the centralization of the state apparatus (its drift from a liberal democratic to a Bonapartist state), and the UNP's open economy approach — made a decisive contribution to the ethnic divide in the island. Thus there was ethnic violence on an ever-increasing scale in 1977, 1981 and 1983.

India's concerns in the Sri Lankan crisis

The eruption of ethnic violence in Sri Lanka in the early years of the 1980s affected India directly and quickly. There was the natural sympathy and concern of the Tamils of Tamil Nadu for their ethnic brethren across the Palk straits, and particularly so because one-third of Sri Lanka's Tamil population (i.e. 5.6 per cent of Sri Lanka's total population), being of recent Indian origin, are even known as Indian Tamils. India had always maintained an active interest in the fate and prospects of these so-called Indian Tamils in Sri Lanka and had sought a negotiated settlement with Colombo on the question of their legal and political status.[3]

The ethnic violence in Sri Lanka opened a flow of Tamil refugees from Sri Lanka to Tamil Nadu and other south Indian states. The number of such refugees was officially acknowledged in India to be 150,000 by the beginning of 1984. As a consequence, the economic resources and administrative capabilities of Tamil Nadu were strained in managing the refugee influx, and the law and order situation started deteriorating. Tamil Nadu became a live theatre of internecine conflicts and rivalries of the Sri Lankan Tamil militant groups.[4]

Such developments could not but affect local politics in south Indian states, particularly Tamil Nadu. The two major Tamil parties, the Dravida Munnetra Kazhagan (DMK) and the All-India Anna DMK (AIADMK) found it politically expedient as well as compelling to champion the cause of Sri Lankan Tamils in order to expand and consolidate their own respective electoral bases in the state. As a result, competitive economic help and political support started flowing to the Sri Lankan Tamil refugees, as well as to their various militant groups. The ruling AIADMK, which was in alliance with the ruling Congress I at the centre at that time, put pressure on the central government in New Delhi to support the Tamil militant groups and assert itself *vis-à-vis* the Sri Lankan government to bring about a political solution of the ethnic crisis.

In addition, the government of India had its own reasons for becoming directly involved in the Sri Lankan ethnic crisis. Two considerations were critically important in New Delhi's approach to the problem. One was the question of the Sri Lankan government's attitude towards India on the issue of ethnic conflict. It believed that the Jayewardene government's emphasis on a military solution to the ethnic crisis had caused the flow of refugees from Sri Lanka to Tamil Nadu and enhanced militarization of the Tamil movement. The consequences of this impinged adversely on internal peace and stability in India's southern states. In seeking a military solution, the Jayewardene regime approached its Western friends for support and decided to exclude India, assuming that Indian support and sympathies would only be with the Tamils. This calculated indifference proved unacceptable to India. It may be recalled here that even in 1958, in the midst of the language controversy in Sri Lanka, an astute elderly statesman from Tamil Nadu, C. Rajgopalachari had said:

> We in India are not quite uninterested in our neighbour's welfare; nor are events there without their effect across the narrow and shallow waters that divide us; and I beg of the leaders of Ceylon not to treat us quite as aliens and strangers.[5]

Such concern had led India to rush military assistance in April 1971 when the Sri Lankan government faced a major insurgency threat from the Jatika Vimukti Peramuna (JVP), a Sinhala extremist group. Similarly again in July 1983, on the outbreak of ethnic violence, Mrs Gandhi's government expressed India's deep concerns and anxiety.[6] On learning about Colombo's request to the United Kingdom, the United States, Pakistan and Bangladesh for assistance, India's External Affairs Minister in a statement on 2 August 1983 warned all powers to keep out of the ethnic turmoil in Sri Lanka. This, however, did not deter Sri Lanka, and its President Jayewardene cautioned India against interfering in Sri Lanka's internal affairs, and declared further that if his country felt any threat from India, it would seek military assistance from 'the US, the UK and the like-minded powers' in defending its sovereignty and territorial integrity.[7]

With the unfolding of the current ethnic crisis, Sri Lanka's acceptance of military and training support from external sources like Israel, Pakistan, China, British mercenary services and various intelligence agencies became evident. There were also references to the revival of Sri Lanka's Defence Agreement of 1948 with the United Kingdom, which had been lying as a dead letter since 1956.[8] During the visit of the then British Prime Minister Mrs Margaret Thatcher to Sri Lanka in April 1985, President Jayewardene indeed made an oblique suggestion about securing British troops on loan, and this attracted the attention of India's Minister of State for External Affairs.[9] The Americans were also encouraged to have a strategic foothold in Sri Lanka. In December 1983 Sri Lanka renewed an agreement with the United States on the maintenance of a very powerful Voice of America (VOA) relaying station, and a US-linked Singapore firm was a partner to a consortium which won a contract for renovating the oil storage facility in the strategically important port of Trincomalee.[10] Security concerns arising out of these developments drew India into involvement in Sri lanka's ethnic crisis.

No less important than India's security concerns arising out of Colombo's developing strategic links with Western powers and their allies (particularly Israel and Pakistan) was the question of the activities of Tamil militant organizations, which compelled India's direct involvement in the Sri Lankan crisis. The support and material help given to the Tamil militant groups was designed to increase the cost to Colombo of its anti-Tamil military operations and thus to bring the Sri Lankan government to the point of accepting a political and negotiated settlement as a more prudent and desirable alternative to its military option. India's support for Tamil militant organizations can also be seen as a means of gaining influence over these groups so that they could be eventually persuaded to give up the demands for a Tamil Eelam, and instead accept a political and negotiated course of finding a solution to the ethnic problem.

There were several considerations that weighed heavily against the Indian support of a separate and independent Eelam. To begin with, the Tamil militant organizations were seen to be incapable of either creating or managing an independent sovereign state on their own, in view of their limited military capabilities, economic resources, political unity and experience on the one hand, and fierce opposition of the Sri Lankan state on the other. Any attempt on India's part to give direct help to the Tamil militants in their struggle for Eelam — on the lines of the Bangladeshi experience — was ruled out, for that would have invoked forceful condemnation and resistance from the international community. India's stakes were not as strong as in the 1971 Bangladeshi operations, so as to ignore this international dimension.

Moreover, such an action on India's part, even if successful in creating an independent and separate Tamil state, was fraught with other undesirable consequences. They could include a relationship of perpetual hostility and tension between India and post-Eelam Sri Lanka; erosion of India's regional standing and image as a friendly and helpful neighbour and creation of a fragile and vulnerable small Tamil state which could not only rejuvenate the separatist aspirations of the Indian Tamils, but could also easily become a tool in the game of great power competition and rivalry in the Indian Ocean. Any Eelam government would be in a position to bargain with an interested and resourceful extra-regional power for the military use of its strategic location, including the Trincomalee harbour, in exchange for economic and political support for the tiny state.[11] After all, India's experience with Bangladesh, both in terms of bilateral relations and Dhaka's strategic approach, has not been a particularly happy one, especially since the violent overthrow of the Mujib regime.

There were three principal objectives behind India's approach towards Sri Lanka in the context of the crisis created by ethnic conflict there: preservation of Sri Lanka's unity and territorial integrity, i.e. to thwart the creation of a separate and independent Tamil state; securing protection of legitimate interests and aspirations of the Tamils of Sri Lanka; and the preservation and promotion of India's perceived regional security interests by ensuring that no external or adversary power is able to establish a strategic foothold or influence in such a close neighbour as Sri Lanka by exploiting the island's ethnic crisis. The three objectives were closely interrelated.

Indian and Sri Lankan approaches had both points of convergence as well as divergence in regard to these objectives. For instance, preservation of unity and territorial integrity of the island by not allowing the emergence of a separate Tamil Eelam was no less in the Sri Lankan government's interests than in that of India's. In the realm of foreign policy also, there existed a broad national consensus in Sri Lanka in favour of a robust, assertive non-alignment, though the UNP regime had often (since the early 1950s) displayed a tendency to adopt a pro-West stance. There was of course a wide divergence between Indian and Sri Lankan perceptions of how best to secure Tamil interests and aspirations.

India's moves in pursuance of these objectives were essentially reactive, being conditioned by the Sri Lankan government's handling of the ethnic crisis and its foreign policy moves to mobilize support from outside powers. Basically, however, Indian strategy was based upon playing a mediatory role through which both the Tamils and the Sri Lankan government could be persuaded to accommodate each other's concerns. The content and style of this strategy of course fluctuated in practice, depending upon the character of the personalities involved as well as responses to Indian moves by the Tamil militants and the regime in Colombo. For instance, the lack of personal rapport and political understanding between Mrs Gandhi in India and President Jayewardene in Sri Lanka considerably complicated the interaction between their two governments on the ethnic issue. The emergence of Rajiv Gandhi's government in New Delhi in late 1984 and the change of key actors in his negotiating team (from G. Parthasarthy to Romesh Bhandari, Natwar Singh and P. Chidambaram) was generally perceived in Colombo as a positive development, notwithstanding the fact that Rajiv Gandhi's proclaimed style of 'settlement by persuasion' proved as tardy and troublesome as Mrs Gandhi's penchant for exerting pressure on Colombo for compromise.[12]

An important factor for changing styles was also the evolving character of the Tamil struggle, which became rapidly militarized, leading to the emergence of various militant groups and their keen desire to acquire arms and material support for a violent conflict. In the process, Mrs Gandhi's initial policy of supporting the moderate and sober Tamil leadership of the TULF had to take cognisance of a militant, assertive and politically immature young leadership which felt more at home with armed struggle than with political negotiations.

A significant variable that affected the tone and temper of Indo-Sri Lankan interaction on the ethnic issue was the role of the United States. During the early 1980s, the United States sought to enlist Sri Lanka in a broader South Asian strategic consensus in favour of its position on the Soviet intervention in Afghanistan. This was also the time when the United States was interested in a strategic foothold in the island to help strengthen its military presence in the Indian Ocean. After 1984, however, the US posture changed significantly when it placed a reduced value on a strategic foothold in Sri Lanka and instead preferred a calculated and qualified accommodation with India in the Indian Ocean region. The altered US position was clearly reflected in its deliberately ambiguous stand on the unilateral Indian relief supply intervention in the island's ethnic war in May/June 1987 and prompt and enthusiastic support for the July 1987 Agreement.[13] Immediately after concluding this agreement, President Jayewardene mentioned that the United States' lukewarm response towards Sri Lanka's requests for help was one of the factors forcing him to sign this agreement with India.[14]

The Indo-Sri Lankan Accord and its failure

The Indo-Sri Lankan interaction in the island's ethnic conflict reached its climax in the form of the agreement signed in Colombo on 29 July 1987. This was a solemn understanding between two sovereign countries aimed at resolving an extremely volatile and complex problem. It sought to fulfil the three objectives of preserving Sri Lanka's unity, territorial integrity and ethnic harmony; promoting the legitimate interests and aspirations of the Tamil community; and safeguarding the perceived security interests of India (in the regional geostrategic context) and Sri Lanka (in relation to internal peace and stability). In reaching this agreement, India made a major shift from its position of being a mediator to that of a party undertaking far-reaching and unprecedented obligations. The Sri Lankan side, for its part, made significant gestures of accommodation towards Tamil interests and India's security concerns.[15]

Critics account the failure of the accord to many of its infirmities. The agreement was unrealistic in some of its clauses, particularly those relating to the precisely detailed time-scale for surrender of arms by the Tamil militants and devolution of power to the Tamil areas by the Sri Lankan government. The agreement was also vague and ambiguous on the question of the merger of the northern and eastern provinces into one administrative unit, since it was subject to a referendum, as well as on the definition of the devolution package. As regards the devolution proposals, one of the relevant provisions of the agreement said:

> These proposals are conditional to an acceptance of proposals negotiated from 4 May 1986 to 19 December 1986. Residual matters, not finalized during the above negotiations shall be resolved between India and Sri Lanka within a period of six weeks of signing this agreement. (Art. 2.15)

Some of the ambiguity on the devolution issue was removed through subsequent negotiations between the two countries, such as the understanding reached between the two sides on 7 November 1987 on the eve of the adoption of constitutional provisions for the Provincial Councils by the Sri Lankan parliament.

Though the agreement had inherent lacunae, it would be unrealistic to hold these responsible for all the difficulties that appeared in the implementation of the agreement. The two parties, India and Sri Lanka had their respective obligations to fulfil under the agreement. India had to ensure that Sri Lanka's unity and territorial integrity was not violated by the threat posed by the Tamil militants. Accordingly, it had to disarm Tamil militants and bring them into the island's political mainstream. For this purpose, the agreement provided for the stationing of an Indian Peace-Keeping Force (IPKF) in Sri Lanka. India succeeded in disarming five of the six Tamil militant groups. However, the dominant one, the LTTE, did not accept either the agreement or India's plea to join the political process—except perhaps for a brief period of two months i.e. August and September 1987. The LTTE persisted with its dedication to arms and Eelam, and India was compelled by its commitment to the agreement to use force against them. This resulted in imposing a new and difficult role on the IPKF, for which it was not quite prepared. Not only did it have to fight the LTTE guerrillas in an alien territory and in the midst of alien people, but also had to undertake political and administrative responsibilities to maintain peace and order in the Tamil areas. In fighting the LTTE, the IPKF was operating under the severe constraints of appearing to be a friend of the Tamils while fighting the most motivated and ruthless group of their militants.

There was also considerable confusion about the objectives of the IPKF, i.e. whether it was to defeat militarily the LTTE or just to weaken and force it to come to the negotiating table. These were the factors that delayed an outright IPKF victory over the LTTE. More so, because when after breaking the LTTE's back, the IPKF was about to subdue them, the Sri Lankan government under the new regime of President Premadasa, changed its tactics and built bridges of political and material support with the LTTE. This change on the one hand emboldened the LTTE, and on the other built up political pressure on the IPKF to suspend its operations and withdraw completely from Sri Lanka.

The failure of the agreement is not India's fault alone. The Sri Lankan government and the LTTE have been equally to blame. The Sri Lankan government's obligation under the agreement was to devolve power to the Tamil areas. The process of devolving power proved to be extremely slow and hesitant because of strong political pressures from Sinhala chauvinistic sections in general and the ever-growing JVP insurgency in particular. The result of all this was that the long-term co-operation and cordiality between India and Sri Lanka, which was expected to result from this agreement, did not emerge. Instead there were mutual frustrations, misunderstandings and apprehensions.

Notes

1. Jonathan Wilkenfeld (ed.), *Conflict Behaviour and Linkage Politics*, New York, 1973; Astri Suhrki and Lela Garner (eds), *Ethnic Conflict in International Relations*, Praeger, New York, 1977; Joseph Rothschild, *Ethnopolitics: A Conceptual Framework*, New York, 1981; Kumar Rupesinghe, 'Theories of Conflict Resolution and Their Applicability to Protracted Ethnic Conflicts', in *Bulletin of Peace Proposals*, vol. 18, no. 4, 1987, pp. 527-39.
2. Some scholars have indicated that Sinhala nationalism on the language

issue was mainly directed against English language and missionary education, but its actual fallout against Tamils was most serious and lasting.

K.M. de Silva, 'Nationalism and the State in Sri Lanka', in K.M. de Silva *et al.* (eds), *Ethnic Conflict in Buddhist Societies: Sri Lanka, Thailand and Burma*, Westview Press, Colorado, 1988.
3. S.U. Kodikara, *Indo-Ceylon Relations Since Independence*, Colombo, 1965.
4. Dagmar Hellman-Rajanayagam, 'The Tamil Tigers in Northern Sri Lanka: Origins, Factions, Programmes', in *Internationalize Asienforum*, vol. 17, (1986), no. 1/2 pp. 63-85; also her 'The Tamil Militants: Before the Accord and After', *Pacific Affairs*, vol. 61, no. 4, pp. 603-19.
5. *The Hindu*, 25 September 1958.
6. Indian Foreign Minister Narasimha Rao's statement in the Indian Parliament on 27 July 1983; immediate official concern was expressed earlier in New Delhi on 25 July, and on 28 July Rao rushed to Colombo.
7. Jayewardene's statement on 18 August 1983, *The Hindu*, 19 August 1983.
8. *The Times of India*, 9th April 1984.
9. Gurbachan Singh, 'The Ethnic Problem in Sri Lanka and Indian Attempts at Mediation', in Satish Kumar (ed.) *Year Book on India's Foreign Policy*, 1984-5, New Delhi, 1987, pp. 127-8.
10. S.D. Muni, 'Sri Lanka's Strategic Connections', in *Patriot* (New Delhi), 7 June 1984; Jasjit Singh, 'U.S. Transmitters in Sri Lanka', *The Times of India*, 6 March 1985; James Manor and Gerald Segal, 'Causes of Conflict: Sri Lanka and the Indian Ocean Strategy', *Asian Survey*, vol. 25, no. 12, December 1985.
11. Such a proposition had in fact been advanced by the LTTE's patrons among the expatriate Tamils in the United States; personal interviews in Washington, February-March, 1987.
12. Romesh Bhandari, 'Sri Lanka: Settlement by Persuasion', *The Hindustan Times* (New Delhi), 29 June 1987. For an account of India-Sri Lanka talks on the ethnic question between 1983 and 1987, see Partha S. Ghosh, *Cooperation and Conflict in South Asia*, Manohar, New Delhi, 1989, pp. 154-213.
13. S.D. Muni, 'Indo-Sri Lanka Agreement: Regional Implications', *Mainstream*, vol. 25, no. 48, September 1987. Also, 'Indo-Sri Lanka Agreement: An Assessment', a paper submitted at a seminar on this subject held in JNU, New Delhi, on 30 January 1988.
14. *The Hindu*, 11 August 1987.
15. S.D. Muni, 'Indo-Sri Lanka Agreement: An Assessment', op. cit. Also his 'The Indian Peace Keeping Force Issue in India-Sri Lanka Relations' (an unpublished seminar paper, December 1989). Kumar Rupesinghe, 'The Indo-Sri Lanka Agreement 1987, and Conflict Resolution in Sri Lanka', *South Asia Journal*, vol. 2, no. 3, January-March 1989, pp. 271-94. Ralph R. Premdas and S.W.R. de A. Samarasinghe, 'Sri Lanka's Ethnic Conflict: The Indo-Lanka Peace Accord', *Asian Survey*, vol. 28, no. 6, June 1987, pp. 676-90.

9 INTERNATIONAL ASPECTS OF THE THAI MUSLIM AND PHILIPPINE MORO ISSUES: A COMPARATIVE STUDY

Aruna Gopinath

I

Introduction

Muslim separatism has threatened to undermine the territorial integrity of both Thailand and the Philippines. The political violence that has plagued the southern Malay Muslim provinces of Thailand and the southern Philippines for over forty years continues. The emergence and escalation of ethnic nationalism among the Muslims in Thailand and the Philippines can be related to both internal and external factors. The latter include the struggles for independence in Malaysia and Indonesia in the 1940s and the recent rise of ethnic nationalist movements in other parts of the world, particularly in the Islamic World. The support offered by some Muslim countries to the Muslims in the Philippines and Thailand has further encouraged the struggle for autonomy.

This chapter examines the historical development of Muslim separatism in both Mindanao and southern Thailand and its transnational implications, highlighting the structural and ideological orientations of the major Muslim separatist movements, the role played by Malaysia, and other external factors in the processes of internationalizing ethnic conflict in the Philippines and Thailand.

As far as the separatist movements in the southern Philippines and southern Thailand are concerned, the internationalization process has far-reaching implications. The two have been able to attract external attention on the basis of ethnic affinity, religion and ideology. Suhrke and Noble state:

> Ethnic conflicts have peculiar characteristics that place them in the area where domestic and international politics interact. They seem to link internal and external forces of conflict and cooperation and, to some extent, to result from such interaction; consequently they must be understood in this context.[1]

Since the turn of the century, political leaders in Indonesia, Malaysia and the Islamic World generally have been concerned about the fate of their 'Muslim brothers' in the southern Philippines and southern Thailand. The Islamic concept of *ummah*, the universal community of believers, has linked the Malay minority groups with the wider world of Islam. As Islamic consciousness rose dramatically during the last decade, the plight of the Muslim minorities was taken up by such organizations as the Organization of Islamic Conference, the Islamic Foreign Ministers' Conference and the Islamic Summit Conference.

Ideological factors have also been important. In the confrontation between the Communist bloc of Indochina and the ASEAN countries the issue of Muslim and other minority groups has been of particular interest to the contending parties, in that they can destabilize national governments and adversely affect intra-ASEAN relations. Malaysia and other ASEAN members would prefer to regard separatist issues as an internal affair and not interfere. Events have shown, however, that solidarity among conservative Muslim elements has bypassed the call for non-interference.

II

The Philippines: 'the Moro problem'

Since the seventeenth century, the history of the Moros has been one of continuing struggle by a minority *bangsa* (nation) against the various historical forms of colonialism bent on weakening or destroying the religious, cultural and politico-economic traditions and characteristics of Moro society.[2] Having resisted both Spanish and American dominance, the Moro struggle has much in common with that of tribal Filipinos; both reflect the determination of a people to preserve their independence and identity. The contemporary movement for autonomy or secession thus revives earlier assertions of independence and historic rights that were either suppressed or ignored.

The coming of Islam in the late thirteenth century had three fundamental effects on the ethnic communities of the Philippines.[3] First, it introduced a new concept of Islamic consciousness, the *ummah*: all who believe in Islam belong to a universal community of believers bound by their common spiritual ties. Second, it marked the establishment of a political institution, the sultanate, first in Sulu and subsequently in Mindanao. Third, there was a blending of Islamic and ethnic elements. Thus, there emerged during the pre-colonial era a

Muslim community bound by a unifying universal consciousness, held together by a sophisticated political institution, but pursuing a socio-cultural life ethno-Islamic in orientation.

Three hundred years of Spanish rule demonstrated that the Muslims were able to withstand the challenge of colonial conquest. Spanish attempts at colonizing the southern Philippines tended to bring independent Muslim groups into a united front against colonialism. It also accelerated the process of Islamization to the extent that by the eighteenth century there had developed Islamic institutions, such as the *madrassah*, Arabic language and literature, and the *sabilallah* or holy warrior, as Muslim answers to attempts at Hispanization and Christianization.

With the close of Spanish rule in 1898 and the beginning of American control over the Philippines, the Muslim struggle began to adopt a defensive rather than offensive posture. The Muslims rejected the American claim to sovereignty in Mindanao and resisted American efforts to subdue them. From 1903 to 1913 a Moro Province set up by the Philippine Commission functioned independently and exercised *de facto* autonomy.[4] However, with the signing of the Kiram-Carpenter Agreement in 1915 the Muslim armed struggle against colonialism ended.

With the abolition of the Moro Province in 1913, a Department of Mindanao and Sulu was created under the immediate jurisdiction of the governor-general of the Philippines and the Philippine Commission. In turn, the Department of Mindanao and Sulu was abolished in 1920 and a Bureau of Non-Christian Tribes established. In this bureau, American officials relinquished direct control over Moro affairs, though the American governor-general retained veto power over the Filipino administration. This gave the Muslims some measure of national recognition, and Muslim appointees were made to the Senate in 1916. By 1920 the Sulu Sultanate, led by Dayang Piandao, was ready to renounce its claims to authority by accepting positions under American authority.[5] They were followed by Muslim leaders in Lanao and Cotabato to such an extent that the Muslim political leadership became the strongest supporter of America's rule in the islands.

During the Commonwealth period (1935–41) a rapid institutionaliza-tion of the government was inaugurated and attempts were made by President Manual Quezon to integrate the Muslims and Christians through various policies, including resettlement in Mindanao.[6] However, without meaningful changes to the social and economic foundations of the community, such changes were largely cosmetic.

In 1946 a new era dawned with Philippine independence and the reins of government shifted from American hands to Filipinos. But the new republic maintained the American approach to the development of Mindanao. Resettlement was intensified and the penetration of foreign and big local capitalists continued unabated. The net effect of this was the systematic dispossession of the Moros and other minority nationalities of their ancestral lands, and a slow but continual erosion of Moro identity and culture. What upset the Muslims specifically about integration was the unmistakable link between Filipinism and Christianization, the latter often equated with modernization. Such a blending of religious and secular aims and purposes presented a serious psychological problem to Muslim integration.

In 1957 a Commission on National Integration (CNI) was established and greater educational opportunities were given to deserving Muslims by way of scholarships. However, like many government programmes, the CNI achieved little apart from dispensing scholarships. Indeed Muslim discontent was at such a point that by the time Marcos assumed the presidency in 1965, autonomy or secession appeared to be the only way to go.

This was the road Muslims took in 1968 when Udtog Matalam organized the Mindanao Independence Movement (MIM). The MIM declared independence from the Republic of the Philippines. In response to the MIM's call for secession, there began a programme of intensive training for ninety recruits in the forests of Malaysia along the Thai border, allegedly with a few Palestinians. Some of the trainees belonged to the youth section of the MIM. They had progressive ideas and sought ways to analyse the Moro situation. To this group belonged Nur Misuari, Commander Clay, Commander George, Commander Dimas, Abu Khayr Alonto, Jimmy Lucman, Al Caluang and others who later formed the Moro National Liberation Front (MNLF) and the Bangsa Moro Army (BMA), and occupied positions of leadership in the contemporary Muslim struggle.[7]

In retaliation against the MIM, certain anti-Muslim Christian politicians from Cotabato came together in September 1970 to launch the Ilaga movement, a self-defence organization with overtones of fanatical and hostile anti-Muslim sentiments. The split between the Christian and Moro ruling élites culminated in the Manila massacre of June 1971. This added a specifically religious dimension to the Mindanao conflict.

It was during this period that Nur Misuari convened a special Moro assembly in Zamboanga City to assess the position of the Moros and their claim to their lands. The most important resolution of the assembly was the founding of the MNLF with Misuari as chairman. To achieve the goal of liberating their homeland, the newly organized Moro Front unanimously adopted two forms of resistance: parliamentary participation and armed struggle.

Between July and November 1971 violent encounters escalated into a war between BMA soldiers and the Ilagas. Local elections in November 1971 added to the problems. Many Moro footholds were lost to Christian politicians and there followed another massacre of Muslims in Lanao del Norte. This prompted President Marcos to declare martial law on 21 September 1972. Thousands were arrested and imprisoned as democratic rights were suspended, the mass media silenced and the Philippine Congress abolished.

For Muslims, the imposition of martial law precluded any hope of struggle by peaceful means. The declaration of martial law and the concomitant programme of creating a 'New Society' or *Bagong Lipunan*[8] were interpreted as an imposition of a Christian totalitarian social order to subvert the Moro politico-economic and socio-cultural identity, depriving Muslims of not only their traditional sources of livelihood but also their Islamic and indigenous culture, supplanting them with Christian culture. The proclamation of martial law thus precipitated a new revolutionary consciousness among the Muslims and the rise of the MNLF/BMA with their goal of self-determination. At its peak in the early 1970s, the MNLF was said to have had between 5,000 and 30,000 guerrilla fighters, some of whom were trained at camps in Malaysia, Libya, Syria and Egypt, and with the Palestine Liberation Organization. Ideologically, the fundamental concern of the MNLF was the achievement of autonomy for the Muslim areas of Mindanao, Sulu and Palawan within the framework of an Islamic state.[9]

The rise of the separatist movement among the Muslim minority was a reflection that the dominant non-Muslim majority had become a barrier to the achievement of the Islamic social order, or *taritib*, which every Muslim must observe and defend, by *Jihad-ul-asghar* (holy war) if necessary.[10]

The role of Malaysia

Financial support for the MNLF has come principally from abroad, particularly Libya. The first ninety trainees were trained under British tutelage with support from Tun Mustapha of Sabah. The Malaysian government has been involved in providing assistance to the MNLF, partly out of sympathy with their Muslim cause, and partly for reasons relating to the Philippines' claim to Sabah.[11]

Tun Mustapha himself was born in a *kampong* in the Kudat district of Sabah. However, he claims paternal lineage from the Sultans of Sulu. Just prior to the formation of Malaysia in 1963, Mustapha formed the United Sabah National Organization (USNO). Although USNO's constitution allows for all native peoples of Sabah to become members, from the beginning its membership drive and appeal were mainly addressed to the Muslim peoples of the state and its leadership was also overwhelmingly Muslim.

One of Tun Mustapha's dominant characteristics was his strong commitment to Islam and his firm belief in the desirability of propagating the faith among the non-Muslims of Sabah. It was for these reasons that Mustapha opened Sabah's door to Filipino Muslims, who came in large numbers after the imposition of martial law in 1972 and the destruction of Jolo in 1978. The numbers amounted to 20,367, while the census of 1980 put the figure at round 47,400.

Apart from the religious factor Sabah was facing severe manpower and labour shortages. This provided another powerful factor determining the Sabah government's accommodative policy towards the Filipino arrivals. In November 1979 the Malaysian Ministry of Home Affairs noted that Sabah's labour force in the internal and remote areas had been considerably increased by the Filipino refugees.[12]

The international dimension

In June 1971 two Muslims were killed in a mosque in Barrio Manili, Carmen, North Cotabato. Philippine Constabulary troopers were implicated and accused of collaboration with the Ilagas in the killings. The 1971 Manili killings had important international ramifications. Libyan leader Colonel Muammar Qaddafi, on hearing of them, expressed his concern to the Philippine government and began a programme of aid and religious activities for Muslim refugees, which subsequently expanded to military and diplomatic support for the Muslim cause.[13] In 1972 Misuari left for Sabah and then Tripoli. MNLF offices were established in Damascus, Jeddah and Teheran. Misuari campaigned to secure the support of the international community in the Middle East. The internationalization of the Moro struggle thus had an important influence on the movement and on its relationship with the

Philippine government. Through the Organization of Islamic Conference (OIC) and with support from Tengku Abdul Rahman of Malaysia (who was the secretary-general of the OIC in 1972), Misuari was able to represent the MNLF's cause to the king of Saudi Arabia and to Qaddafi. The OIC pressured the Marcos government to negotiate with the MNLF over its demands for autonomy and provided material assistance.[14]

The MNLF also sought the support of the Islamic Foreign Ministers' Conference. Speaking for the 'five million oppressed Bangsa Moro people, wishing to free ourselves from the terror, oppression and tyranny of Filipino colonialism', the MNLF declared the establishment of a free and independent Bangsa Moro Republic in Mindanao, Basilan, Sulu and Palawah.[15]

The MNLF asked for political, economic and military aid from the Islamic foreign ministers. Specifically, it wanted formal recognition of the republic, support for the MNLF in the United Nations and in Third World fora, military assistance for the Bangsa Moro army, the channelling of all refugee aid through the MNLF, and the breaking of all diplomatic, economic and cultural ties with the Philippines. It identified an oil boycott as being of primary significance. Subsequently, both Saudi Arabia and Iran briefly suspended exports of oil to the Philippines to show their support for the MNLF. The boycott following the Middle East War in 1973 had greatly reduced the Philippines' military operations against Muslims, and the pro-Arab diplomatic initiatives that had resulted in the lifting of that boycott were motivated solely by opportunism.

The Islamic foreign ministers did not give formal recognition to or support for an independent Muslim state; they did not call for military support for the Bangsa Moro Army; and they did not agree to break diplomatic, economic and cultural ties with the Philippines. However, they condemned as inadequate the socio-economic measures proposed by the Philippine government as a solution to the Muslims' problems, called on the Philippines to negotiate a political and peaceful solution 'to the plight of Filipino Muslims within the framework of the national sovereignty and territorial integrity of the Philippines', and identified the MNLF as an appropriate participant in negotiations. They also appealed to 'peace loving states and religions and international authorities' to use their good offices to ensure the safety and liberty of Philippine Muslims.[16]

Thus the Kuala Lumpur meetings in 1974 gave both the MNLF and the Philippine government the intent and extent of Islamic Conference involvement. In subsequent months, while the MNLF consolidated its military organization and extended the scope of its military operations against the rapidly augmented Philippine armed forces, the Islamic Conference continued to take initiatives designed to resolve the conflict. The Conference's secretary-general made several trips to Manila, and succeeded in arranging a meeting between the MNLF leadership and a Philippine delegation in Jeddah in January 1975. The meeting ended in a deadlock and a four-member committee (with members from Saudi Arabia, Libya, Somalia and Senegal), was appointed by the Islamic foreign ministers to prepare a draft agenda for further negotiations.

Negotiations did not take place immediately. The MNLF had agreed to give up independence as a goal, substituting instead a demand for an internally sovereign, politically 'autonomous' Bangsa Moro state that would include all of Mindanao, the Sulu Archipelago, Basilan and Palawan.[17] This state would have its own security force and exclusive responsibility for maintaining internal order, and it would be loosely associated with the Philippines. The foreign ministers' agenda (which the MNLF supported) provided for Islamic self-government in the territory owned by Muslims before 1944, including that taken from Muslims since then; Christians and non-Christian minorities historically present in Islamic territories would have the status of minorities in a Muslim land. The Marcos plan, in contrast, involved the creation of four 'autonomous' regions in the southern Philippines, to be headed by commissioners appointed by the president and directly responsible to him; the appointment of Muslims to economic and social welfare offices; and the absorption of high-ranking Muslim defectors into the armed forces. In short, there was agreement on the use of the word 'autonomy' but not on its substance.

By 1975 the Islamic foreign ministers meeting in Kuala Lumpur and the negotiations with the MNLF in Jeddah had provided a new focus. Marcos had already created two regional offices in areas of heavy Muslim population and appointed commissioners to head them. Western Mindanao (Region 9) included the five provinces of Sulu, Tawi-Tawi, Basilan, Zamboanga del Norte and Zamboanga del Sur. Region 12 (Central Mindanao) included North Cotabato, Maguindanao, Sultan Kudarat, Lanao del Norte and Lanao del Sur.

Negotiations finally resumed in Tripoli in December 1976 after talks between Imelda Marcos and Qaddafi. The Philippine government's position was that these two regions, and the ten provinces they included, should constitute the 'autonomous' area. The MNLF and the Islamic foreign ministers' team had proposed twenty-one provinces and a single autonomy for the Muslims. The Philippine government also agreed that it would use 'all necessary constitutional processes for the implementation of the entire agreement'.[18] These included a referendum and elections for public officials.[19]

The Tripoli talks ended in deadlock. The Philippine government charged the MNLF with reverting to earlier demands for a separate state and insisted on a referendum, which the MNLF considered unnecessary. Finally, Imelda Marcos flew to Tripoli to work out another compromise. Her efforts produced an exchange of cables between Qaddafi and Marcos on 8 and 19 March 1977. Despite objections from Qaddafi, the Islamic Conference's secretary-general and Misuari, the Philippine government held the referendum it wanted, with the questions of its choice. A majority vote rejected the merger of the thirteen provinces into one region (which had been agreed to at Tripoli), as well as other proposals based on a MNLF draft prepared for negotiations.[20] Instead the majority approved a proposal that the administration of the 'autonomy' be under the general supervision and control of the Philippine government, with ten provinces clustered in two regions. Representatives from the Islamic Conference, the MNLF and the Philippine government then met in Manila in an attempt to save the negotiations. The talks ended in April with mutual recrimination. Thereafter, the Philippine government proceeded to implement the Tripoli Agreement as it chose.

Subsequently in 1977 the Islamic Conference, at the initiation of Qaddafi, gave the MNLF observer status at the Conference. The following year it recognized the MNLF as the legal representative of the Muslim movement in the southern Philippines; requested Islamic states to support the MNLF; and entrusted the secretary-general with the task of holding consultations with the Islamic states with a view to providing emergency assistance to the Muslims in the southern Philippines.

1977 was a crucial year for the MNLF. Misuari declared the Tripoli Agreement 'null and void' and resumed his earlier demand for a fully-independent Bangsa Moro Republic. Many members of the Bangsa Moro army had by then gone to Sabah or the Middle East as refugees. Several others surrendered under the Marcos government's amnesty programmes. By this time, also, the movement was showing signs of fragmentation.

The split in the MNLF organization seems to run along tribal and ethnic lines. Nur Misuari's group is predominantly Tausug, while Salamat's Moro Islamic Liberation Front (MILF) is basically Maguindanao, and Lucman and Pundato represent the Maranaos. The centuries-old tribalism remains a formidable barrier to uniting the different Muslim groups in the Philippines, a fact which has grave implications for the issue of autonomy in Mindanao.

To the Philippine government, the division in the rank and file of the MNLF served as a convenient excuse for its failure to implement the Tripoli Agreement, since it claimed it was not possible to identify the right MNLF group with which to negotiate the implementation of the accord.

In January 1981 the MNLF appealed to the Third Summit Conference of Heads of States in Mecca for recognition and support of the Bangsa Moro people's right to self-determination, and won sympathy from the Muslim world.

After 1980 the MNLF's clamour for secession was supported by the Communist National Democratic Front (NDF). The NDF's declared commitment to 'support the nation's minorities, in their struggle for self-determination and democracy' was reiterated at a session of the Permanent Peoples' Tribunal in Belgium in 1980, where specific charges against the Marcos regime and US imperialism in the Philippines were heard.[21] The threat of armed secessionist struggle continued till 25 February 1986 when the dictatorial government of Marcos was overthrown by the 'people power' movement, and Corazon Aquino was installed as the seventh president of the Philippines.

The major step was taken by the Aquino government to hold peace talks with Nur Misuari in Jolo in September 1986, in the hopes of ending the fourteen-year Muslim struggle. A negotiated cease-fire was called for, coupled with an amnesty for returning guerrillas. Secession, however, did not appeal to the new government, who still saw autonomy as the sole answer. A compromise was achieved with the signing on 4 January 1987 of an autonomy agreement (the Jeddah Accord) between the Philippine government and the MNLF. This prompted hopeful but premature reports that the Muslim struggle was coming to an end. The main significance of the accord, which proposed to grant autonomy to all of Mindanao, including the island provinces of Tawi-Tawi, Basilan and Palawan, lay in the seal it set on Misuari's apparent abandonment of demands for full independence for the Bangsa Moro people.[22]

The Jeddah Accord spoke of granting autonomy to a large area, 'subject to democratic pressures'. The resumption in April 1987 of peace talks between the central government and the MNLF was on the basis of a draft executive order on the proposed autonomous government, which covered the existing ten provinces in the Muslim autonomous regions.[23] The MNLF demanded full autonomy for the entire twenty-three provinces in Mindanao and the islands of Basilan, Sulu, Tawi-Tawi and Palawan.

Subsequently, the Aquino government created a Regional Consultative Commission which assisted Congress in drafting an Organic Act. President Aquino signed it as a bill on 1 August 1989.[24] A plebiscite was held on 19 November 1989, but it did not produce the desired results. Provisions relating to the territory of Muslim Mindanao, national defence affairs, representation in the national government, the judicial and educational systems, powers of taxation, and economic and financial affairs were not acceptable to the Muslim majority. In the event only four provinces voted for autonomy. Meanwhile the MNLF has threatened the Aquino government that if the autonomy issue is not resolved, it will revert to armed struggle.

III

Southern Thailand: Malay-Muslim separatism

The problem of Malay Muslim separatism in Thailand has its origins in the days when the traditional polities of South-East Asia continually battled with one another to establish their respective spheres of political control and order.[25] Thai–Malay confrontation begins at the time Sukhotai began to exert its political power in the southern parts of the Malayan peninsula. From the mid-fourteenth century, the empire of Ayudhaya met military resistance from the Malay Muslim sultanates of Patani, Kedah, Kelantan, Trengganu and Malacca. The tributary relationship which had linked the Malay Muslim sultanates of Patani, Kedah, Kelantan and Trengganu to the Thai empire was political in nature. In all other respects they were able to cherish their separate and distinctive Malay characteristics. Malay culture and Islam continued to flourish even after the fall of Ayudhaya to the Burmese in 1767.

It was only in the late nineteenth and early twentieth centuries that relations between Bangkok and the Malay Muslim states were restructured, following Bangkok's move to consolidate its territorial and political control of the kingdom.[26] The Anglo-Siamese Treaty of 1909 relinquished Thai control over the Muslim states of Kedah, Perlis, Kelantan and Trengganu but the province of Satun (within Kedah and Patani) was retained within Thailand and the role of the traditional Malay Muslim ruling aristocracy in Patani and Satun became nominal. With the introduction of a bureaucracy that was directly responsible to Bangkok, the Malay Muslims became alienated. The majority of the

Malay Muslims in the Patani region tried to minimize their contacts with the Thai authorities and found sanctuary in Islamic religion and culture. *Pondok* education flourished and those who were not happy living in Thailand crossed over to settle in Malaya. Similarly, the kin relationships, cultural ties, commercial contacts, and exchange of ideas between the Malay Muslims of Patani and the Malays of Kedah, Perak and Kelantan, and the Malay Muslims of Satun and Songkhla and the Malays in Perlis, Kedah and Perak were sustained.

In the 1930s, when the Phibun Songkrem government decided to revive the Thai-ization of the Malay Muslims, the latter aligned themselves with the Malay world, encouraged by the emergence of Malay nationalism in Malaya and Indonesia. At the end of World War II, they turned to the British to liberate them from Thailand. When British support was not forthcoming, the Malay Muslims opted for a physical confrontation with the Thais. This gave birth to Malay Muslim separatist movements which sought to pursue their objectives politically and militarily until full independence was granted. Four separatist movements can be identified: the Gabungan Melayu Patani Raya (GAMPAR), the Barisan Nasional Pembesan Patani (BNPP), the Barisan Revolusi Nasional (BRN) and the Patani United Liberation Organization (PULO).

Gabungan Melayu Patani Raya (GAMPAR)

The first formal Malay Muslim political organization founded in the post-war period. GAMPAR, or the Association of Malays of Greater Patani, aimed at promoting and protecting Malay Muslim interests in Malaya and Thailand.[27] The Association was launched under the auspices of the leftist Malay Nationalist Party in Kota Bharu, Kelantan in 1948. Its specific aims were to unite all Malay Muslims and their descendants living in Malaya; to establish closer contacts with their homes and relatives in Siam; to improve living standards; to co-operate with one another, and to improve their education and revive Malay culture among them. The leadership of GAMPAR was assumed by the Malay Muslim religious and royal exiles in Malaya.[28]

The Barisan Revolusi Nasional (BRN)

When Malaya obtained independence in 1957, the resurgence of Malay nationalism rekindled Malay Muslim hopes of realizing their own independence. Although the Emergency in Malaya curtailed the activities of the Malay Muslims living in Malaya, the need for an organized political movement was felt. The BRN was formed in 1960 and it claimed to be the first political organization to have been launched from within the Malay Muslim provinces.[29] It was not just a separatist movement but harboured pan-Malay nationalist aspirations.

The BRN was prepared to co-operate with any other ideological group, international or regional, opposed to Thai colonialism. It espoused armed revolution. Its main objectives were, first, to bring about the complete secession of the four Muslim provinces of southern Siam, including the western section of the province of Songkhla, in order to reconstruct the sovereign Malay Muslim state of Patani, completely independent from Thailand; and second, to incorporate the independent state within a wider Malay nation from Patani to Singapore and across the Straits of Malacca from Sabang to Merauke. The leaders of the BRN were mainly the religious leaders and élite of the Muslim provinces. Branches of the BRN soon mushroomed all over the south receiving support from the Malay Muslims who sought to liberate themselves from Thai rule. The BRN staged a revolt against the Thai authorities in 1961 but it was nipped in the bud; several leaders were arrested while others fled to neighbouring Malaya.

However, the formation of Malaysia in 1963 helped boost the BRN's morale. It set out again to reassert its demands for independence from Thailand, pursuing the Partai Socialis Rakyat Malaya line. However, confrontation with Indonesia brought about a rift in the BRN, splitting the conservatives and those pursuing radical and revolutionary goals. The first breakaway group of the BRN founded the Partai Revolusi Nasional (PARNAS) in 1965, while the conservative Islamic group founded the Barisan Nasional Pembebasan Patani (BNPP).

The Barisan Nasional Pembebasan Patani (BNPP)

The BNPP, Patani National Liberation Movement, was formed in 1971 in Kelantan under the leadership of Tengku Abdul Jalal (Adun Na Saiburi). Its platform was Islamic in orientation and its political objectives were to liberate all Muslim areas in the south from Thailand and to establish an independent and sovereign Islamic state of Patani.[30] The BNPP undertook psychological warfare by undermining law and order in the south; it was hoped that this would persuade the Thai authorities to give greater concessions to the Malay Muslims and strengthen the case for secession. It also waged a guerrilla war, claiming a guerrilla force of around 3,000.[31] Many of its members underwent military training abroad (although leaders do not disclose the countries concerned, Moro sources in the Philippines refer to the 'Patani brethren in Libya') and obtained modern weapons from Indochina after the American withdrawal from Vietnam. The BNPP possesses a good international network with representatives in many Arab countries and organizations, including the Islamic Secretariat, the Arab League, and the Palestine Liberation Organization (PLO).[32]

The Patani United Liberation Organization (PULO)

PULO, launched in 1967, comprises mostly foreign-educated Malay Muslims. Its ideology is '*Ubang tapekema*', an acronym derived from *Ugama, Bangsa, Tanah Air* and *Perikemanusian* (Religion, Race, Homeland and Humanitarianism).[33] PULO believes in the long-term goal of secession. While the BRN represents pan-Malay socialist interests and the BNPP is basically religious and conservative in outlook, PULO stresses education. It also sanctions the use of force in seeking to bring about secession and recognizes the need to intensify international publicity on the plight of the Malay Muslims. A military wing known as PULA, or Putani United Liberation Army, has been set up to promote armed separatist insurgency in Thailand. PULA cadres receive training abroad. Support comes principally from Malay Muslim students studying overseas.

Besides these organizations there are other splinter militant movements such as the Black December (1902) Movement, the Sabilallah Group and the United Patani Freedom Movement.[34] These groups are committed to accelerating the pace of confrontation with the Thais by resorting to urban terrorism. Their aim is to bring about secession. They engage in extortion, violence, kidnapping, sabotage, and attacks on high government officials.

The role of Malaysia

The Malay Muslims believed that the Malays in Malaya/Malaysia would come to their rescue, due to their common religious, ethnic and cultural backgrounds. Moreover, the geographical contiguity with the northern states of Malaya gave the Malay Muslims easy and immediate access to Malay sympathy and support for their cause. Many Malay Muslim exiles in various parts of Perak, Kelantan and Kedah helped form political organizations to challenge or at least embarrass the Thai government. Neighbouring Malaya/Malaysia became a safe sanctuary for their political and military organizations. Furthermore, the Malaysian media has given wide and sympathetic coverage to the Malay Muslim plight in Thailand,[35] and many Malaysian political parties and personalities have shown sympathy towards the Malay Muslims.

Generally, the Malays in Malaysia have supported the Muslim plight in Thailand. In response to a questionnaire survey of Malaysian attitudes toward the Muslim problem in southern Thailand in 1977, a majority supported a policy of active Malaysian governmental intervention in favour of the Malay Muslims.[36] This concern still exists today. In 1981, when 1,178 Malay Muslims fled into Kelantan, the present prime minister, Datuk Seri Dr Mahathir Mohammed, threatened 'to study the background of this mass exodus'.[37] Since late 1980, Thai officials have pointed out that 'Muslim separatists have been wearing jungle fatigue and using tinned rations and equipment similar to those used by Malaysian forces'.[38] Conservative Malays have also pressed the Malaysian government to support the Patani cause.

The Thai government has always been apprehensive of Malaysia's involvement in southern Thailand. The Thai English-language daily, *The Nation*, also identified Malaysia as a prime supporter of separatists. The journalist, Termsak C. Palanupap, stated that 'the Malaysian government has hardly made any serious attempt to stop these separatist terrorists and Thailand's repeated pleas for help have largely been ignored'.[39] A similar commentary appeared in the *Daily News* of 20 June 1974. The Thai daily *Prachaathibpata* claimed in its issue of 17 June 1974 that Tun Abdul Razak, the Malaysian premier, 'secretly supported the movement'.[40] This allegation was repeated in another newspaper: *Daaw Siam* which claimed that Malaysia was trying to encourage the Malay Muslims to assume dual citizenship for political purposes.[41] Although the prevailing good relations between Thailand and Malaysia have helped to defuse the crisis, it is unlikely that sentiments in favour of the Malay Muslims will disappear.

The international dimension

The Thai government's unsympathetic attitudes towards the Malay Muslim separatists' demands have led them to seek an international platform to voice their grievances. They have been helped by a number of factors. The resurgence of Islam has been to the advantage of the Malay Muslim separatists. The growth of international Muslim institutions and organizations and the emergence of an Islamic bloc in the world political community have made it easier for Malay Muslim grievances to reach international fora. Malay Muslim exiles in Saudi Arabia continue to maintain an interest in the affairs of their homeland.[42] They are instrumental in organizing Malay Muslim political and diplomatic opposition to the Thais, and are a useful source of finance, organization and manpower. The *haj* (pilgrimage to Mecca) provides an invaluable channel of communication between separatist organizations abroad and the Malay Muslims from the southern provinces, despite the fact that Thai authorities have imposed strict restrictions on the pilgrims.

Foreign-educated students are also a major source of recruitment into the separatist ranks. A large number of Malay Muslim youths prefer to go abroad for tertiary education, especially to the Middle East, India and Pakistan. For example, PULO is led by Bira, a political science graduate who left his native province of Patani twenty-one years ago to study in India. He later established himself at Tumpat in Kelantan and in 1967 dedicated himself to transforming Muslim-dominated Patani into an autonomous Islamic state. He spends much of his time commuting between Malaysia, Saudi Arabia and Syria, and he has been successful in bringing the southern minority issue before international Islamic fora. In so doing, he has received substantial financial aid from left-wing Arab regimes in Syria and Libya (though assistance has declined since 1978). Separatist recruits also include village-educated youths who go abroad specifically for short-term military-cum-political training.[43] In addition, the PULO is well supported by more than 8,000 Patani Muslims in Mecca. One level of policy organization is located in Mecca; a second level, responsible for political affairs, has its headquarters in Tumpat.[44]

Muslim organizations have been identified as sources of support for the separatists. The Thai press has alleged that Palestine has given military training to Malay Muslim guerrillas in the southern provinces,[45] and that Libya is the chief financier of the separatists.[46]

The separatists have also sent observer-delegates to successive Islamic Foreign Ministers' Conferences and have been represented at the Muslim World League Conference, the Asian Islamic Conference and the Arab League Conference. At the First Asian Islamic Conference held in Karachi in 1978 the issue of Patani was an important item on the agenda.

At the Fifth Islamic Foreign Ministers' Conference in Kuala Lumpur the delegates tried to generate a discussion of the political problem of the Malay Muslims but their call for an oil embargo against Thailand was ignored. At the Sixth Conference a resolution was passed calling for a discussion of the problems of Muslim minorities all over the world. This was taken up at the Seventh Islamic Foreign Ministers' Conference in 1976 and again at other international Islamic meetings in London, organized by the Islamic Council of Europe in 1978. Meanwhile, King Abdul Aziz University in Jeddah founded an Institute of Muslim Minority Affairs.

From time to time, leading international Muslim personalities have called on Thailand to make greater concessions to the Malay Muslims in the southern provinces to enable them to have a greater role in the administration of their region.[47] There have also been visits from international Muslim missions which have undertaken fact-finding tours of the Muslim provinces. One such visit, in 1978, was by Dr Enamullah Khan, secretary-general of the World Muslim Council. The United Arab Emirates and the Islamic Secretariat have also promised funds for the development of southern Thailand.[48] Clearly, religion is seen as the essence of the Malay Muslim issue in Thailand, and has made the issue an object of serious concern for the international Muslim community. It is in this context that the impact of Islamic revivalism in Mindanao and southern Thailand should be studied.

Islamic revivalism

In the face of external threats, any minority group, particularly a religious minority group, seeks to consolidate its power by strengthening its members' group identification. In the case of the Muslims in the Philippines and the Malay Muslims of southern Thailand, all five factors (race, language, religion, customs and the consciousness of a separate identity) have been mobilized to consolidate group solidarity against attempts at integration and assimilation by the central governments. The most effective tool in strengthening the ethnic bond has been the growing tendency towards Islamic revivalism. Islam is able to generate a tremendous moral, spiritual and emotional strength for both Muslim communities. It has been able to instill a sense of religious solidarity among its believers. External threats are hence seen as a direct threat to the existence of the *religious* community.

There are at least two reasons why Muslim Filipinos and Malay Muslims turn towards Islamic revivalism. First, there is a genuine desire to preserve the form of Islamic practice which has been handed down through generations, a realization that a return to the more fundamental teachings and principles of Islam would also strengthen the community's will to survive as an entity separate and distinct from the mainstream of Thai or Filipino society. The current social, economic and political ills faced by the community are seen by some as due to a lax attitude towards the practice of the Islamic faith. The central government's encroachment on the religious and social institutions of the community signals a great danger to the cultural values and religious ideals sacred to the Muslims. The best form of defence against such encroachment lies in the reinforcement of the community's moral values. Hence the traditional leaders turn towards Islamic revivalism. Second, there is a need to justify the violence being employed in the struggle against integration. Islam becomes the vanguard of the *jihad* (holy war) and violence is used in the name of Islam.[49]

These two factors have been responsible for the growth of Islamic militant groups in both countries and the development of the *dakwah* (missionary) and *tariqah* (mystical) movements, particularly in southern Thailand. The *dakwah* leaders promote religious values through public preaching. They feel that the steady erosion of traditional values is the reason for the emergence of social problems such as drug addiction, sexual promiscuity and lack of interest in Islam. They oppose the integration programmes of the central government. The *dakwah* movement is very popular in Malaysia and has encouraged Malay Muslims across the border to strengthen their identity and Islamic consciousness. Malaysian-based *tabligh* groups have ventured into Thailand and the Philippines during the last decade to participate in mass meetings to propagate the faith and to support religious education.[50]

While the *dakwah* movement is a new phenomenon, the *tariqah* movement has been a permanent feature of Malay Muslim and Muslim Filipino society since Islam came to Thailand and the Philippines. *Tariqah* is the esoteric path of Islam that emphasizes the ultimate aim of spiritual perfection. People who choose to follow such a way of life are called *sufi*, or Muslim mystics. The *tariqah* movement has been lending support to the separatists in both southern Philippines and southern Thailand. Its religious activities have drawn 'fundamentalist' groups from neighbouring countries, especially from Kelantan in Malaysia. Generally the *gurus* (*to' khru*), who are involved in the pursuit and propagation of esoteric knowledge and participate in various religious circles, belong to the *tariqah* movement.

In the Greater Patani Region, three sects of the *tariqah* movement can be identified: the *Baju Hiyao* (Green Robe), the *Sheikh Usman* Order and the *Baju Marah* (Red Robe).[51] These orders do not have a political ideology of their own, but they support separatist organizations. They have been supported by *sufis* from Kelantan, the Middle East and Pakistan.

Apart from the *dakwah* and *tariqah* movements, Islamic revivalism is manifested in a number of militant groups operating with the sole purpose of defending Islam against idol-worshipping Thai Buddhists or Filipino Christians. These militant groups do not have an ideological orientation and claim no affiliation with any organized movement. They claim to have drawn their inspiration from the verses of the Holy Qur'an. In southern Thailand, two groups are prominent: the Sabilillah and the Gerakan Islam Patani (GIP). The Sabilillah (The Path of God) was formed in December 1975 and is committed to violent measures against government control of the Malay area. It is responsible for a number of bomb attacks on railway stations and the bombing of Bangkok's Don Muang International Airport in 1977.[52]

The GIP, on the other hand, is a relatively new militant organization of foreign origin. It was set up in Kota Bharu, where a sizeable number of Patani Malays reside, and has been under the patronage of some Malay elements within the state of Kelantan. The group has been active in recruiting members from among Patani students studying in Malaysia and Indonesia. It keeps close ties with Malay politicians and conservative elements in the Middle East.

In the Philippines, the split in the MNLF has been associated with Islamic revivalism. The splinter group of the Moro National Liberation Front Reformist Group, under the aegis of Dimas Pundato, is spearheading a conservative Islamic revivalist movement. The militant nature of these groups can be seen in their support for the communist wings of the National Democratic Front and its military arm, the New Peoples' Army. These militant groups have attracted attention from Muslims in Southeast Asia and in the Middle East.

IV

Conclusion

The ethnic separatist movements in Thailand and the Philippines have many common features. Both have been characterized by an increasing level and intensity of violence since the 1970s. In both cases Islamic revivalism has brought the wider Islamic world into the power conflict between the minority Muslims and the central government. Strict adherence to Islamic precepts is now advocated in order to raise religious consciousness and strengthen the ethnic identity of the people. Religious institutions such as the mystical *tariqah* and the missionary *dakwah* have been revived to meet the challenges of the present day.

Steps towards integration by the Philippines and Thai governments have brought about cleavages. Possessing different languages, cultures and religions, the Muslim minorities in both countries perceive integration programmes as interference in their religious domain. Consequently, political protests have sought to defend Islam and Malay culture against outside interference. A process of 'religious purification' coincided with the heightened political consciousness of the Muslims. What the central governments have been up against are the forces of Islam and Malay ethnicity seeking to gain autonomy.

Ethnicity is an extension of a dialectic between political and economic life; it is shaped and moulded by political and economic forces, but politics and economics themselves can be heavily influenced by ethnicity. Ethnicity cannot be treated in isolation, but treating it solely as the product of other forces will not do it justice. According to Max Weber, ethnicity implies a sense of shared common descent extending beyond kinship, political solidarity *vis-à-vis* other groups, and common customs, language, religion, values, morality and etiquette. It always has a political dimension.[53]

This Weberian analysis is illuminating in trying to understand the situation of the Muslim minorities in the Philippines and Thailand. While they are a part of the nation-state, they also possess a sentiment of 'ethnic solidarity' that tends to be viewed by the dominant group as a challenge to the authority of the state, and thus threatens the nation's security. This ethnic sentiment has defied the Philippine and Thai governments' efforts to bridge the cleavages that exist between the Muslims and the two governments. In the process much conflict and violence has ensued. In the face of the political encroachment of the Thai and Philippine administrative apparatus, ethnic solidarity developed as a reaction. The Moros and the Malay Muslims turned to their distinctive cultural features and accentuated them in order to maintain 'ethnic boundaries' between themselves and the ever-increasing presence of the bureaucrat.

It is these boundaries that sustain the separate identity of the Moros and the Malay Muslims and continue to give impetus to separatist movements. This identity will not fade away and will continue to be manipulated for political purposes. With the international call for Muslim solidarity, the Muslim autonomy question in both the Philippines and Thailand remains potentially explosive.

Notes

1. A. Suhrke and L. Noble (eds), *Ethnic Conflict in International Relations*, New York, Praeger Publishers, 1977.
2. E.R. Mercado, 'Culture, Economics and Revolt in Mindanao: The Origins of the MNLF and the Politics of Moro Separatism', in Lim Joo-Jock and S. Vani (eds), *Armed Separatism in Southeast Asia*, Singapore, Institute of Southeast Asian Studies, 1984, pp. 151–75.
3. N. Saleeby, *The History of Sulu*, Manila, Filipiana Book Guild, 1963.
4. Peter G. Gowing, *Mandate in Moroland, The American Government of Muslim Filipinos 1899–1920*, Quezon City, New Day Publishers, 1983.
5. Teopisto Guingiona, 'A Historical Survey of Policies Pursued by Spain and the United States towards the Moros in the Philippines'. Report submitted to the Japanese Research Commission of the Philippines, Manila, 1943.
6. Aruna Gopinath, *Manuel L. Quezon: The Tutelary Democrat*, Quezon City, New Day Publishers, 1987.
7. Lim Joo-Jock and S. Vani (eds), *Armed Separatism in Southeast Asia*, op. cit., pp. 156–7.
8. Ferdinand Marcos, *Marcos of the Philippines*, Manila, n.p. 1979.
9. R.J. May, 'The Moro Movement in Southern Philippines', *Ethnic Studies Report*, 1988, 6 (2), pp. 52–64.
10. Nagasura Madale, 'The Future of the Moro National Liberation Front (MNLF) as a Separatist Movement in Southern Philippines', in Lim Joo-Jock and S. Vani (eds), op. cit., pp. 176–89.
11. Lela Garner Noble, 'The Moro National Liberation Front in the Philippines', *Pacific Affairs* 49 (3), 1979, pp. 405–24.
12. *New Straits Times*, 20 November 1979.
13. Lela Garner Noble, 'The Philippines: Autonomy for the Muslims', in John L. Esposito (ed.), *Islam in Asia*, New York, Oxford University Press, 1987, pp. 97–124.
14. R.J. May, 'The Moro Movement in Southern Philippines' op. cit.
15. Appeal Letter to the Islamic Foreign Ministers' Conference, Kuala Lumpur, 21 June 1974.
16. *The Straits Times*, 26 June 1974.
17. Noble, op. cit., 1987.
18. Lela Garner Noble, 'Muslim Separatism in the Philippines 1972–1981: The Making of a Stalemate', *Asian Survey* 21 (11), 1981, pp. 1097–1114.
19. Department of Foreign Affairs (Republic of the Philippines), *The Southwestern Philippines Question*, Manila.
20. National Council on Multilateral Cooperation for Southern Philippines, *Regional Autonomous Governments, Southern Philippines: A Primer*, Manila, 1980.
21. Abdurasad Asani, 'A Case for Self Determination', in *Philippines: Repression*

and Resistance. *Permanent Peoples' Tribunal Session on the Philippines*, London, Komite ng Sambayanang, Philipino, 1981, p. 225–33.

22. James P. Clad, 'Autonomy and Acrimony', *Far Eastern Economic Review* (FEER), 15 January 1987.
23. *The New Straits Times*, 9 April 1987, p. 12.
24. *Aide Mémoire on the Mindanao Peace talks*, June 1987.
25. Omar Farouk, 'The Historical and Transnational Dimensions of Malay Muslim Separatism in Southern Thailand', in Lim Joo-Jock and S. Vani, op. cit., pp. 234–57.
26. Tej Bunnag, *The Provincial Administration of Siam 1892–1915*, Kuala Lumpur, Oxford University Press, 1977.
27. Ramli Ahmed, 'Pergerakan Pembebasan Pattani', paper prepared for Department of History, University of Malaya, (1975–6).
28. Ibid.
29. *The New Straits Times*, 26 November 1961.
30. Barisan Nasional Pembebasan Patani (BNPP), *The Muslim Struggle for Survival in Southern Thailand, 1976*, n.p.
31. Ibid.
32. Ahmed, op. cit.
33. Ibid.
34. Margaret Koch, 'Patani and the Development of a Thai State', *Journal of the Malayan Branch of the Royal Asiatic Society*, 50 (part 2), 1977, pp. 69–88.
35. Noordin Mohd Sopiee (compiler), *The South Siam Secession Movement and the Battle for Unification with Malaya: A Historical Source Book*, Kuala Lumpur, 1977.
36. The questionnaire survey was carried out in 1977 in the states of Kedah, Perlis, Perak, Penang, Kelantan, the Federal Territory and Trengganu in Malaysia. The number of Malays used as a sample in the survey was 56. Out of this number, 46 or 82 per cent stated that they would support a policy of Malaysian government intervention in southern Thailand favouring the Malay Muslims. Another 9 per cent objected to any kind of Malaysian interference, while the remaining 9 per cent were neutral.
37. *Impact*, 24 April 1981.
38. P. Sricharatchanya, 'The Muslims Move In', *FEER*, 9 October 1981, pp. 23–4.
39. *The Nation*, 5 June 1974.
40. *Prachaathibpta*, 17 June 1974.
41. *Daaw Siam*, 26 June 1974.
42. Malay Muslims have been emigrating to Saudi Arabia since the beginning of the twentieth century. There is a large number of them in Mecca and Jeddah, many of whom possess Saudi citizenship.
43. Farouk, op. cit.
44. Surin Pitsuwan, *Islam and Malay Nationalism. A Case Study of the Malay-Muslims of Southern Thailand*, Thai Khadi Research Institute, Thammasat University, Bangkok, 1985.
45. *Siam Rath*, 18 June 1974.
46. *The Nation*, 5 June 1974.
47. *Prachaathibpata*, 3 July 1974.
48. *The Bangkok Post*, 3 August 1974.

49. H. Gerth, C.W. Mills, *From Max Weber: Essays in Sociology*, Oxford University Press, New York, 1958, pp. 159-74.
50. Omar Farouk, 'Malaysia's Islamic Awakening. Impact on Singapore and Thai Muslims', *Conflict*, 1988, 8: pp. 157-8.
51. S. Pitsuwan, op. cit.
52. A. Forbes, 'Legacy of Resentment', *FEER*, 20 June 1980, 21-2.
53. Gerth and Mills, op. cit., pp. 159-74.

10 THE INTERNATIONALIZATION OF ETHNIC CONFLICT: THE WORLD ACCORDING TO THE THAI MUSLIMS

Chaiwat Satha-Anand

This chapter seeks to assess the transnational aspect of Muslims in the Thai polity by looking at the way in which they view outside events. Because of the inherently transnational character of Islam, the relationship between the international context and the Muslims themselves is of paramount importance. In Thai society, where Muslims constitute an important minority group, Muslims' views on world events, as reflected in the pages of independent Muslim magazines and newspapers, can be used as an indicator of how they perceive the world. The Thai Muslims' perception of the world can be properly understood on the basis of three important and interconnected factors: the power of the contemporary Islamic resurgence; the proximity of Thailand, especially the four southernmost provinces, to Malaysia; and the ethnic origins of Muslims in Thailand.

This study examines news about the world as reported in the pages of *Islamic Guidance Post (IGP)*, a well-known Muslim news magazine in Thailand. This magazine was chosen for the present review for two reasons; first, because it states explicitly that it tries to view the world from the 'Islamic perspective'; and second, because its staff are mostly young college-educated Muslims who are quick to present relevant issues facing Muslims in Thailand. The *IGP* also publishes a monthly *Islamic Guidance Post: an analytical issue*, which focused on topical issues of the day, such as the killing of Iranians in Mecca in July 1987,[1] or the crisis that occurred in Malaysia when the Malaysian government arrested a number of people including opposition politicians and intellectuals in late October 1987.[2] Financial constraints forced the magazine to stop publishing these analytical editions in 1988. In addition to issues of the day, the *IGP* includes columns on international events and world news.

The world according to Islamic Guidance Post

Four important events reported in the journal are reviewed here. These concerned Burmese Muslims, Palestinians, Afghans, and the assassination of President Zia ul Haq of Pakistan.[3]

The *IGP* gave particular emphasis to Burmese Muslims, publishing two full-length articles about them as well as two brief news reports. The reasons given included the fact that, while events in such places as Afghanistan and Palestine were usually considered remote by Muslims in Thailand, Burma is a neighbouring country. Both articles began with historical accounts of Muslims in Burma. The October issue of the *IGP* claimed that contrary to the view of Western historians, Islam came to Burma a hundred years after Prophet Muhammad passed away, being established first in Arakan and later spreading all over Burma. However, the 'official history' of Burmese Muslims began 300 years ago when more than 3,700 Muslim families migrated to Burma by invitation to serve the Arakan king. Then, under British colonial rule, Muslims in Burma again made their presence felt because Abdul Razak Muslim was a high-ranking member of the 'Anti-Fascist Peoples Freedom League' under the leadership of Ong Saan (Aung San); a Muslim writer, U Jo Wae Mong, played an important intellectual role, and Muslims dominated the Burmese economy.

At present, Muslims constitute 18 per cent of the total population of Burma. Most of them live in big cities, including Rangoon, the capital city of one million people of whom approximately 43 per cent are Muslim. In Rangoon alone there are seventeen *pondok* (religious schools), and throughout the country there are round 4,000 mosques.

The *IGP* pointed out that since Burma accepted Buddhism as its state religion in the early 1960s, other ethnic groups such as the Karens, who are mostly Christian, were facing discrimination. In 1961, when the Ne Win government confiscated private industries, most of the Muslim economic élite were severely affected. Muslims became third-class citizens because they were not ethnically Burmese and, consisting as they did of several ethnic groups, could not easily be characterized in ethnic terms. In addition, many Muslims were killed, their women raped, and their land confiscated; some were rehabilitated; and many migrated to Bangladesh and Thailand. In 1983 the Ne Win government tore down seventeen mosques to build roads. Laws were passed restricting the recruitment of Muslims to the civil service, and Islamic names had to be changed to an indigenous Burmese form. Naming four Muslim political organizations, the *IGP* claimed that the official Yamiat Al Ulama Burma, whose leader is an adviser to the head of state, merely serves as a government puppet.

It is interesting to note how a recent incident in Burma was reported by the Muslim press. On 10 July 1988, one day after the curfew was lifted, Buddhist monks went into Muslims' shops for alms in Tong Yi, the capital of Shan State. This caused consternation among Muslims and resulted in clashes between the latter and Buddhists. The communal violence lasted for four days and led to the death of three people. The Muslim press portrayed this incident as a contributing factor in prolonging the subsequent mass uprising in Burma.[4]

The role of Muslims in the uprising was highlighted. The *IGP* reported that the mass uprising for democracy on 8 August 1988 began with students from vocational colleges, universities and 'four *pondok* uncontrollable by the Shaikh-ul-Islam'. The central mosque in Rangoon was the centre of the demonstration and Muslims were thought to constitute 15 per cent of almost a million people who took to the streets on 24 August.[5] The active role of Burmese Muslims in fighting for democracy, given marginal importance in other papers, was highlighted in the Muslim press.

Reporting on the Palestinian struggle,[6] the *IGP* used a highly emotional headline: 'Palestinians fight extremely fiercely — Jewish Minister of Defence almost perishes'. The reference was to an incident which took place on 22 September 1988, when Ishtak Rabin, Israel's Minister of Defence, was very nearly killed while touring a town in the Gaza Strip. A huge concrete block was dropped from a nearby building, missing him by five metres. In its obvious sympathy for the Palestinian struggle, the *IGP* elevated the dropping of a concrete block to 'an extremely fierce struggle'.

Turning to the Afghan resistance to the Soviet invasion, the *IGP* raised the issue of drug addiction among the Soviet troops. Many Soviet soldiers took heroin and LSD before engaging in battles with the *mujahideen*. They bought drugs from the Afghans and used them to reduce their anxiety when fighting. Approximately 20 per cent of the Soviet soldiers were introduced to drugs while in the army. This has been going on for the past twenty years and is similar to the drug-related problems of American soldiers in Vietnam. Citing *Pravda*, the *IGP* concluded this news item by mentioning that drugs were a serious social problem in the Soviet Union and that there were more than 130,000 drug addicts in the country. The clear implication was that the Russian army faced a destiny similar to that of the Americans. Not only did they face defeat, but social problems would arise in their own society as well.

The death of General Zia ul Haq, President of Pakistan, was dealt with in great detail while other cases, such as an attempt to overthrow Imam Khomeini of Iran or the violation of human rights by the

Egyptian government in actions against Muslims, were simply reported as news.

The *IGP* asked whether the death of Zia was an accident or murder. Zia was favourably portrayed by the Muslim media. Several possible reasons for the assassination of Zia were suggested by the *IGP*. First, India was a prime suspect, because of its long history of hostility to Pakistan. An article in the *IGP* traced the relationship between the two countries back to the days of the raj. The death of Liyaqat Ali Khan at the hand of an assassin, thought to have been under orders from India in 1948, was highlighted. Zia's death might also have been the result of border disputes: he had gained support from the leadership of Western Kashmir, and also, India accused Pakistan of interference in the Punjab. Thus India had reasons to see him gone. The article underscored the fact that two days prior to Zia's death, Rajiv Gandhi warned, 'Zia will learn to regret what he did'.[7] Second, the *IGP* suggested, Zia might have been assassinated because the Shi-ite group in Pakistan disagreed with his pro-Sunnah style. In 1987 a Sunni scholar by the name of Ihsan Ilahi was killed after publishing works critical of Shi-ite belief.

It was also possible that Zia's death was an act of revenge — a former Shi-ite political party leader had been murdered secretly twelve days earlier — though the article concluded that this was a quite remote probability. Third, it was suggested that the Soviet Union might be the culprit. It is no secret that Pakistan was helping the *mujahideen* to fight the Soviet invaders by allowing American weapons to pass through its territory into Afghanistan, and Pakistan allowed Peshawar to be used as a sanctuary for the *mujahideen*. Fourth, two Pakistani political parties also had their reasons to kill him. The Pakistan People's Party (PPP) may have wanted to kill him to avenge the execution of Zulfiqar Ali Bhutto. Thus the latter's family had sufficient reason to be deeply hostile to him. While referring to the Bhutto era as an age of moral degradation and submission to materialism, the *IGP* cited Benazir Bhutto describing her father's death as 'a judicial' assassination. A fifth possibility was that Zia was killed by the Pakistan Muslim League because he had deposed former Prime Minister Junejo, one of the leaders of the party. The *IGP* commented that 'although the Pakistan Muslim League has a beautiful name, it does not employ Islamic theory in administering the party nor formulate its policies by using Islamic teaching as its core'.[8] Sixth, Zia might have been killed on the orders of his own military top men. One military leader narrowly escaped the explosion because he did not embark on that fateful plane with the rest of Zia's party. After Zia's death a major reshuffle took place in the military leadership.

Finally, the *IGP* questioned whether the attempted use of Islamic law in Pakistan resulted in Zia's death because there were some who disapproved of Zia's strong Islamic orientation. In this context, the United States became a prime suspect. *IGP* supported this speculation by citing the very critical attitude of the American press to the introduction of Islamic law in Pakistan. The death of an American diplomat along with Zia was described as a ploy to divert suspicion from the American government. Thus the *IGP* article portrays Zia's death as an assassination stemming from his assertiveness in promoting policies of Islamization. The underlying assumption is that those who have supported Islamization have frequently fallen victims at the hands of those who fear it.

The main actors in the world-view of the *IGP* are Muslims. They act and are acted upon. Sometimes the actors are nation-states; sometimes they are political leaders. Those who are against them are considered 'unislamic'. In a recent book Bernard Lewis has explained the powerful attraction of Islam: 'In most Muslim countries Islam is still the ultimate criterion of group identity and loyalty. It is Islam which distinguishes between self and other, between insider and outsider, between brother and stranger.'[9]

The *IGP*'s firm commitment to Islam is quite evident. This commitment leads it to criticize Muslim leaders or countries that seem to deviate from the path of Islam as understood by it. The world, in their perception, is not defined by countries or even by ethnicity, since there are times when the line between one's ethnic and religious identities is very thin. Islam serves to blur that line. As Lewis aptly states:

> There is a recurring tendency in times of crisis, in times of emergency, when the deeper loyalties take over, for Muslims to find their basic identity in the religious community; that is to say, in an entity defined by Islam rather than by ethnic origin, language, or country of habitation.[10]

Whether the blurring of lines which is taking place in the world according to the Muslim press in Thailand, is a result of crisis, is a question that requires further study. 'Crisis' itself can be a problematic concept. Suffice it to say that such a portrait of the world can be explained by a major phenomenon of our time: Islamic resurgence.

Factors explaining the portrait of the world according to the Muslim press

The world-view of the Muslims who publish the *Islamic Guidance Post* is influenced by a number of interrelated factors specifically, time, geography and ethnohistory.

Time

Muslims today live in a time of what many call an 'Islamic resurgence'. It is not intended to examine this highly controversial notion here. Nevertheless we need to point out that Islamic resurgence generally assumes one of two forms.[11] One falls back upon Islamic tradition as far as possible, seeing any change as being for the worse. The solution is to hold fast to Islamic tradition either by withdrawing from the processes of Westernization or by preserving the Muslim legacy in the areas of culture, knowledge and institutions. The other sees the preservation of the past as inadequate. What is needed is a creative, positive response to the Western challenge by trying to understand its nature and to offer an alternative to it. The Islamic resurgence endeavours to prepare itself for all-out confrontation with the Western challenge and to offer Islam as the alternative basis for culture and civilization.[12]

From the pages of the *IGP*, it is clear that its editors ride the tide of Islamic resurgence. The fact that they positively and publicly use Islam as a basic perspective in viewing the world is honest and courageous. For them, Arabs as an ethnic group appear to be monolithic in religious terms: it is difficult for them to conceptualize Christian Arabs or Christian Palestinians also fighting Israeli occupation.

It would be misleading to overemphasize the commonality of phenomena resulting from Islamic resurgence all over the world. Indeed one of the most salient features of contemporary Islamic resurgence is that it manifests local characteristics, sectarian differences and indigenous accents.[13] In the case of Thailand, the power of both geography and history are vital in shaping the Muslims' view of the world.

Geography

The Thai state regards the problems in the four southernmost provinces, where the majority of Muslims live, as very sensitive security issues. Even economic development is closely related to security measures without which, the Thai policymakers think, the private sector will be discouraged from investing in the region.[14] The Muslims in the south are seen as a security problem by the Thai government partly because the way of life of the Muslims, who belong to the Malay cultural world of South-East Asia, is clearly different from that of the Thais. The proximity of Thailand to Malaysia, and especially of the four southern provinces, Yala, Patani, Narathiwat and Satun, to the northern states of Malaysia contributes to this closer identification.[15]

In addition, the Malay Muslims in southern Thailand take pride in Malaysia as the epicentre of their world and view events there positively. So, with the rise of Islamic resurgence in Malaysia,[16] Malaysian-based *tabligh* (propagation) groups, who have ventured into Thailand over the past decade or so, are very eagerly received by the Muslims in southern Thailand.

The development of Islam in Malaysia is particularly significant for the Malay Muslims of the Thai south, due among other things, to their cultural affinity.[17] This helps explain why the *IGP* included an interview with Uztaz Hadi Awang, a leading PAS (Malaysian Islamic Party) member, in September 1988, concerning the impact of the global religious rift on Muslim activism among younger generations.[18] The same issue reported that the Thai governor of Narathiwat admitted that young Muslims in the south prefer to continue their studies in Malaysia, because of their religious faith.[19]

This geographical proximity is conducive to ideas travelling between the two countries, and ensures that the impact of Islamic resurgence in Malaysia will be felt by Muslims in Thai society. However, geographical proximity alone cannot explain the feeling of affinity Muslims in Thailand share with those as far away as Iran, Pakistan or Afghanistan. The strength of faith cannot be denied.

Ethnohistory
Malay Muslims are not the only Muslim group in Thai society. It is believed that the first Muslims came to Thailand from Persia some 700 years ago.[20] They came first as traders. Later, during the Ayudhaya period at the turn of the seventeenth century, some of them decided to enter government service. Abandoning Islam and turning to Buddhism, this group later became quite powerful, reaching the height of its powers towards the end of King Rama IV's reign in 1868.

The largest group, however, is the Malay Muslims who constitute the majority of the population in the four southern border provinces. They did not migrate to Thailand but were incorporated when the Thai state defeated the rulers of Patani. Most of them continue to live in the south, though some came to Bangkok and tilled the soil as farmers. With urbanization, the value of their land has increased significantly. Other Muslims came to Bangkok in the reign of King Rama IV from Indonesia, and became famous as gardeners and businessmen.[21]

Another group came from Cambodia some time between 1656 and 1688. They moved to Bangkok at the dawn of the Chakkri dynasty. About two hundred years ago, King Rama I gave a piece of land in the Phya Thai district, called 'Ban Krua', to these Cambodian Muslims, who continue to live there today. Their community of 3,000 people is famous for weaving Thai silk under the brand name of Jim Thompson. Despite this most of them are poor.[22]

Some Muslims came to Thailand from the Indian subcontinent. There are Pathans, who generally earn their living by raising cattle outside Bangkok, especially in the north-east, and Indian Muslims who came to Bangkok in the reign of King Rama IV and live near Chinatown in the Rajawong area where they have been traders, especially in textiles and precious stones. There are also Chinese Muslims in the north who came to Thailand when Chiang Kai Chek fled mainland China for Formosa (Taiwan). Most of them are in the field of commerce.

This brief sketch illustrates the complex picture of Muslims in Thai society. Many are not eager to recall their distinctive lineages, but most are aware that their roots are in other lands. The declining significance of individual lineage is consonant with a strengthening of collective Muslim identity. At a time of Islamic resurgence their Muslim identity is emphasized. In a country where Muslims constitute a minority, and follow a different way of life from the majority in the society, they do not perceive that their being different from the mainstream Thais is wrong. In fact, for some Muslims this may be something to be proud of. When they trace their own histories, they soon realize that their origins are different from those of others. This realization of existential and historical differences constitutes a particular world-view that, in turn, provides a condition for seeing the world as depicted by the *IGP*.

Conclusion

By examining international news published by the *IGP*, it is possible to characterize a Muslim world-view. Muslims everywhere are at the centre of the world stage. Their movements constitute the rhythm of the world that is relevant to the Muslims. At a time when the wave of Islamic resurgence is apparent, an Islam-oriented perspective becomes more relevant. However, it is not faith alone that dictates the strong feeling between Muslims in Thai society and their co-religionists elsewhere in the world. The fact that Thailand is close to Malaysia allows for easy interaction between Muslims in the two countries so that information on Islam and matters related to the Muslims can be exchanged easily. In addition to psychological affinity resulting from common faith and geographical proximity, a common legacy between Muslims in southern Thailand and those in northern Malaysia is also significant in shaping the Muslims' perception of the world. Since there are different lineages of Muslims in Thailand, they can also feel affinity with Muslims elsewhere. The passage of time may have reduced the power of distinctive lineages; in fact, it may be argued that the fading memory of distinctive lineages is somehow responsible for the strengthening of the collective awareness of being Muslim, which transcends national or ethnic boundaries. It is the configuration of these important factors, among others, which can explain the portrait of today's international order as seen by some Muslims in Thai society.

Notes

1. *Islamic Guidance Post* (*IGP*), August–September 1987.
2. *IGP*, November–December 1987.
3. It goes without saying that the Muslims are not the only people who fight for the Palestinian state. Many Christian Arabs have taken part in this struggle for a long time. However, this aspect of the Palestinian struggle is not normally highlighted by the Muslim press, more perhaps out of ignorance than out of malice.
4. Ibid., October 1988, pp. 20–1.
5. Ibid., November–December 1988, p. 16.
6. Ibid., October 1988, p. 49.
7. Ibid., October–November 1988, p. 16.
8. Ibid., p. 17.
9. Bernard Lewis, *The Political Language of Islam*, Chicago and London, The University of Chicago Press, 1988, p. 4.
10. Ibid., 1988, p. 4.
11. The terms 'revivalism' and 'reassertion' are sometimes used in the same context. See Chandra Muzaffar, 'Islamic Resurgence: A GlobalView', in Taufik Abdullah and Sharon Siddique (eds), *Islam and Society in Southeast Asia*, Singapore, Institute of Southeast Asian Studies, 1986, pp. 5–39; and his *Islamic Resurgence in Malaysia*, Petaling Jaya, Penerbit Fajar Bakti, 1987. See also Chaiwat Satha-Anand, '*Hi jab* and Moments of Legitimation: Islamic Resurgence in Thai Society'. Paper presented at the International Conference on Communities in Question, organized by the Social Science Research Council (New York) and the American Council of Learned Societies, Hua Hin, 1989.

12. Kurshid Ahmad, 'The Nature of Islamic Resurgence', in John L. Esposito (ed.), *Voice of Resurgent Islam*, New York, Oxford University Press, 1983, pp. 18–29.
13. Amin Saikal, 'Islam: Resistance and Reassertion', *The World Today* 43 (11), 1987, pp. 191–4.
14. *Bangkok Post*, 15 April 1985.
15. Chaiwat Satha-Anand, *Islam and Violence: A Case Study of Violent Events in the Four Southern Provinces, Thailand, 1976–1981*, Tampa, Florida, USF Monographs in Religious and Public Policy, 1987, pp. 23–8.
16. Chandra Muzaffar, *Islamic Resurgence in Malaysia*, Petaling Jayan, Penerbit, Fajar Bakti, 1987.
17. Omar Farouk, 'Malaysia's Islamic Awakening: Impact on Singapore and Thai Muslims', *Conflict*, 1988, 8, pp. 157–68.
18. *IGP*, op. cit., 1988, pp. 17–18.
19. Ibid.
20. Prayoonsak Chalayondecha, *Muslims in Thailand*, Bangkok, Tonson Mosque, 1988, p. 6 (In Thai).
21. Peerayot Rahimmula, 'Thai Muslims in Thailand', *Kao Son*, 1 (3), 1979–80 (In Thai).
22. Ibid., p. 48.

11 SOURCES OF EXTERNAL SUPPORT FOR THE WEST PAPUA MOVEMENT

R.J. May

In August 1945, two days after the defeat of Japan in World War II, nationalist leaders in the Netherlands East Indies proclaimed the independent Republic of Indonesia. Four years later, after protracted negotiations between the Dutch and the Indonesians, the federal Republic of United Indonesia was formally recognized. The new republic did not have an easy birth. Within twelve months the federal structure had been replaced by a centralized state but centrifugal forces were challenging the authority of the central government in the outlying regions, notably in Aceh, in South Sulawesi and in the South Moluccas. The Aceh and South Moluccas rebellions continued into the early 1960s.[1] A Republic of South Moluccas government-in-exile was subsequently established in the Netherlands, from where it continues to campaign for a free *Maluku Selatan.*

Initially, there was apparent disagreement among Indonesia's founding fathers about whether the republic should include the Melanesian territory of Netherlands New Guinea.[2] By 1949, however, not only did Indonesia's political leaders claim to be heirs to the whole of the former Dutch territory, they justified their demands by reference to a historical 'Greater Indonesia' (*Indonesia Raya*) which extended well beyond the boundaries of the Netherlands East Indies.[3] The Indonesian claim to Netherlands New Guinea was pursued, with little effect, during the 1950s. In the Netherlands, denial of Indonesia's claims was motivated by a mixture of territorial self-interest, national pride, and genuine belief in the moral right of self-determination for the Melanesians. In neighbouring Australia, whose colony Papua New Guinea shared a common border with Netherlands New Guinea, there was concern, on strategic grounds, about Indonesia's expansionist ambitions, and there were some who entertained the idea of an eventual independent Federation of Melanesia.[4] At the United Nations, Indonesia was unable to gather the necessary support for its demand.

Eventually, around 1960 the Indonesian government began looking towards a military solution to its West New Guinea claim. A $US450 million low-interest loan for the purchase of military equipment was received from the USSR, which supported the Indonesian claim to West New Guinea, and plans were developed for the infiltration and invasion of the island by a force under the leadership of General Suharto. This culminated in 1962 in a brief naval engagement between the two countries. By this time, however, the international climate had changed and pressure was put on the Netherlands (notably by the United States, but with Australia acquiescing) to reach a settlement of the issue. The outcome of this was an agreement, signed in New York in 1962, under the terms of which West New Guinea was placed under a UN Temporary Executive Authority (UNTEA), pending an 'act of self-determination in accordance with international practice'. Already in 1962, however, there was a substantial Indonesian military presence in West New Guinea, and by May 1963 Indonesian authorities had effectively taken over the administration of the territory. Over the next few years political activity among Melanesians was proscribed, Melanesians were substantially displaced from government positions, and there were numerous reports of abuses against the Melanesian population. President Sukarno made no secret of his opposition to the act of self-determination, at one stage in 1965 announcing that there would be no plebiscite.[5] A so-called 'Act of Free Choice' (referred to by critics as an 'Act of No Choice' or 'Act Free of Choice') was held in 1969, but rather than a popular vote it was a managed public consultation (*musjawarah*), and the final vote by 1,022 appointed delegates took place amid widespread reports of repression and intimidation.[6] Predictably, the delegates supported the incorporation of West New Guinea into the Republic, and although the report of the UN representative, and reports by visiting journalists, criticized the conduct of the Act of Free Choice,[7] outside West New Guinea there was little real interest in the issue. Despite lobbying by *émigré* West Papuans, with some support from African nations, the outcome of the Act of Free Choice was accepted by the UN and the former Dutch territory thus became formally a part of the Indonesian Republic.

The origins of West Papuan nationalism

Melanesian resistance to Dutch colonial rule can be traced back to the period before World War II, though in this early period, and even much later, anti-colonialism was often associated with millenarian tendencies.[8] Following the Japanese invasion some Melanesian nationalists initially saw collaboration as a strategy to gain independence from Dutch rule.

On Biak, however, members of a millenarian, proto-nationalist movement confronted the Japanese in 1942, declaring their independence and raising a West New Guinea flag; Japanese retribution was severe.

On returning to New Guinea in 1944 the Dutch administration embarked on a programme of rapid economic and political development. Among its first acts was the establishment of a School of Administration, a Police Training School and a Papuan Battalion; nearly all the early West Papuan nationalist leaders came through one of these institutions. In the following years the Dutch administration extended its influence into previously uncontacted areas, embarked on a programme of 'Papuanization' of government jobs, and promoted education. Political participation was fostered through the establishment of regional councils, beginning with Biak in 1947, and in 1961 a New Guinea Council was created, with a mixture of elected and appointed members, mostly Melanesians.

The first 'modern' political organization in West New Guinea, *Suara Rakjat* (Voice of the People) was formed in Biak in 1945 under the leadership of Lukas Rumkorem; its objective was independence for West New Guinea. The Indonesian proclamation of independence in August 1945, however, caused a split among the West New Guinean nationalists. In Hollandia and Serui Indonesian-initiated pro-independence parties (the *Komite Indonesia Merdeka* and the *Partai Kemerdekaan Indonesia Irian*) attracted the support of educated nationalists Lukas Rumkorem, Silas Papare and Marthen Indey. As against these a 'pro-Dutch' group, prominent among whom were Markus Kaisiepo, Abdullah Arfan, Johan Ariks and subsequently Nicolaas Jouwe, denied the Indonesian claim to what Frans Kaisiepo in 1946 termed 'Irian' (Biak-Numfoor means 'hot land') and threw in their lot with the Dutch administration, forming the *Gerakan Persatuan Nieuw Guinea* (New Guinea Unity Movement, GPNG). The GPNG set up branches around the country.

In the period from 1945 to 1962 an emerging sense of Irianese national identity was caught up in the wider Indonesian–Dutch dialogue, including the debate over the future of West New Guinea, but it was fostered also by the growing influx of Eurasian *émigrés* from Java, who competed for jobs and occupied Melanesian land, and by increasing disenchantment with the pace of political devolution. In 1952 a Protestant church-backed Christian Workers' Union (CWNG-Persekding), was launched and quickly attracted the support of Melanesians. Among the political parties which emerged on the eve of elections for the New Guinea Council in 1961, the largest, *Partai Nasional (Parna)*, drew the bulk of its leadership from CWNG-Persekding. The frenzied pursuit in West New Guinea of what van der Veur refers to as 'terminal colonial democracy', from around 1959 to 1962, overcame some of the disenchantment among Melanesian nationalists and, as intended, undermined pro-Indonesian sentiments. However, as Hastings commented in 1969, 'Dutch actions were to breed terrible consequences in frustrated Papuan hopes.'[10] The UN debate over West New Guinea in 1961 prompted a group of some seventy educated Melanesians, mostly from western and northern Irian, to convene a meeting, at which a *Komite Nasional* was established, a nationalist manifesto drafted, and a flag, a national anthem and a name for the country (*Irian Barat*) chosen. In December 1961 the Irian flag was raised alongside the Dutch. The Dutch capitulation in 1962 caused confusion and distress in Irian, but the *Komite Nasional* agreed to accept the New York Agreement, providing the UNTEA recognized the Irian flag and arranged for a self-determination plebiscite by 1963.

In fact, the use of the Irian flag was expressly forbidden by the UNTEA and the terms in which the act of self-determination was specified were not honoured. Even before the UNTEA was established there was an exodus of Dutch citizens and Eurasians from West New Guinea. With them went a number of the pro-Dutch nationalist figures, including Markus Kaisiepo and Nicholaas Jouwe who took up residence in the Netherlands. Others, including in 1963 most of the students of the School of Administration, crossed the border into Papua New Guinea (where the Australian administration sent many back). As economic and political conditions deteriorated in West New Guinea between 1962 and 1969, the exodus increased and opposition to the Indonesian administration mounted, even among those who had earlier been in the 'pro-Indonesia' camp.

Opposition to Indonesian rule and the demand for independence

In 1962 some Irianese still believed that an act of self-determination would take place and that an independent Irian was achievable. It quickly became apparent, however, that Indonesia had no intention of relinquishing control of West New Guinea and that it would not countenance Melanesian nationalist sentiments. In addition to a ban on political activity and restrictions on the movement of people, after May 1963 the Indonesian administration began replacing senior Melanesian officials suspected of nationalist or pro-Dutch sympathies and there were frequent reports of Indonesian military action against dissident local groups. This confrontation intensified after Indonesia's military coup of 1965.

Around 1963, villagers in the Arfak area in the west of the island, under the leadership initially of Johan Ariks and later of Lodewijk and Barend Mandatjan and Perminas Awom, launched a rebellion against Indonesian rule, subsequently declaring a 'Free Papuan State' in the region. They were met with heavy military resistance. Ariks was captured in 1965 and died in prison two years later. The Mandatjan brothers and Awom later surrendered under an amnesty offered in 1969, but the three were apparently executed. In 1967 Silas Papare, then a member of the government-appointed People's Consultative Committee, complained that villages in the Arfak area were being strafed and that casualties were heavy. In Biak in 1965 Melanesian nationalists attacked Shell Oil Company installations, and in the lead-up to the 1969 vote there were uprisings also in Waghete, Enaratoli and Paniai. By 1969 there were reports that several thousand Melanesians had been killed in clashes with Indonesian troops, and there were several hundred political prisoners.

Meanwhile, in the Netherlands a West Papuan government-in-exile, headed by Jouwe, Markus Kaisiepo and Herman Womsiwor, campaigned against the incorporation of West New Guinea into the Indonesian Republic. The group's office in Delft distributed propaganda (including Free West Papua flags and emblems) and published an occasional magazine in Dutch, Indonesian and English, and through a small office in New York it lobbied UN members, notably the 'Brazzaville Group' (comprising mostly former French territories in Africa) who gave some support. Later the overseas group also opened an office in Dakar, where Ben Tanggahma was supported by the government of Senegal's Leopold Senghor. In the Netherlands the group received apparently small amounts of financial and logistic assistance from sympathetic private individuals and groups, including the conservative Protestant *Door de eeuwen trouw* (Eternal Faith) foundation, which was also a major supporter of the South Moluccan government-in-exile. It is also said to have received overseas support from American and Japanese ex-servicemen.

Some time around 1965 the anti-Indonesian nationalist forces within West Papua, coalesced around the *Organisasi Papua Merdeka*,[11] suggested that 'The West Irianese resistance movements were loosely controlled by the West Papuan government-in-exile in Delft',[12] but in fact it seems that the groups engaged in a guerrilla campaign against the Indonesian government operated largely independently of the government-in-exile. In 1971 the OPM, from its secret headquarters at 'Markas Viktoria' in Irian Jaya, announced the formation of a Provisional Republic of West Papua New Guinea, and proclaimed the territory's independence. Since 1971, despite frequent predictions by Indonesian authorities and foreign observers of its imminent demise, the West Papuan movement has continued to fight for a Free West Papua, even though there have been divisions, frequently bitter, within the movement, both in Irian Jaya and abroad.[13]

Sources of support for the OPM

European and African connections

The exodus of West Papuan nationalist leaders to the Netherlands in the early 1960s created a sizeable community of West Papuans there, who interacted with other refugee groups from Indonesia, particularly (as noted above) the South Moluccan government-in-exile, representatives of the Aceh National Liberation Front, and sympathetic Dutch and Eurasian ex-colonials hostile towards Indonesia. The relationship with the RSM and Aceh communities does not appear to have been very close, however, and as the RSM turned to terrorism in Europe the West Papuan community appears to have distanced itself from it. Most of the support (and that largely moral support) for the West Papuan cause in the Netherlands came from church (especially Protestant church) sources and academics, initially centring on Delft, where the West Papuan government-in-exile was located, and more recently on Nijmegen. From Nijmegen the Stichting Werkgroep Nieuw Guinea published a bi-monthly *West Papuan Observer*, which serves as a propaganda vehicle for Dutch-based groups.

An office of the West Papuan government-in-exile was also established in the 1960s in Stockholm, where support came from Swedish academics. In 1978 when OPM leaders Jacob Prai and Otto Ondowame were arrested and deported from Papua New Guinea it was the Swedish government which eventually provided a home for them. Support from Sweden is currently co-ordinated through Föreningen Ett Fritt Papua (FFT), a support group of which Prai is president.

In London, TAPOL, the British Campaign for the Defence of Political Prisoners and Human Rights in Indonesia, provided a sympathetic coverage of developments in West Papua (and East Timor) through its widely disseminated *Tapol Bulletin* (published quarterly since the early 1970s). TAPOL also published a partisan but well-documented account of the West Papuan issue, *West Papua: The Obliteration of a People* (1983 but subsequently reprinted) and has acted as a distributor for other publications critical of the Indonesian regime. In the 1970s the OPM also maintained a small office in London, run by an Australian former student at the University of Papua New Guinea, which distributed news releases from West Papua.

The office in Senegal, run by Ben Tanggahma, reflected the somewhat tenuous links established with the Brazzaville Group during the 1950s and 1960s and relied on a sentiment of shared '*negritude*', for which President Senghor was a leading spokesman. However, although it served as a useful point for propaganda distribution in Africa, it achieved little in terms of securing concrete support.

After the Indonesian invasion of East Timor in 1975, there was some contact between the OPM and Fretilin, but the East Timor group found the factionalized West Papuans difficult to deal with and interaction between the two has been slight (Jose Ramos Horta, interview 1988).

The strength of the movement in the Netherlands has been depleted since the early 1970s by divisions within the West Papuan movement, by distance from events in Irian Jaya, and eventually by the passage of time. Although there is still a strong emotional commitment to West Papua among the *émigré* community — as evidenced in the organization of a West Papuan 'summit' meeting at Oetgeest in 1982 and the creation of a Co-ordination Group of West Papuan Organizations in the Netherlands in 1984 — the nationalist leaders of the 1950s and 1960s are getting older, having seen little response to their demands, and a younger generation has grown up mostly with no personal contact with their ancestral place. In Dakar, too, support for an independent West Papua has diminished, especially since the death of Senghor, and in London the OPM Office appears to have closed after its representative shifted to Spain, though TAPOL still covers West Papua. Nevertheless, West Papuan leaders in Europe continue to attend conferences and workshops and to present their case to generally sympathetic audiences.

Relations with Papua New Guinea[14]

The emergence of a nationalist élite occurred at about the same time in West New Guinea and Papua New Guinea — more slowly, in fact, in the latter where Australian colonial policy was specifically against the creation of an élite. With the signing of a joint Australian–Netherlands Co-operative Agreement in 1957 there was some limited contact between the Dutch and Australian colonial administrations and their Melanesian protégés. The idea of a Melanesian federation, extending at least from West Papua to the Solomon Islands, was also floated, unofficially, but the idea seems to have appealed more to expatriate residents and Australian observers than to Melanesians, who were primarily concerned with their own more narrowly defined nationalist aspirations.

In 1962 members of Papua New Guinea's legislative council voiced concern about the future of West New Guinea and supported an immediate referendum on self-determination. A group of Papua New Guineans, including John Guise (who became Papua New Guinea's first governor-general), wrote to the United Nations, expressing their dissatisfaction with the UN's actions. Subsequently, with large numbers of Irianese refugees crossing the border into Papua New Guinea, and Australian officials putting pressure on them to return, Papua New Guinean members of parliament expressed sympathy with the refugees and concern at the UN's failure to organize a vote on self-determination. Early in 1969 student and church leaders led a protest march in Port Moresby which condemned Indonesian actions in West New Guinea and Australia's tacit support of Indonesia, and there was further condemnation following the 'Act of Free Choice'. Participant commentator Davis[15] compared Papua New Guinean student involvement in the West Papuan issue at this time with Australian student involvement over Vietnam. However, if West Papuan leaders expected substantive support from their Melanesian brothers, they were to be disappointed. As early as 1968, while expressing their sympathy for the West Papuans, prominent Papua New Guinean politicians made it clear that they did not want West Papuan refugees to make trouble for Papua New Guinea, whose relations with Indonesia must be kept friendly.[16] Indeed, it was made a condition for the granting of residence visas to West Papuan refugees that they did not take part in political activity directed against Indonesia.

In 1973 Chief Minister Michael Somare, acting on behalf of the Australian administration, signed an agreement on border administration. This covered such matters as traditional land rights and movement across the border, health and quarantine in the border area, and border liaison, but it also contained a provision which bound both parties to prevent the use of their respective territories for hostile acts against the other. This last provision was in specific recognition of the fact that the OPM forces had been taking sanctuary and establishing base camps in the dense jungle on Papua New Guinea's side of the border.

After independence in 1975 Papua New Guinea broadly maintained the policy lines laid down by the colonial administration: successive governments have acknowledged Indonesian sovereignty in Irian Jaya; they have attempted to deny the OPM access to the border area (though they have refused to engage in joint military action in the border area); they have discouraged movement across the border, and where residence visas have been granted they have insisted that the visa-holders refrain from political activity directed against Indonesia, in several instances repatriating or deporting refugees who have violated this condition.

Nevertheless, there has been an underlying tension between what I have described elsewhere as the public attitudes and the private feelings of Papua New Guinea's leaders.[17] Such tension has been exacerbated by the often high-handed and even dishonest position Indonesia has adopted in its dealings with Papua New Guinea.

In 1973 Foreign Minister Albert Maori Kiki initiated 'secret diplomacy' with OPM leaders from within Irian Jaya and overseas in an attempt 'to mediate between the rebels and the Indonesian Government and bring about conditions where the two could have come together for constructive consideration of the means of peaceful reintegration of the rebel groups into the Irianese community'.[18] Talks were held over several years but failed to bring the West Papuans and Indonesians to the conference table, largely, according to Kiki, because of divisions within the West Papuan movement.

The duality of Papua New Guinean attitudes towards West Papua/Irian Jaya became more apparent during the second half of the 1970s. In late 1976 Papua New Guinea's National Broadcasting Commission relayed a report from the official Indonesian newsagency ANTARA that talks had begun between the Papua New Guinea and Indonesian governments over the extradition of 500 Irianese residents in Papua New Guinea. Although the report was denied by Prime Minister Somare, the subject was raised as a matter of public importance in the National Parliament where several speakers criticized Indonesia and the UN, recalling the invasion of East Timor, and demanded independence for Irian Jaya. One of the parliament's more colourful members, Pita Lus, told the House:

> the United Nations is not doing its job to recognize the West Irian cause. I think it is made up of lazy ——! If only this country could send me to the United Nations...I would tell the United Nations to give West Irian its freedom.[19]

And Kiki said: 'The West Irianese are our neighbours and friends ... the government has no intention of selling our brothers.'[20] Earlier in the year, however, in denying a statement by the Netherlands-based Revolutionary Provisional Government of West Papua New Guinea (RPGWPNG) that Australian officers in the Papua New Guinea defence forces had been involved in joint action with Indonesian troops on the border, in which 1,600 villagers had been killed, Kiki and Somare expressed anger at those who had helped publicize the story and threatened to prosecute Papua New Guineans and to deport Irianese residence visa-holders who were actively supporting the OPM. A spokesman for the Irianese community in Port Moresby responded with a statement that 'threats of Government action against dissidents must not go unchallenged' and that the Irianese may be forced to seek Communist aid. However, after Kiki accused the group of breaching the conditions of their residency and threatened them with deportation, the community's spokesman retracted and the subject was dropped. Such tensions became increasingly evident in the following years as conflict between the OPM and the Indonesian military intensified and hundreds of Irianese began crossing the border into Papua New Guinea. Expressions of concern by the Papua New Guinean government were met by the Indonesian response that 'tribal fighting' in Irian Jaya was no concern of Papua New Guinea. However, this interpretation of the situation was scarcely consistent with Indonesian demands that the Papua New Guinean government act against critics of Indonesia within Papua New Guinea and that it take effective action to deny the OPM access to the Papua New Guinea border area. Relations between the two countries deteriorated early in 1978 when an Indonesian diplomat in Port Moresby accused Papua New Guinea of 'double standards' on the West Papuan issue, and after an Indonesian patrol had raided a village on the Papua New Guinea side of the border.

Relations between the Papua New Guinean government and the Irianese community also deteriorated during this period. The Irianese community in Papua New Guinea was a channel for OPM propaganda — including a press release in 1978 which, to the embarrassment of the Papua New Guinean government, named the ministry of the RPGWPNG, and included among the eighteen names were six Papua New Guinean citizens, two holders of residence visas, and two people serving gaol sentences for illegal entry who had given notice of intent to apply for political asylum. However, in 1977 it was also reported that the West Papuan movement intended to use terrorism in the Pacific to draw attention to its demands. Threats were later made against certain Papua

New Guinean politicians and public servants. The Papua New Guinean government responded by announcing a tougher line on border crossing, by threatening to cancel the entry permits of those supporting the RPGWPNG, and by arranging a meeting with OPM leaders Jacob Prai and Seth Rumkorem and telling them to remove the camps on the Papua New Guinea side of the border or have them burned. According to a *Post-Courier* report,[21] Prai and Rumkorem 'were told that PNG did not want to act against other Melanesians, but at the same time the Government could not afford to fall out with Indonesia'. When, towards the end of 1978, Prai and several of his deputies crossed into Papua New Guinea and were arrested they were denied residence visas; after unsuccessful attempts to find homes for them in Australia, New Zealand, Fiji, Solomon Islands, Tonga and Western Samoa, the refugees were eventually given asylum in Sweden. As activity along the border increased during 1977-8 Somare announced his government's decision to deploy extra police and troops in the area but he refused to grant Indonesia the right of 'hot pursuit' across the border and resisted suggestions for joint patrolling.

The Papua New Guinean government thus found itself squeezed on three sides: by Indonesia, who sought a firm commitment against Irianese rebels; by OPM leaders, who threatened military action against Papua New Guinea if it attempted to close the border; and by an increasingly vocal group within the country, led by church and student groups, and politicians from the border area, who demanded sympathy towards their Melanesian brothers and a firmer stand against Indonesian actions along the border.

In 1980 Papua New Guinea's incoming prime minister, Sir Julius Chan, on the eve of an official visit to Indonesia, was reported as saying that his government did not recognize the OPM and that if guerrilla activities along the border increased it would consider military action after consultation with Indonesian authorities. Chan's statement drew a sharp reaction within Papua New Guinea, and the national executive of Chan's coalition partner, the Melanesian Alliance, strongly criticized the prime minister and 'declared its support for the Irian Jaya freedom movement'.[22] The following year University of Papua New Guinea students staged a solidarity march 'to assess the public's support for the West Papua freedom movement' and collected K2,000 to support the OPM. Subsequently the students organized a Melanesian Solidarity Week, as part of which a South Pacific Human Rights Tribunal was convened to consider charges that Indonesia had violated international laws on human rights. A prominent member of the tribunal was Bernard

Narokobi, then an acting national court judge and currently Minister for Justice in the National Parliament and deputy chairman of the Melanesian Alliance. Indonesia appears to have pressured the Papua New Guinean government to stop the hearings but Prime Minister Chan declined to intervene, describing the tribunal as 'an expression of our people's rights to express themselves'.[23] Nevertheless, shortly after the tribunal completed its proceedings, it became known that three Irianese refugees who had presented evidence—including former Irian Jaya Governor Eliezer Bonay, who had crossed to Papua New Guinea seeking asylum in 1979, and Dean Kafiar—were to be deported. Bonay and Kafiar were sent to Sweden, but a third West Papuan supporter was concealed from police by students and the government's deportation order aroused strong criticism from a number of sources. This did not, however, prevent the government from repatriating another three OPM supporters to Indonesia the same month.

Shortly after this, in commenting on a government White Paper on Foreign Policy, and referring specifically to recent military activity in Irian Jaya which had led to new border crossings into Papua New Guinea, Deputy Prime Minister Iambakey Okuk said that 'Indonesia must realize the people of Irian Jaya were Melanesians—not Indonesians' and that Indonesia 'should be ashamed that its own people were crossing the border to live in Papua New Guinea'.[24] Okuk's statement provoked a series of heated exchanges with Indonesian officials, but there was support for Okuk, especially after a series of border violations by Indonesian troops and aircraft in late 1981 and early 1982, which Indonesian officials refused to acknowledge. There were calls for the closure of the Indonesian embassy in Port Moresby. Nevertheless, when in 1982 OPM leader Seth Rumkorem was taken into custody in Papua New Guinean waters with nine of his deputies, allegedly en route to Senegal via Vanuatu, he was refused asylum in Papua New Guinea, and with Vanuatu also unwilling to accept him he was subsequently sent to Greece.

Had the West Papuans, or at least the West Papuan community in Papua New Guinea, shown more solidarity, they might have been able to exert more influence on public opinion in Papua New Guinea. As it was, they were fractious. When in 1978, for example, an officially-sanctioned visit by Nicolaas Jouwe was organized, a faction calling itself the South Pacific Group opposed it. Factional conflict within the OPM escalated in 1981 and the three West Papuans, members of the Melanesian Socialist Party, who were deported that year were accused by the Papua New Guinean government of 'orchestrating... recent armed clashes between OPM rebel factions' on the border.[25] The same year several West Papuans were arrested after an attempted abduction of self-styled OPM spokesman Henk Joku in Port Moresby. (Joku was an early *émigré* from Irian Jaya who had acquired Papua New Guinean citizenship.)

Early in 1984, in an apparent upsurge of OPM activity, an abortive attempt was made by OPM supporters to raise the West Papuan flag on the provincial assembly building in Jayapura. Two West Papuans were killed in the incident and, according to West Papuan sources, 'hundreds' detained in subsequent Indonesian military reprisals. Although the Indonesians initially insisted that the situation in the province was normal, refugees soon began crossing into Papua New Guinea in large numbers. By the end of April 1984 there were some 4,500 refugees in camps along the border. Despite attempts by Papua New Guinean officials to discourage border crossing, and to persuade those who had crossed to return, by the end of the year the number had risen to about 12,000 — almost 1 per cent of Irian Jaya's total population. There were also during 1984 further border incursions by Indonesian troops and aircraft.

As on previous occasions, Indonesia's failure to deal seriously with Papua New Guinea's calls for explanations of what was happening along the border, and its intransigence on the issue of repatriating refugees (specifically refusing to guarantee the safety of those who might be repatriated), frustrated and eventually angered Papua New Guinea's leaders, who found themselves under increasing domestic pressure to deal sympathetically with the refugees and to stand up to Indonesia. On a visit to Indonesia in April 1984 Foreign Minister Namaliu lodged 'a very strong formal protest' about Indonesian violations of Papua New Guinea's territorial sovereignty, and complained that with reference to the refugee situation, his government was having 'to deal with the effects of problems not of our making': 'The people and government of my country have a very real interest in ensuring that Irian Jaya is administered in an orderly and peaceful way and that development takes place in the interests of the people who live there,' the minister said.[26] Indonesia's foreign minister found Namaliu's comments 'offensive' and 'provocative'[27] and the military commander in Irian Jaya countered by accusing Papua New Guinea of 'harbouring, giving sanctuary, to the OPM'.

Nevertheless, in Papua New Guinea there were many who felt that the government had not gone far enough. United Party leader Torato urged that diplomatic relations with Indonesia be cut and that Papua New

Guinea support West Papuan demands at the UN. A similar call for the government to 'support UN moves to enable the people of Irian Jaya to determine their own future' came from the premier of Western Province and in a resolution of the Sandaun provincial assembly—these being the two provinces sharing the border with Irian Jaya. There were even suggestions (for example, by the Sandaun deputy premier in 1983 and by the *Post-Courier's* defence correspondent in 1985) that people in Papua New Guinea's border villages were joining or giving sanctuary to the OPM. Mission stations in the border area were also under suspicion in some government circles of harbouring OPM guerrillas and passing on intelligence. The Papua New Guinean government stopped well short of supporting the West Papuan cause, but in October Namaliu did inform the UN General Assembly of developments along the border and said that his government had not been satisfied with Indonesian responses to its diplomatic representations. 'It was', said Osborne,[28] 'the first time that PNG had internationalised the matter.'

Once again, however, the OPM failed to take advantage of the considerable popular sympathy in Papua New Guinea, which was manifested in a widespread opposition to forced repatriation of refugees. The kidnapping of a Swiss pilot in Irian Jaya and a subsequent ransom demand, which came from Henk Joku, was condemned by most of the Irianese community (and did little for Joku's credibility), and further threats by the OPM against several Papua New Guinean politicians and officials and against the big copper/gold mine at Ok Tedi (close to the border), should repatriation proceed, angered the government, which once again threatened to withdraw residence visas and to charge those violating Papua New Guinea's laws. There was also a move to place restrictions on the activities of foreign journalists, and the ABC representative in Papua New Guinea was expelled as a result of a controversial ABC-TV interview with OPM leader James Nayaro.

There remains in Papua New Guinea a great deal of popular sympathy for the situation of the West Papuans, particularly among church and student groups and in villages along the border. However, there has been little inclination to translate the sympathy for West Papuans into active support for a free West Papua. Papua New Guinean governments, pragmatically, have seen a free West Papua as worthy but unrealistic, and have been concerned predominantly with maintaining cordial relations with their large neighbour to the west. In this respect the signing of a Treaty of Mutual Respect, Friendship and Co-operation between the two countries in 1986 was taken by many as evidence of a closer relationship between Papua New Guinea and Indonesia, even though the Treaty says little that has not been said before.²⁹ Disunity within the Irianese community in Papua New Guinea—reflecting the discord within the larger Irianese community—and the occasionally belligerent attitude the OPM has adopted towards Papua New Guinea, have further acted against the emergence of an effective pro-West Papuan lobby in Papua New Guinea.

Vanuatu, Libyan connections and the South Pacific Forum
In 1980, as part of an independent foreign policy initiative, the Vanuatu government of Fr Walter Lini invited an Irianese refugee in Papua New Guinea, Rex Rumakiek, to open an information office in Port Vila. Rumakiek, a former OPM guerrilla, is a graduate of the University of Papua New Guinea and a former student activisit. Papua New Guinea authorities responded to this by cancelling Rumakiek's travel documents and threatening to deport him to a third country (his appointment was also opposed by Jacob Prai), but eventually he was allowed to leave for Vanuatu where he became director of a Vanuatu Pacific Community Centre, from where he distributed OPM propaganda.

In 1984 the ruling Vanuaaku Party voted to recognize the OPM and to take up the West Papuan cause at a forthcoming Commonwealth Heads of Government Regional Meeting and at the South Pacific Forum, but Lini was dissuaded from this by Papua New Guinea's Prime Minister Somare, who suggested that Vanuatu's Melanesian sympathies might be better served by accepting refugees (Vanuatu had refused to accept Rumkorem in 1982 and was no more co-operative during the refugee crisis of 1984). The same year several overseas Irianese activists were invited to Vanuatu, and residence visas were granted to the Black Brothers rock group, whose members—all OPM supporters—had left Indonesia in 1979 and spent periods in Papua New Guinea and in Holland. In 1985 Vanuaaku Party General-Secretary Barak Sope managed to bring together in Vila the leaders of the major OPM factions, including Prai and Rumkorem, who agreed to settle their differences and signed a reconciliatory Declaration of Port Vila.

About this time, also, there appears to have been some contact between the Vanuatu and Libyan governments.³⁰ Formal diplomatic links between the countries were established in 1986 and several Ni-Vanuatu, and Rumakiek, subsequently attended training courses in Libya. An OPM delegation also attended a World Conference of Liberation Movements in Libya in early 1986. Rumkorem later said that Libya had offered the OPM financial assistance,³¹ and an OPM spokesman in Papua New Guinea claimed in 1987 that a group of Irianese freedom fighters had recently returned to the border area after training in Libya and that another group was currently undergoing training.[32] As against this, an OPM commander in Irian Jaya said that the freedom fighters in the bush had seen nothing of Libyan assistance, and in an ABC interview in 1988 Rumakiek stated that 'so far we have nothing concrete [from Libya]'.[33]

Osborne[34] suggests that from around 1984 the OPM attempted to gain increased support from the South Pacific and to rely less on European sources. If this was the case, however, the strategy had little success. Although it has been vocal in support of Kanak independence in New Caledonia, the South Pacific Forum and the member states, other than Vanuatu, have been silent on the West Papua issue.

In mid-1988, following a dispute between Lini and Sope which resulted in rioting in Port Vila and an attempt to remove Lini from office, some of Sope's supporters were arrested. The residence visas of the Black Brothers and their families were revoked. Unable to leave the country (with no rights of residence elsewhere), they were arrested and subsequently deported. (The group currently has temporary residence in Australia.) Rumakiek, who was out of Vanuatu at the time, has not returned. The Irianese community in Vanuatu has thus effectively disappeared and Rumakiek's office has closed.

Australian support for West Papua

Since the capitulation to Indonesian demands and international pressure in the 1960s, Australian governments have displayed no interest in the West Papua cause, being far more concerned with avoiding any rift in relations with Indonesia. At its annual conference in 1969 the Australian Labor Party (ALP) passed a resolution that

> conference believes that the people of West Irian have an inalienable right to determine their own form of government and that the recent undemocratic action by the government of Indonesia is inconsistent with any act of free choice by the people.

However, by the time the ALP came to office in 1972 this resolution had conveniently lapsed. The Liberal Party's Minister of External Territories at the time, Gordon Freeth, was less equivocal, saying that it would be immoral for outsiders to incite the Papuans on a course of resistance for which they would receive no outside backing.[35] Australia has, however, provided financial assistance to Irianese refugees in Papua New Guinea, through the UNHCR, and in recent years has reluctantly granted a small number of Irianese refugees temporary residence visas.

A more sympathetic attitude has existed outside government, among organizations of the Left critical of the right-wing regime in Indonesia, and among human rights groups, church groups and NGOs. A list of such organizations include Australia Asia Worker Links, CARPA (Committee Against Repression in Pacific and Asia), Asian Bureau Australia, the Catholic Commission for Justice and Peace and The Australian Council for Overseas Aid. Many of these organizations have overlapping memberships and have espoused a number of regional causes including East Timor, Kanak independence, a nuclear-free Pacific, the anti-Marcos movement in the Philippines and Australian Aboriginal land rights. In 1984 Henk Joku attended a conference in Australia of the World Council of Indigenous Peoples, where he made contact, amongst others, with the Aboriginal Land Rights Support Group and other Aboriginal activists. Individual criticism of Indonesian rule in Irian Jaya has also come from journalists and academics, including a number of Indonesian specialists and people who have spent time in Papua New Guinea. The arrest and subsequent murder, in 1984, of Arnold Ap, well known to many outside Irian Jaya as curator of the Cendrawasih University museum and a member of the Mambesak cultural group, brought condemnation of Indonesia from academics and others who had previously tended to discount allegations of repression in Irian Jaya.

In the 1970s an office of the South Pacific News Service was maintained in Sydney and there has been regular contact between TAPOL and sources in Australia. Books by Australians, such as Nonie Sharp,[36], Robin Osborne,[37] Julie Southwood and Patrick Flanagan,[38] and the late Bob Mitton,[39] have publicized the West Papuans' grievances against Indonesia, as has the Melbourne-based quarterly magazine *Inside Indonesia*.

The refugee crisis which emerged in 1984, and was well publicized in Australia, provoked criticism of Indonesian rule in Irian Jaya and a questioning of its transmigration targets in relation to the province. A delegation of the Australian chapter of the International Commission of Jurists visited the refugee camps in Papua New Guinea and issued a report which criticized both Indonesian policies which had created the refugee problem and the Papua New Guinean government's handling of the situation, eliciting the comment from Somare: 'The ICJ does not run this country.'[40] The Refugee Council of Australia added its support to the ICJ findings. At about the same time a Friends of West Papua organization (later renamed the Australia–West Papua Association) was launched in Melbourne, with contacts in Canberra and Sydney; it publishes an occasional newsletter and serves selectively as an outlet for OPM publicity.

While these various groups have provided moral support for the West Papuan movement, they do not appear to have provided any significant financial or logistic support to the OPM. In 1984 an Australian former mercenary soldier with contacts in Papua New Guinea was arrested in Sydney, accused of attempting to supply arms to OPM guerrillas, and a Papua New Guinean permanent resident who visited Australia and applied for asylum there was said to have been sent to Australia by the OPM to organize military and financial support for the movement. However, these appear to have been isolated instances without concrete effect.

International links
The Left. Commenting on the early failures of the West Papuan nationalists, an Australian commentator concluded:

> The history of the national liberation struggle in West Irian is to a large extent the story of the misfortunes of the educated petty-bourgeoisie; their successive attempts to make linkages with a variety of foreign elements: the Dutch colonialists, the Indonesian 'middle strata' colonisers and political exiles in Dutch New Guinea, the UNTEA, and the Indonesian pre-1969 administration.... Finally, left with nowhere else to turn, elements of the educated petty-bourgeoisie have turned inwards and sought to make linkages with the peasant and proto-peasant masses.[41]

If the pseudonymous Savage — himself an active supporter of the OPM in Port Moresby in the late 1970s — saw a role for external support, it was in the context of the international class struggle and the solidarity of the Left. It is true that around this time a (West) Melanesian Socialist Party was formed among elements of the movement and that (somewhat inept) attempts were made to obtain arms from the USSR and Cuba.[42] Later a student activist from the University of Papua New Guinea was to visit North Korea to seek assistance. Nevertheless, earlier West Papuan nationalists remembered that the Communist Party of Indonesia (PKI) and later the USSR and China had supported Indonesia's claims to West New Guinea and that the Eastern bloc countries had supplied arms, and they were suspicious of left-wing support. Others, of a fundamentalist Christian persuasion, opposed 'communist' tendencies in the movement from a religious viewpoint. The issue of whether or not to approach the

Eastern block countries for arms was in fact a major element of the split which developed in the movement in the late 1970s, with Prai accusing Rumkorem of being a communist. (Nevertheless, Prai himself visited Moscow in 1984.) At least up till 1984, overseas supporters of the West Papuan movement, especially in Australia and Sweden, were, like Savage, largely of the political Left. There was never a well-developed solidarity, however, partly because of attitudes within the OPM and partly because the Left has had some difficulty dealing with a largely non-ideological and somewhat erratic movement.

The Church. While the West Papuan movement has not had the specifically religious orientation that some separatist movements have displayed, there has been a strong (and sometimes fundamentalist) Christian element in the movement, which is explicit in the constitution and has been especially clear in statements by Prai and later Nyaro. The movement's Papua New Guinea-based spokesman, Henk Joku, was for some time secretary of the Bible Society in Papua New Guinea. However, though the Christian church may have been expected to show concern for the plight of the largely Christian Melanesian population in a predominantly Islamic country (particularly in view of reports of Indonesian troops desecrating churches), the missions in Irian Jaya have avoided a confrontation which might threaten the continuation of their work in Indonesia and neither the Catholic nor the Protestant church overseas has shown the religious solidarity that, say, the international Muslim community has shown for Muslim minorities in non-Muslim countries. Indeed, when Pope John Paul II visited the Asia–Pacific region in 1984, as Robin Osborne[43] records: 'In Thailand, he expressed his compassion for the mostly non-Christian Indochinese; in PNG he declined the opportunity to visit refugee camps when Church services were a part of daily life and where his own Catholic priests had become active in relief work'.

Human rights and indigenous peoples' groups. In the absence of an international 'patron', and unable to capitalize on class or religious solidarity, the West Papuan movement has been able to secure some publicity for its grievances and its demands through a network of international human rights and indigenous peoples' organizations. In 1979 the London-based Minority Rights Group published a MRG Report on 'West Irian, East Timor and Indonesia' by an Australian academic and human rights activist,[44] and in 1984 it protested to the World Bank about the Bank's funding of transmigration in Indonesia.

The Anti-Slavery Society, another London-based organization, also published a critical report in 1983. Allegations of human rights abuses have also been made in Amnesty International reports, and Survival International has criticized Indonesian developmental policies from an environmental as well as a human rights perspective. With growing international support for the rights of indigenous peoples, the West Papuans have found additional fora: as noted, Joku attended a Pacific Region Conference of the World Council of Indigenous Peoples in Australia in 1984, attended also by representatives of Fretilin and the Kanak Independence Front. In the same year West Papuan *émigré* Adolf Jombo addressed the UN Working Group on Indigenous Populations in Geneva. The following year the Dutch Research Institute of Oppressed Peoples[45] published a report on 'The tragedy of the Papuans and the International Political Order', and in 1986 the US Center for World Indigenous Studies published an occasional paper (referring to the Treaty of Mutual Respect, Friendship and Co-operation) entitled 'A Treaty for Genocide'.

How much support?

Superficially, this survey suggests extensive support for the West Papuan movement. Looked at more closely, however, and from the viewpoint of Irianese demands for a Free West Papua, the support does not appear to add up to much. *Émigré* West Papua communities in the Netherlands, Papua New Guinea, Senegal and elsewhere are neither sufficiently well off nor, for the most part, sufficiently well placed in terms of migration status to provide substantive assistance to the OPM forces in Irian Jaya. They are, moreover (notwithstanding the Declaration of Port Vila), split across regional, personal and ideological divides and becoming increasingly out of touch with events on the ground in Irian Jaya. West Papua's 'Melanesian brothers' have expressed sympathy and perhaps given some covert support, but Papua New Guinea has its own problems in living with a large, sometimes truculent neighbour, and Vanuatu's support, when placed in the context of Vanuatu's domestic politics, has proved fickle. Moreover, as fewer and fewer Irianese speak English or Tokpisin, even basic communication between the people on the two sides of New Guinea (except in villages along the border) has become more difficult. Moral support from groups and individuals in the Netherlands, Australia and elsewhere has been comforting but has done little if anything to shift

Indonesian attitudes (except *perhaps* in relation to transmigration targets), which remain totally opposed even to any degree of autonomy and continue to display an attitude of cultural superiority towards the Melanesian population.

The events of 1984 focused wider attention on the situation in Irian Jaya, especially as the international media sought to talk to OPM leaders. Indeed, there is evidence that the OPM encouraged movement across the border to draw attention to their cause. One outcome of this was a petition from Australian and British groups to the IGGI (the organization of major aid donors to Indonesia) urging (without success) that continued aid be contingent upon an improvement in Indonesia's human rights record. However, soon other world events overshadowed the West Papuan struggle and it is doubtful whether the increased interest generated in 1984 had any lasting effect. The fact remains that the countries most likely to be able to influence the situation—the United States, Australia, and perhaps Papua New Guinea—have themselves strong strategic and/or commercial reasons for maintaining good relations with Indonesia, which are seen to outweigh the interests of West Papua's Melanesian population.

Consequently, the West Papuan movement within Irian Jaya has had to rely essentially on its own meagre local resources, mobilizing the local population against a militarily vastly superior and generally repressive regime in Jakarta. In this context, achievement of a Free West Papua seems an impossibility, though the struggle is likely to continue for years to come. For the West Papuans the harsh reality has been that it is difficult to internationalize an issue, however just, when the strategic interests of potential supporters are best served by ignoring it.

Notes

1. Kuntjoro-Jakti Dorodjatun and T.A.M. Simatupang, 'The Indonesian experience in facing non-armed and armed movement: lessons from the past and glimpses of the future', in Kisuma Snitwongse and Sukhumbhanl Paribatra (eds), *Durable Stability in Southeast Asia*, Singapore, Institute of South-East Asian Studies, 1987, pp. 96–116.
2. Netherlands New Guinea became West New Guinea, West Irian (Irian Barat) and finally, as a province of Indonesia, Irian Jaya. The nationalist movement initially coined the name 'Irian' but has since adopted 'West Papua'. The indigenous Melanesian people have been referred to as Papuans, West Papuans or Irianese. Since the separatist movement which is the subject of this study has generally used 'West Papua' and has referred to its people as 'West Papuans', these terms will be generally adopted in this

chapter, except where the context suggests that 'Irian Jaya' and 'Irianese' are more appropriate. K. Lagerberg, *West Irian and Jakarta Imperialism*, London, C. Hurst, 1979.

3. J.A.C. Mackie, (1974), *Konfrontasi: The Indonesia–Malaysia Dispute 1963–1966*, Kuala Lumpur, Oxford University Press.

4. June Verrier, *Australia, Papua New Guinea and the West New Guinea Question 1949–1969*, unpublished doctoral dissertation, Monash University, 1976.

5. J.M. van der Kroef, 'West New Guinea: the uncertain future', *Asian Survey* 8 (8): 1968, pp. 691–207.

6. R.C. Bone, *The Dynamics of the West New Guinea (Irian Barat) Problem*, Ithaca, Modern Indonesia Project, Cornell University, 1958; P. van der Veur, 'Political awakening in West New Guinea', *Pacific Affairs* 36 (1), 1963, pp. 54–73; 'The United Nations in West Irian: A Critique', *International Organization* 18 (1), 1964, pp. 53–73; Peter Hastings, *New Guinea: Problems and Prospects*, Melbourne, Cheshire, 1969; J. Ryan, *The Hot Land: Focus on New Guinea*, Melbourne, Macmillan, 1970. June Verrier, op. cit., 1976; Robin Osborne, *Indonesia's Secret War. The Guerilla Struggle in Irian Jaya*, Sydney, Allen & Unwin, 1985.

7. Peter Hastings, op. cit., 1969; Brian May, *The Indonesian Tragedy*, London, Routledge & Kegan Paul, 1978.

8. P. Worsley, *The Trumpet Shall Sound: A Study of 'Cargo' Cults in Melanesia*, London, MacGibbon and Kee, 1957.

9. Veur van der, op. cit., 1963.

10. Peter Hastings, op. cit., 1969, p. 219.

11. The term OPM refers to a group of nationalist organizations or factions which have not always gone under the banner of the OPM. For a discussion of 'definitions' of the OPM, see Blaskett and Wong (1989: 46–7). Also see Hastings's discussion on the OPM as 'state of mind' (in May 1986: 218–31), and Osborne (1985).

12. Peter Hastings, op. cit., 1969, p. 233.

13. R. Osborne, op. cit., 1985; Beverley Blaskett (forthcoming), 'A brief history of the OPM', in G.W. Trompf (ed.), *Island States and Micro-nationalism*.

14. This section draws heavily on a more detailed account of Papua New Guinean relations and the OPM, in May 1986, chapter 5.

15. M. Maunsell Davis, 'Student hang-ups and student action: student political activity at the University of Papua and New Guinea', in Marion W. Ward (ed.), *The Politics of Melanesia*, Canberra, The Research School of Pacific Studies, The Australian National University and the University of Papua New Guinea, 1970, pp. 285–302.

16. R.J. May, (ed.) *Between Two Nations, The Indonesia–Papua New Guinea Border and West Papua Nationalism*, Bathurst, Robert Brown & Associates, 1986.

17. R.J. May, 'Living with a Lion. Public Attitudes and Private Feelings', in R.J. May (ed.), *The Indonesia–Papua New Guinea Border: Irianese Nationalism and Small State Diplomacy*. Research School of Pacific Studies, Australian National University, Department of Political and Social Change, Working Paper no. 2, 1979, pp. 80–107.

18. *Post-Courier*, 23 February 1976.
19. *National Parliamentary Debates*, (I(8), 9 December 1976, pp. 2400–10.
20. Ibid.
21. *Post-Courier*, 28 April 1978.
22. *Post-Courier*, 12 December 1980.
23. *Post-Courier*, 29 May 1981.
24. *Age*, 11 November 1981.
25. *Post-Courier*, 28, 30, 31 July 1981.
26. *Nius Niugini*, 16 April 1984.
27. *Post-Courier*, 23 April 1984.
28. R. Osborne, op. cit., 1985, p. 187.
29. R.J. May, '"Mutual Respect, Friendship and Co-operation"? The Indonesia–Papua New Guinea border and its effects on relations between Papua New Guinea and Australia', *Bulletin of Concerned Asia Scholars* 19 (4), 1988, pp. 44–52.
30. D. Hegarty, 'Libya and the South Pacific'. Research School of Pacific Studies, Australian National University, Strategic and Defence Studies Centre, Working Paper no. 127, 1987.
31. *Age*, 7 April 1987.
32. *Age*, 13 May 1987.
33. Australian television interview with Paul Murphy, 7 June 1988.
34. R. Osborne, op. cit., 1985, p. 108.
35. Ibid., p. 50.
36. Nonie Sharp, *The Rule of the Sword. The Story of West Irian*. Malmsbury, Vic., Kibble Books, 1977.
37. R. Osborne, op. cit., 1985.
38. Julie Southwood and Patrick Flanagan, *Indonesia: Law, Propaganda and Terror*, London, Zed Press, 1983.
39. Robert Mitton, *The Lost World of Irian Jaya*. Melbourne, Oxford University Press, 1983.
40. *Nius Niugini*, 5 October 1984.
41. P. Savage, 'The National Struggle in West Irian: The Divisions within the Liberation Movement', *Australian and New Zealand Journal of Sociology*, 14 (2), 1978, pp. 142–8.
42. R. Osborne, op. cit., 1985.
43. Ibid., p. 184.
44. Keith Suter, *West Irian, East Timor and Indonesia*, London, Minority Rights Group Report, no. 42, 1979.
45. Research Institute of Oppressed Peoples, *The Tragedy of the Papuans and the International Political Order*, Amsterdam, RIOP Report, no. 1, 1985.

12 THE INTERNATIONALIZATION OF BURMA'S ETHNIC CONFLICT

Bertil Lintner

The Union of Burma has had not only forty-two years of independence from Britain, but also as many years of civil war, strife and insurgency. The young republic was hardly born when the Communist Party of Burma (CPB) went underground and resorted to armed struggle; army units rose in mutiny and ethnic minorities took up arms against the central government. The fighting since independence has been little more than a continuing stalemate. Over the past two years, however, this situation has undergone fundamental changes and South-East Asia's longest civil war has reached a turning-point. The Burmese army is well on the way to achieving a goal that has been out of reach for more than four decades: the expulsion of ethnic minority forces from nearly all key trading-points on the border with Thailand. At the same time Burma's decades-long communist insurgency has ended. In March–April 1989, the ethnic rank and file of the CPB rose in a mutiny and drove the party's ageing, mostly Burman Maoist leadership into exile in China. The military government quickly, and shrewdly, exploited the CPB mutiny and managed to turn a previously hostile, 10–15,000-strong guerrilla army into a paramilitary militia force. While these dramatic changes have enabled Rangoon to exert firmer control over the country than perhaps at any time since independence, two main issues have followed in the wake of the changing battlefield pattern: a stream of refugees to neighbouring countries, primarily Thailand, and an unparalleled upsurge in drug-trafficking from the Burmese sector of the Golden Triangle where the ex-CPB forces are active. Seen in this perspective, the Burmese regime now, also for the first time, has to cope with an internationalization of its previously solely internal conflict. This may, in the long run, prove counterproductive for the regime. This chapter discusses the events that led to the present situation in Burma's traditionally rebellious frontier areas and their implications for the future.

The Thai-Burmese border

Ironically, the Burmese military's new, unprecedented iron grip on the country is a direct outcome of the massive anti-government protests which swept Burma during 1988, and the isolation of the new regime that followed. When the military decided on 18 September to step in and reassert power after more than a month of daily demonstrations in Rangoon and elsewhere, many observers saw it as a desperate act of an old regime which had reached the end of the rope. The general public had rejected twenty-six years of military rule, and the carnage resulting from the crackdown on unarmed demonstrators, which came in the wake of the September takeover, had been condemned by the world's democratic community. Virtually all foreign aid programmes had been suspended and trade was down to a trickle. Burma's foreign debt stood at an estimated $US5 billion, requiring $US238 million a year to service. Its reserves of foreign hard currency were down to $US10–12 million.[1] If foreign governments had kept up the squeeze, it would have been only a matter of months before the government totally depleted its foreign exchange reserves—and ran out of bullets.

Then, on 14 December 1988, the Thai army commander, General Chaovalit Yongchaiyuth, undertook a one-day visit to Rangoon. Accompanied by an entourage of eighty-six people, including army officers, Thai pressmen and staff from the Burmese embassy in Bangkok, he was the first foreign dignitary to visit Burma after the coup.

Hardly by coincidence, some unprecedented business deals were signed between the Burmese authorities and several Thai companies shortly afterwards. By early 1989, a stampede of logging concerns, most of whom had close connections with business-oriented Thai army officers, were entering deals with Rangoon. A document written by the military government's Timber Corporation in February said that twenty concession areas had been contracted along the Thai–Burmese border with total exports of 160,000 tonnes of teak logs and 500,000 tonnes of other hardwood logs authorized. The corporation estimated revenues of $US112 million a year from the logging, a bonanza by the scale of Burma's trade.

Two Thai fishery companies, the Atlantis Corporation and Mars & Co., each received permission to catch 250,000 tonnes of fish in Burmese waters. A small firm, the Thip Tharn Thong, signed a contract on 17 December 1988 to barter used cars and machinery in exchange for Burmese gems, jade and pearls. The logging deals especially were timely for Thai interests; following a mudslide caused by deforestation in southern Thailand in late November, the government in Bangkok introduced a ban on logging throughout the country.

The Burmese regime boosted its nearly depleted foreign exchange reserves almost overnight. It survived the unofficial blockade imposed by the United States, the countries of the European communities and Japan. Perhaps even more important, General Chaovalit was ideally placed to resolve the main obstacle that had prevented official cross-border trade in the past: to evict the Karens, the Mons and other ethnic rebels who for decades had been ensconced in the forest areas along the Thai-Burmese border where these new concessions were located.

The Burmese army had begun an offensive against the Karen and Mon rebels in 1984, but was never able to hold territory at the end of tenuous supply lines from Moulmein and other coastal towns through the June–October rainy season. The rebel armies were well trained and equipped with strong fortified bases in the border areas. The Thai authorities had long turned a blind eye to their border smuggling and black market arms purchases, reasoning that the rebels formed a convenient buffer against Thailand's historical enemy, the Burmese. Thai timber companies and gem merchants also had business deals with the Karens, the Mons and other ethnic minorities, and the Thai army's special forces had assigned advisers to some of the rebel groups, especially the Karen National Union (KNU). The rebel New Mon State Party (NMSP) had longstanding ties with the large Mon community settled in Thailand.

In addition, several thousand dissident students had fled to the border areas in the wake of the September 1988 military takeover and the massacre of virtually unarmed demonstrators which followed. On 5 November 1988, they had set up the All-Burma Students Democratic Front (ABSDF) during a meeting at the Karen rebel camp of Wangkha near the Thai border. Although they vowed to fight against the SLORC, the ABSDF soon discovered that their hosts, the ethnic rebel armies along the Thai border, did not have any significant amounts of arms and ammunition to share with the Burmese students. They stayed in their camps along the border and concentrated most of their efforts on international publicity. Thailand's initial policy towards these dissident students had been rather lenient; on 22 November the Thai government had even granted temporary asylum to them.

All this changed soon after Chaovalit's visit to Rangoon, which coincided with the start of a dry season offensive launched by the Burmese army. Now, rice and other commodities could be bought from across the border in Thailand, and Burmese forces were no longer held back from crossing into Thai territory and attacking the rebel camps from the rear, using their newly acquired heavy mortars, rockets and artillery. The Thai government also decided to let Burmese aircraft use Thai airspace to take aerial pictures of border areas 'until 31 March 1989'.[2]

On 21 December 1988 the KNU stronghold of Mae Tha Waw was in government hands, and the Burmese army then made a clean sweep south along the Moei river which delineates the Thai–Burmese frontier around the border town of Mae Sot. Klerday, another camp that had been under siege since 1984, was captured on 19 January 1989, followed by Maw Pokay on 26 March and Mae La on 18 April.

As part of the deal between the Thai and Burmese military, a reception centre for students who wanted to return to Burma 'voluntarily' was also set up near the provincial airport at Tak on 21 December 1988 and a similar camp was attached to the 11th Infantry Regiment's camp at Bangkhen, a northern Bangkok suburb. The first batch of eighty Burmese students from the border areas was repatriated five days later, followed by several hundred over the weeks that followed. On 5 January 1989 the US State Department said it had received reports that as many as fifty Burmese students who had returned via the 'reception centres' set up by the Burmese Army close to the Thai border had been arrested and some had been killed in custody. There was also fear for the safety of the 'absconding and misled students' (to use the SLORC's terminology) whom the Thais were sending back by air. However, human rights issues had taken a very definite back seat in Thailand's refugee policy in view of the lucrative business deals which the Burmese military were now offering their Thai counterparts.

The forced repatriation proved embarrassing for the Thai as well as for the Burmese authorities. In a feeble attempt to show the increasingly concerned international community that the students who had been repatriated from Thailand had not been arrested or maltreated, which several press reports had claimed, the SLORC in mid-January 1989 made the unexpected move of contacting the Foreign Correspondents' Club of Thailand. Forty-six Bangkok-based journalists were invited to visit Burma; it was the first press tour of its kind since the military takeover in 1962. The unprecedented press tour went to Rangoon, Loikaw, Taunggyi, Meiktila and Pagan, but was strictly guarded by both uniformed military police and plain-clothes DDSI agents—easily distinguishable in their dark sunglasses and with their stern looks. Helen White, one of the participants of the tour, wrote in the Asian Wall Street Journal shortly afterwards:

The military regime's initial public-relations efforts were far from convincing ... the military refused journalists' requests to visit markets, or to stroll through city streets ... however, there was little the government could do to limit the damage to its image when several students interrupted a government spokesman in Taunggyi. The spokesman was explaining that the mass shootings in the city by government troops last September came in response to aggression by demonstrators. The room, which was filled with student returnees and their parents, erupted in applause as the students shouted that the slaughter—which they said killed about 74 people—was unprovoked.[3]

The entire repatriation programme came to a halt in late March, following the adverse publicity which the press tour had generated as well as a vigorous protest from the United Nations High Commissioner for Refugees (UNHCR) in Geneva. The offensive against the border camps also slowed down when on 20 May several hundred Burmese government troops entered Thailand opposite the KNU base of Wangkha and burned down a Thai border village. Several Thai politicians protested and the independent Thai daily, *The Nation*, published a strongly-worded commentary, headlined 'Border incident shows army's ties with Burma going too far'.[4] The commentary said:

How could 400 Burmese troops march into ... [a] Thai border village to launch a battle against the Karen base ... across the river and cause the razing of some 200 houses without any resistance from the Thai security forces? ... with the support of the Thai military, the Rangoon regime is able to breathe against the condemnation and boycott from Western countries.

However, such protests from critical Thai voices had no impact on the close co-operation between the Thai army, allied timber companies, and the military in Rangoon. As soon as the rainy season of 1989 was over, the offensive began again. On 29 December Burmese government troops using Thai territory as a springboard to attack from the rear, overran Phalu, one of the KNU's best-fortified camps on the Moei river. On 20 January Burmese government troops captured the KNU's Mawdaung camp opposite Prachuap Khiri Khan in Thailand, and four days later Thay Baw Bo, a camp further up the Moei river which the KNU shared with the ABSDF, fell to Rangoon's forces. On 31 January, Walay, a KNU base to the south, was also captured and on 11 February, a major offensive in the Three Pagodas Pass area led to the fall of the NMSP's headquarters. During the latter battle, intelligence sources assert that Burmese government troops attacked from the Thai side and that some troops had been transported in Thai trucks provided by a Bangkok-based timber merchant (interview with Nai Aung Tin from the

Mon Refugee Committee, Three Pagodas Pass, 8 April 1990). Thai timber companies were also reported to have been involved in the assault on Phalu in December.

With the onset of the rainy season of 1990 the fighting subsequently died down again. Only a few camps remain in rebel hands—and a steady flow of Thai timber trucks cross the international frontier almost every day. While that may be welcome, the successes of the Burmese army along the border have also resulted in a big influx of refugees into Thailand. About 20,000 Karens were in camps in Thailand already before the latest offensive, most of them having fled when the Burmese army began its first major operation against the KNU in 1984. In early 1990, however, the number of refugees had risen to over 40,000.[5] This figure includes Karens, Mons, Karennis, Burmese dissident students and ordinary Burmese who have fled after the government troops press-ganged them into becoming porters for their assaults on the ethnic rebels.

Thailand's policy towards these refugees thus far has been inflexible on the issue of asylum and international protection, so as not to upset the new and therefore still delicate ties with Rangoon. Instead, Thailand has arrested and deported more than 3,200 Burmese refugees since 1988 and refuses to allow international agencies like the UNHCR and the International Committee of the Red Cross to provide humanitarian aid or other forms of protection to the refugees. In a remarkable statement, Chalerm Suppamorn, the governor of Thailand's Rangong Province, said, 'we are in a hurry [to send back the refugees] because the Burmese army sought our co-operation, saying it needs the [illegal] immigrants for the military', i.e. to act as forced labour.[6]

Despite this resistance from the Thai authorities, however, the refugee question had become an international issue already when the Thais began repatriating Burmese students in December 1988. Several non-governmental organizations soon also became involved with assisting the refugees along the border and in November 1989 the US government decided to contribute $US250,000 to the effort. International relief agencies, US politicians and others started to criticize openly Thailand's dealings with Burma. *The New York Times*, for instance, wrote in a recent editorial: 'At a minimum the US and others need to urge Thailand to condition its commerce on elementary standards of civilized conduct.'[7]

Eventually, on 24 April 1990 the US Senate unanimously approved a bill that would prohibit US purchases of any goods of Burmese origin. The United States is the main export market for several Thai furniture companies and gem merchants who now import most of their products from Burma. The bill has to be approved by the US House of Representatives and it must be signed by the president before it becomes law. If that happens, General Chaovalit's rush into Burma in December 1988 will be proved to have been strongly counterproductive, and the effort on the part of the Burmese military to break its isolation will have back-fired. The civil strife in Burma—first, the 1988 massacres in the towns and cities, and later, the escalated civil war in the frontier areas—has very clearly become an international issue.

The Sino–Burmese border

The drastic changes along the Thai–Burmese border since 1988 have been paralleled by no less dramatic events in the far north of Burma, where the country's strongest rebel armies traditionally have been active. Unlike the situation along the Thai border in the south, the groups in the north controlled large tracts of land with their own administration and infrastructure. These groups in the remotest areas of Burma, however, never received anything like the same publicity as the easily accessible rebel armies along the Thai–Burmese border.

The strongest group in the north was the CPB, which in the late 1960s and early 1970s had wrested control over a 20,000 sq km area adjacent to the Chinese frontier. This communist base had a population of approximately 300,000 people and included middle-sized towns, villages, and wild mountain ranges where the local hill-tribe population grew opium poppies. Young recruits from these hill-tribes, mainly Wa, made up almost the entire rank and file of the CPB's 10–15,000 strong rebel army. The party leadership, however, was predominantly Burman; communist veterans from Rangoon, Mandalay, Pyinmana and other towns in central Burma who, with Chinese help, had established their base in these remote border regions. From there, they hoped to reinfiltrate Burma itself and to re-enter the CPB's old strongholds in central Burma: the Pegu Yoma mountain range north of Rangoon, the Irrawaddy delta south of the capital, the Pinlebu region of northern Sagaing Division and other former base areas which had been overrun by the government's army in the 1970s.

Then, on 12 March 1989, CPB units from Kokang, a district in the communist area dominated by ethnic Chinese, decided to break with the Burmese-dominated and ideologically-motivated party leadership. Led by the local chieftain, Pheung Kya-shin, and his younger brother,

Pheung Kya-fu, the Kokang Chinese discarded Marxism-Leninism and set up their own Burma National Democratic Front (BNDF). The mutiny spread rapidly across the CPB's base area, and later on 16 April Wa troops stormed the party's general headquarters at Panghsang near the Chinese border. The entire Burmese leadership of the CPB fled in disarray to China in the early hours of 17 April. The CPB split up into a number of smaller rebel armies based on ethnic lines.[8]

The events which led to the mutiny in 1989 originated in the Chinese decision ten years earlier to reduce drastically aid to the CPB. From 1968 to 1978 the Chinese had provided the CPB with nearly everything it needed: arms, ammunition, medicines, uniforms and even foodstuff. The party's annual budget totalled 56 million Kyats when the Chinese changed that policy in the late 1970s.[9] An official CPB breakdown shows that 67 per cent of this amount came from trade (i.e. taxation of the cross-border trade with China), 25 per cent from 'the centre' (Chinese aid); 4 per cent from 'the districts' (house tax on people living in the base area); 1 per cent from contributions made by army personnel; and 2 per cent from other unspecified sources.[10] When the Chinese decided that the CPB had to be 'self-reliant', they directed all cross-border trade through communist-controlled toll gates along the Sino-Burmese frontier. The most important was Panghsai (or Kyu-hkok) where the Burma Road crosses the international frontier into the Chinese town of Wanting. The tax levied by the CPB at Panghsai amounted to 27 million Kyats, or nearly 50 per cent of the CPB's budget in the late 1970s. Black-marketeers from government-controlled areas, as well as other rebel groups (for instance the Kachin Independence Army (KIA) in the northern Kachin state, which at this time also traded in Chinese-made consumer goods), had no choice but to trade through the CPB.

In 1980, however, China announced a new open-door trade policy and soon there were about seventy unofficially approved 'gates' along the border through which Chinese goods entered Burma. The KIA could now trade directly with China; in addition some goods crossed the frontier at the only point then controlled by the government: a narrow corridor from Nongkhang in Burma to Man Khun in China, between the two CPB-controlled enclaves of Khun Hai and Man Hio opposite Namkham on the Shweli river. The government had access to a small stretch of the border opposite Muse as well, but that area was considered too insecure because of the proximity of the CPB garrison at Panghsai only a few kilometres to the east.

The communists found it increasingly difficult to practise this new policy of 'self-reliance': due to the reduction of revenue on the cross-border trade, they turned their attention to the few resources available to them in the north-eastern base area. Unlike the KIA's territory in Kachin state where the soil is rich with jade, rubies and sapphires, there are almost no minerals in Kokang, the Wa Hills and other CPB areas. The only cash crops were tea in Kokang, and plenty of opium in Kokang, the Wa Hills and the so-called 815 Region north-east of Kengtung, near Laos. An estimated 80 per cent of all poppy fields in Burma were already under the CPB's control, but party policy until the late 1970s had been to curb the production. With Chinese assistance, new varieties of wheat had been introduced, but few among the hill-tribe population knew how to prepare these new crops. The CPB's crop-substitution efforts ended in 1976, after an invasion of rats in the southern Wa Hills, which wiped out much of the area's crops. The CPB assisted the famine victims by distributing 60,000 Indian silver rupees (still the most commonly used hard currency in the Wa Hills) and 1,600 kg of opium. When the crisis was over, many families had reverted to growing poppies, which are less vulnerable to pests than the substitute crops. With the reduction of Chinese aid in 1979, there was naturally even less incentive for the CPB to pursue its crop-substitution programme.

The CPB now began showing increased interest in the potentially lucrative drug trade—certainly an unorthodox alternative for a party claiming to be communist. Thousands of viss (1.6 kg) of opium were stockpiled at Panghsang. From there the party transported the drugs via M ng Paw in the CPB's Northern Kengtung District to the bank of the Nam Hka river, then on by bamboo raft down to the junction of the Salween and downriver to Ta-Kaw. There it was loaded onto mules and porters and carried to the Thai border via M ng Pu-awn and M ng Hkok. Thus, the CPB became directly involved with remnants of the Kuomintang, and drug kingpin Chang Chifu, alias Khun Sa, who were based along the Thai–Burmese border where they refined the opium into heroin. The CPB also allowed increasing numbers of heroin refineries to operate within its own base area. These refineries were run by the same syndicates as those along the Thai border, and they had to pay 'protection fees' and other taxes to the CPB. Such refineries were soon established near Panghsang, in the 815 Region and near the Salween river in the Kokang area.

The CPB's official policy was confined to collecting 20 per cent of the opium harvested in its base area. This opium was stockpiled at local district offices, where the CPB's 'trade and commerce departments' sold it to traders from Tang-yan, Nawng Leng, Lashio and other opium-trading centres in the goverment-controlled area west of the Salween. In addition, there were a 10 per cent 'trade tax' on opium that was sold in the local markets and a 5 per cent tax on any quantity leaving the CPB's area for other destinations (interview with Mya Thaung, political commissar of the CPB's Northern Wa District, M ng Mau, 4 December 1986). The funds derived from these sources were viewed as legitimate, but several local commanders became increasingly involved in other private trading activities as well as the production of heroin.

At the same time the CPB's once rather efficient civil administration began to break down. Schools and clinics had to close because of lack of funds, and party cadres showed less motivation for their work. The main preoccupation of the civil administrators out in the districts became tax collection for the party; they also engaged in trade in order to support themselves and their families. Ironically, the area controlled by the orthodox Marxist-Leninists of the CPB became a haven for free trade in then socialist Burma. The economy remained thoroughly capitalistic and the CPB never even tried to implement a land reform in the north-east, in sharp contrast to the dramatic land distribution schemes which the party had carried out in central Burma in the early 1950s. Communist ideology became a hollow concept without any real meaning to the people in the north-eastern base areas.

Despite the strength of the CPB army, the actual party organization remained weak. In 1977 there were only 2,379 party members in Namkham, Kutkai, Kokang, Northern Wa, Southern Wa, Panghsang and Northern Kengtung districts, of whom, significantly, only 888 came from the then 23,000-strong army. In addition, there were 115 party members in Tenasserim and 26 in the central '108 War Zone'. The party's youth organization claimed a membership of 2,315, and various 'peasant unions'— the basis of the CPB's 'people-power' structure in the north-east—enlisted 87,608 members in 882 different local organizations (CPB 1979: 104). However, these 'mass organizations' existed only on paper. By the mid-1980s, the CPB had in effect ceased to function as a properly organized Communist party.

In late 1985 the CPB decided to launch a 'rectification campaign' with the aim of 'improving discipline and political as well as military training of soldiers and cadres, rebuilding the civil administration, improving relations with other rebel armies and punish [*sic*] cadres involved in illegal activities'. In directives related to the last item, the CPB said that any party member found to be involved in private opium trading would face severe punishment, and anyone caught with 2 kg or more of heroin would face execution.[11] The CPB's involvement in the drug trade had become an embarrassment to the party's ageing, ideologically-motivated leadership. It is also plausible to assume that the 'campaign' had been launched under Chinese pressure. The spillover of drugs from the CPB's area into China was becoming a problem, and increasing amounts were also being smuggled via Kunming to Hongkong. Subsequent to the decision in 1985 to clamp down on the drug trade, party agents were sent out to check up on local cadres and report any wrong-doing to the centre at Panghsang. While this did not affect the illiterate rank and file of the CPB, it nevertheless caused severe frictions between the top party leadership and several local commanders who had begun to act as warlords in their respective areas.

In addition, another, separate development had a tremendous impact on the rank and file as well as the hill-tribe population in the areas under the CPB's control. In April 1985 a delegation from the non-communist umbrella organization, the National Democratic Front (NDF), which then comprised nine different ethnic resistance armies, left the Thai border for a long trek north. After an arduous seven-month journey, the NDF delegates reached Pa Jau, the headquarters of the Kachin rebels in the far north of the country. A meeting was held at Pa Jau and the NDF decided to discard separatism once and for all in favour of advocating a federal system of government in Burma, and in a significant break from past policies they also decided to contact the CPB in order to co-ordinate military operations against the government in Rangoon. From Pa Jau the delegation proceeded to Panghsang, where a second meeting was held on 17–24 March 1986. The NDF and the CPB decided to set up a united front, modelled on the anti-Vietnamese coalition in Kampuchea.[12]

Despite a great deal of initial enthusiasm, surprisingly little came out of this agreement, mainly because the pact was opposed by the second largest member of the NDF, the staunchly anti-communist KNU, which refused to co-operate with the CPB under any circumstances. The impact of the meeting was immediately felt in the CPB's base area. The NDF delegation trekked through M ng Ko, Kokang and over the Wa Hills before they eventually reached Panghsang. For the first time, the various ethnic minorities in the CPB's base area came into direct contact with leaders and troops from non-communist ethnic resistance armies. The NDF delegation also included a young representative from the Wa National Army (WNA) and almost overnight he became somewhat of a national hero in the Wa Hills. In what was possibly a naïve attempt to placate the increasingly restless Was, the CPB allowed the WNA to set up a liaison post at Kang Hs inside the base area in the northern Wa Hills. The outcome was that several of the rank and file CPB soldiers began wearing WNA caps and badges. The first signs of an ethnic consciousness now appeared among the Was in the CPB's area, in contrast with the Marxist-Leninist ideology with which they had been fed for years.

The disillusionment with the old leadership increased after a series of military defeats during the 1986-7 dry season. On 16 November 1986, the CPB attacked a government outpost on Hsi-Hsinwan mountain between M ng Paw and Panghsai. Nearly 1,000 CPB troops were mobilized for the operation, the largest the CPB had mounted in many years. The attack was launched partly because government troops had been able to disrupt the lucrative trade route to Panghsai from their mountaintop positions. However, another motive was that, with the NDF becoming popular even in the CPB's own base area, the communists were losing momentum; they wanted to show the smaller, ethnic rebel groups that they were still the strongest force and the only one able to launch a spectacular attack on a major Burmese army camp. The Chinese, no doubt, supported the CPB, at least during the initial stages of the fighting, since they were also suffering from the slackening trade to Panghsai.[13]

The outpost was overrun, but only to provoke a determined counteroffensive from the Burmese army. Thousands of troops, supported by heavy artillery and aircraft, moved in on Hsi-Hsinwan. The CPB was forced to evacuate the mountain on 7 December, and on 3 January 1987 the government forces pushed down from Hsi-Hsinwan and captured M ng Paw, a major market village at the foot of the mountain range. The onslaught continued with a massive attack along the Burma Road. Panghsai fell on 6 January.[14] When the threat posed by the CPB forces in this strategic border town had been removed, the government's troops crossed the Shweli river on 13 January and recaptured Khun Hai and Man Hio, two enclaves north of the Shweli river opposite Namkham, which had been in communist hands since 1968. At that point, persistent reports claim that China allowed the Burmese troops to use its territory to attack these two enclaves, which indicates that the Chinese had simply decided to side with the force they thought was going to win the battle for the border area. From then onwards, the government controlled a 60-km long stretch of the border, from Namkham to Panghsai, and official surface trade between Burma and China was re-established.

In terms of actual territory, the government's gains were small, while the price it had to pay for the victory was enormous according to all independent sources. Government losses were estimated to be at least 1,000 dead and wounded. Nevertheless it was a major victory over the CPB, both strategically and in terms of prestige. The communists had lost their most important toll gate along the border with China; financially, the CPB had suffered another setback, and the morale of its army was shattered. The CPB had used disastrous human-wave tactics resulting in at least 200 deaths.[15] Resentment towards the old leadership became even more intense than before.

Then, in the following year, the pro-democracy movement swept across Burma as anti-government demonstrations shook nearly every town and city throughout the country. The CPB paid minimal attention to the uprising. Its 3rd Party Congress in 1985 had reiterated the Maoist doctrine of capturing the countryside first, then surrounding the cities and moving into urban areas later. Anything else was considered 'adventuristic' and not in accordance with 'Marxism-Leninism, Mao Zedong thought'.

On 19 and 20 May 1988 the CPB's clandestine radio station, the People's Voice of Burma had carried a surprisingly accurate account apparently based on an eye-witness report of the first anti-government demonstrations in March.[16] However, that was almost the extent of the CPB's 'involvement' in the pro-democracy movement in Burma of 1988.

The policy of the CPB's leadership towards the popular nation-wide uprising for democracy was, however, discussed at a Politbureau meeting on 10 September. Apparently, some of the party's younger members were encouraged by the urban rising and wanted to link up with it. However, after discussing in general terms the movement's demand for the formation of an interim government in Rangoon, the ageing Burmese Maoists concluded:

> The No. 1 point I would like to say is not to let them [i.e. the younger cadres] lose sight of the fact that we are fighting a long-term war. It is impossible for us to make attacks in the towns taking months and years. That is possible only in our rural areas.[17]

In accordance with this line, the CPB launched an all-out attack on Möng Yang, a small, remote garrison town near the Chinese fronties in eastern Shan state. The CPB's forces managed to capture the town on 24 September and the commanding officer of the Burmese Army's 11th Battalion, Major Soe Lwin, was killed in the battle along with 130 of his men. At least a hundred government soldiers were wounded and nine were captured alive. The government forces, however, immediately launched a counteroffensive and on two consecutive days aircraft strafed and bombarded the town, reducing parts of it to rubble. After a few days of heavy fighting, the CPB's troops withdrew from Möng Yang.[18] The battle for Möng Yang was the last major engagement between the Burmese army and the CPB.

When large numbers of students fled Rangoon and other cities for the border areas after the military takeover on 18 September, only 50–60 went to the CPB's territory.[19] The CPB's failure to link up with the biggest popular uprising in modern Burmese history annoyed the few young intellectuals within the party as well as some of the better-educated, Burmese-speaking minority cadres who had heard about the uprising in central Burma on the BBC's Burmese service. The vast majority of the CPB's hill-tribe rank and file was, however, unaware of the fact that there was a mass uprising in the first place.

Friction within the CPB intensified, reaching a climax by the beginning of 1989. By this time, the Chinese had signed several trade agreements with these Burmese authorities, and Chinese pressure on the CPB to reconsider its old policies was becoming more persistent. Already in 1981 the Chinese had begun offering asylum to party leaders and high-ranking cadres. This offer included a modest government pension (Rmb 250 a month for a Politbureau member; Rmb 200 for a member of the Central Committee, Rmb 180 for any other leading cadre; and Rmb 100 for ordinary party members), a house and a plot of land, on the condition that the retired CPB cadres refrained from political activity of any kind in China. The old guard, especially the many veterans who had lived in China during the days of the Cultural Revolution and been close to Mao Zedong, saw the offer as treachery, although they never criticized China openly. The offer was repeated in 1985 and again in 1988. Some of the younger, lower-ranking CPB cadres accepted the offer, but none of the top party leadership did so except Than Shwe, a member of the CPB's central committee who went to China in 1985.

In early 1989 the Chinese once again approached the CPB and tried to persuade the leadership to give up and retire in China. A crisis meeting was convened on 20 February at Panghsang. For the first time Thakin Ba Thein Tin lashed out against the Chinese. In an address to the secret meeting he referred to

> misunderstandings in our relations with a sister party. Even if there are differences between us, we have to co-exist and adhere to the principle of non-interference in each other's affairs. This is the same as in 1981, 1985 and 1988. We have no desire to become revisionists.[20]

The minutes of the secret meeting were leaked, however, and this may have encouraged the disgruntled rank and file to rise up against the old leadership. A major reason why the mutiny did not happen earlier was that the ordinary soldiers and local commanders were uncertain of China's reaction to such a move. After all, the CPB leaders still went to China every now and then—and they were always picked up at the border by Chinese officials in limousines; the complexities of regional politics were beyond the comprehension of most CPB soldiers.[21]

Even so, by early 1989 the friction within the CPB had reached a point of no return. The mutiny broke out and within a month of the initial uprising in Kokang the CPB had ceased to exist—almost fifty years after its formation in Rangoon on 15 August 1939, and forty-one years since it had decided to resort to armed struggle against the government shortly after Burma's independence in 1948.

Initially, it was believed that the NDF would exploit the mutiny, especially through its Wa component, the WNA. But instead it was the SLORC, the military junta, that managed to strike deals with the ex-CPB mutineers. In these efforts, Rangoon managed to solicit the support of Lo Hsing-han, a former opium warlord from Kokang who now lives in Lashio. He had visited Kokang on 20–21 March 1989, about a week after the Pheungs had initiated the mutiny in that area but a few weeks before the other ethnic components of the CPB had joined the uprising. On 22 April, when the mutiny had spread all over the CPB's north-eastern base area, then Brigadier-General Khin Nyunt, the director of military intelligence, and Colonel Maung Thint, the chief of the Burmese army's north-eastern command in Lashio, travelled to the town of Kunlong near Kokang.[22] Using Lo Hsing-han as an intermediary, they met Pheung Kya-fu and made the initial contact with the ex-CPB forces.

Step by step, marriages of convenience were forged between the Burmese army and various groups of ex-CPB mutineers, and Brigadier-General Khin Nyunt himself paid several highly-publicized visits to Kokang. Then, on 11 November 1989, the leader of the Was, Chao Ngi Lai, and some of his officers were taken by helicopter from the Wa hills to Lashio to meet Khin Nyunt, Maung Tint, the Taunggyi-based eastern commander, Brigadier-General Maung Aye, Brigadier-General Tin Oo from the ruling junta, and four other high-ranking army officers. A 'border development scheme' had already been launched officially by Rangoon and, according to government figures, 70 million Kyats ($US10.7 million) has been spent so far on building roads, bridges, schools and hospitals in these previously neglected frontier areas.

Diesel, petrol, kerosene and rice have been distributed in the former CPB areas.[23]

The agreement with the Was was followed by unofficial peace talks in Rangoon from 16 November to 6 December 1989 between the government and the remaining ex-CPB units. This team was led by Pheng Kya-fu and included another prominent former-CPB commander in Kokang, Liu Go Chi, as well as representatives from the former 815 Region, now controlled by Pheung Kya-shin's son-in-law, Lin Ming Xian.[24]

Although recent, these agreements are not unprecedented in modern Burmese history. In 1963 the Rangoon authorities had authorized the setting-up of the Ka Kwe Ye (KKY) home guards, a local militia which was given the right to use all government controlled roads and towns in Shan State for opium smuggling in exchange for fighting anti-Rangoon rebel forces in the area. Among the home guard commanders who became rich on that deal were Lo Hsing-han, then leader of Kokang KKY, and Khun Sa, who commanded the KKY unit in his native Loi Maw region. These KKY commanders, however, had by 1973 grown too strong for governmental control and the entire scheme was abandoned.

Now, the SLORC appears to have revived the idea, albeit in a different form. Following the cease-fire agreements with the former CPB forces, some of them have attacked ethnic rebel armies in Shan State, and the opium now flows unabated down from the poppy fields in the north-east to the refineries along the Thai border.

Narcotics officials describe the northern Burmese city of Mandalay as the 'hub' for Burma's drug traffic. Chemicals, mainly acetic anhydride which is needed to convert raw opium into heroin, are smuggled in from India at Tamu-Moreh on the border between Burma's Sagaing Division and the north-eastern Indian state of Manipur. The chemicals are trucked down to Sittaung on the Chindwin and from there river boats carry them to the railhead of Monywa west of Mandalay. Communications from Mandalay are quite well developed by Burmese standards. There is an airport, and roads and railways connect Mandalay with various places in Shan State. A US intelligence source said his reports indicated that Burmese army vehicles were used to transport chemicals as well as drugs.[25]

Intelligence sources also claim that there are now at least seventeen refineries in Kokang and the adjacent former-CPB territory west of the Salween river in the north-easternmost corner of Shan State: four in the vicinity of what used to be the CPB's northern bureau headquarters at M ng Ko, six at M ng Hom about 20 km to the south, two at Nam Kyuan, one at Kang Möng south of the Hsenwi-Kunlong road and four inside Kokang itself, east of the Salween.

For trading purposes, the Kokang group has divided itself into two groups in charge of different drug routes and markets. The first group is led by Lo Hsing-han himself and includes the Pheung brothers as well as Liu Go Chi. This group controls thirteen laboratories and sends their refined products, mainly pitzu, a brownish-yellowish powder which can be converted into pure white No. 4 heroin if acetic anhydride and other chemicals are added. The second, smaller group is in charge of local distribution in north eastern Shan state and across the border into China. Intelligence sources claim that this group is led by Liu Go Kyin and Pheung Lau San—both ex-CPB officers—and it controls four refineries, all located in the Möng Ko area. In Lin Ming Xian's easternmost area, one *pitzu* refinery has been located at Loi Mi mountain between M ng Yang and the garrison town of Kengtung. The *pitzu* from there is reportedly sent down to a Khun Sa-controlled facility at Pang Tsang near the Thai border, which can produce No. 4 heroin.

Lo Hsing-han's younger brother, Lo Hsing-minh, has been appointed by the Burmese military authorities to maintain liaison with the former CPB forces north of Kengtung. Officially, he has also been permitted to set up a distillery in Kengtung and to maintain a transport company which distributes his liquor down to Tachilek and other towns along the Thai border. Thailand-based narcotics agents say they are convinced the Lo brothers are involved in co-ordinating the drug traffic. Lo Hsing-han, when he is not seen playing golf with Burmese army officers in Rangoon, is reported to spend most of his time in Lashio where a security force of one Burmese army lieutenant and at least six soldiers are permanently posted at his residence for security.

The sudden rise to power of the Lo brothers in the Shan state heroin trade may be cause for concern for the recently indicted Khun Sa. Traditionally, Burma's military authorities have played off one against the other. Khun Sa spent 1969–74 in jail in Mandalay; Lo Hsing-han was arrested in 1973 then released during a 1980 amnesty. This has led to speculation whether Rangoon, while supporting Lo Hsing-han, may be willing to try to capture Khun Sa and hand him over to the US Drug Enforcement Administration (DEA) as a publicity stunt. Despite evidence of official complicity in the drug trade in Burma, the DEA has shown increased interest in co-operating with the Burmese authorities, which is also in defiance of official US policy that is aimed at isolating the Rangoon regime. Evidently, the isolated Rangoon government is desperately trying to be readmitted into the international community by exploiting the highly emotional drug issue, and the DEA has decided to play along.

Since the beginning of 1990, heavy fighting — real this time — has been raging between the Was and Khun Sa's forces along the Thai border. The Wa troops reportedly have been sent down in Burmese army lorries, which seems to lend credence to a suggestion, issued by US senator Daniel P. Moynihan on 22 March, that the Burmese regime 'has done nothing more than change business partners. Turn on Khun Sa and get the "public relations" advantage that the DEA is giving them. Use the former CPB and turn an armed enemy into a willing drug trafficking partner.'[26]

Critics are also quick to point out that official Burmese complicity in the drug trade is nothing new. The old KKY programme was based on semi-institutionalized drug-trafficking agreements, and narcotics-related corruption has always been widespread in Burma. An internal document from the gong an ju, China's public security bureau, on the activities of underground Chinese groups in Burma from 1985, states that a major Mandalay-based drug syndicate 'in 1982...through connections with the Burmese minister for Home and Religious Affairs, Bo Ni, used Kyats 2 million to build a large community hall in Rangoon and move the centre of its activities there'.[27] Bo Ni, who also served as head of Burma's National Intelligence Bureau, was ousted and arrested in the following year — but on completely different charges, and there is nothing to indicate that his imprisonment affected the activities of this syndicate.

Such evidence of long-standing official Burmese involvement with drug traffickers seems to contradict the assumption that Burma 'suspended drug enforcement activities' after the 1988 military takeover and that the drastic increase in production has been caused by Burma's recent political turmoil. This view has been advocated by the present US ambassador to Thailand, Daniel O'Donohue: 'Many Burmese Army troops, previously dedicated to anti-narcotics operations, were withdrawn from the field and redeployed to enforce martial law.'[28]

Intelligence sources say they are unaware of such troop rotations. The forces which were used to quell the demonstrations in 1988 came mainly from the 22nd and 44th Light Infantry Divisions, which are based in Karen state, an area where no poppies are grown. No troops were pulled out of north-eastern Shan state until after a cease-fire agreement had been reached with the ex-CPB forces. These troops have now been redeployed in Kayah and Kachin states where they are engaged in fighting ethnic rebels.

What seems to have happened since 1988, however, is a much more blatant and more thinly disguised involvement with drug-trafficking groups than before. The new willingness on the part of narcotics officials to address corruption, official complicity and other issues, which until recently were considered taboo, clearly reflects international concern over recent developments in Burma's north-eastern border areas. In addressing this problem, however, differences in opinion are also evident. The DEA has begun to lobby for a resumption of US aid to Burma, which was cut off after the September 1988 massacre in Rangoon. On 13 February this year, a Rangoon-based DEA agent, Angelo Sandino, agreed to participate in a SLORC-orchestrated drug-burning ceremony in Rangoon, and said that he had found 'a new willingness by the Burmese government to cooperate with US drug eradication efforts'.[29] Moynihan retorted in a strongly-worded statement: 'The DEA's policy is at odds with the State Department's. And it is repugnant to see.'[30] A State Department spokesman dismissed the drug-burning ceremony as a 'publicity stunt' and reiterated the charge of official collusion with drug traffickers.[31] This was the first time the conflict between the DEA and politicians in Washington came out in the open.

China's reaction to the CPB mutiny and the upsurge in drug-trafficking along its borders has been surprisingly muted, probably reflecting the fact that since the Tienanmen square incident in June 1989 the Chinese hierarchy has been embroiled in its own internal problems. However, at least the local authorities in Yunnan have begun to address the problem—in their own way. Courts in Yunnan sentenced 136 people to death on drug-trafficking charges and another 68 to life imprisonment during 1989. Last year 2,364 people were sentenced to unspecified penalties for drug-trafficking.[32] Yunnan's role as a major route for drugs reaching Hong Kong is bound to increase—and so will friction with the Burmese military authorities, who refer to the Kokang and Wa ex-CPB forces as 'special police units'.

The Indo-Burmese border

Almost forgotten amongst the students who fled the towns in Burma in 1988 were those who headed to the north and the north-west. About 300 Burmese students, mainly from Mandalay, along with about 700 Kachin students took refuge in the KIA headquarters area south-east of Myitkyina in northernmost Kachin state. There seemed to be less friction between these students and the KIA than was the case in the south with the KNU; the students in the far north were immediately allotted their own camp with its own administration. The Kachin guerrillas provided security for the student camp as well as training and some arms. This group in Kachin state became almost the only student contingent that was properly organized along military lines.

Across the Indian border, the authorities there, unlike the Thais, adopted a clear-cut policy at an early stage. One refugee camp was built at Leikhul in Chandel District of Manipur, mainly for Burmese students who had crossed the frontier near Tamu in Sagaing Division. Two more camps for Chin nationals were set up at Champhai and Saiha in Mizoram. From the very beginning, the Indian authorities made it clear that no one would be forced back to Burma and that the refugees would be granted asylum as long as their lives were in danger.

The number of students who had reached India was not more than a few hundred. Of special interest were the students from Burma's western Chin State; the Chins are closely related to the Mizos of Mizoram which made it easier for them across the border in India. However, being unable to secure more than moral support in Mizoram, a few hundred of the more militant Chin activists trekked north to Kachin state, where they set up the Chin National Front (CNF) and received military training from the KIA. Indirectly, the student movement of 1988 thus contributed to the formation of a new ethnic insurgent army among the hitherto quiet Chins.

Already in October 1988, the Burman students along the Indian border had announced the formation of the Freedom Democratic Guerrilla Front (North Burma) and, like their comrades in the ABSDF, vowed to take up arms against the SLORC. However, like their brethren near the Thai border, they were also unable to secure a supply of arms and ammunition. From a political point of view, the Indian connection will most certainly become increasingly important. India was one of the first countries to comment on the Burmese crisis. On 10 September 1988 New Delhi expressed its support for 'the undaunted resolve of the Burmese people to achieve democracy'. India's sympathetic attitude to the movement has been reflected also in the frankness of All-India Radio's Burmese service, which is outspoken in its criticism of the military regime in Rangoon.[33] Recent reports from northern Burma also indicate that the Indian security authorities have established liaison with the KIA, which now maintains a camp on the Indian border near Chaukan Pass; previously, the KIA's only border camps were along the Sino-Burmese frontier in the east and one small liaison post on the Thai border in the south.

Whither Burma's insurgency?

Despite Burmese army successes in its offensives against the country's abundance of ethnic rebel armies, and the CPB mutiny, Burma's civil war is likely to continue. Since seizing power in 1962, the Burmese military has never shown any real interest in settling the conflict by political means. Here, differences in approach between the Thais and the Burmese can also be detected. The Thai position appears to have been to allow Burmese troops to enter Thailand to capture rebel camps, while at the same time recognizing that the dislodged insurgents would try to disrupt the trade with raids behind Burmese lines, which indeed has happened on a number of occasions since December 1988. Hence, a negotiated end to the fighting would be the only permanent solution to the problem. A Thai attempt to mediate and offer such a solution was, however, dismissed by the Burmese military in May 1989: 'We shall fight the insurgents until they are eliminated', a Burmese army spokesman said at the time.[34]

The internationalization of the Burmese civil war, and the increased attention now being paid to it by Burma's neighbours, are bound to affect not only the outcome of the conflict but also the regime's standing in the world community. Also, despite differences within the US administration, the drug issue, and especially the question of official complicity, is bound to prompt Washington and other foreign powers to become more directly involved in the civil war. A comment, typical of the times, concludes a recent report from the US Committee for Refugees: 'The rest of the world [must] come to the aid of the Burmese people who are desperate, and are dying, for peace and democracy.'[35] Such a comment from a Washington-based organization would have been unthinkable only two years ago, which in itself reflects the new era which Burma's decades-long civil war has now entered. There can be no way back to the self-imposed isolation from which the Burmese military benefited for years.

Notes

1. These and other figures from the *Far Eastern Economic Review*, 22 February 1990.
2. *The Nation*, 28 December 1988.
3. *Asian Wall Street Journal*, 23 January 1989.
4. *The Nation*, 25 May 1989.
5. C. Robinson, *The War is Getting Worse and Worse*, US Committee for Refugees, Washington, DC, 1990.

6. *The Nation*, 19 March 1990.
7. *The New York Times*, 25 March 1990.
8. *Far Eastern Economic Review*, 30 March, 1 June 1989.
9. Interview with Soe Thein, political commissar of the north-eastern base area, Panghsang, 5 January 1987.
10. *The Entire Party! United and March to Achieve Victory.* Political report of the CPB, submitted by Chairman Thakin Ba Thein Tin, 1 November 1978, (in Burma) Panghsan, the PCB Press, 1979, pp. 104–5.
11. Interview with Soe Thein, political commissar of the CPB's north-eastern base area, Panghsang, 5 January 1987.
12. *Far Eastern Economic Review*, 26 May 1987.
13. According to my observations at Hsi-Hsinwan, November 1986.
14. *Far Eastern Economic Review*, 19 February 1987.
15. These are estimates made by the author while at the battlefront in north-eastern Shan State from November 1986 to January 1987. Predictably, the Burmese government has released completely different figures.
16. SWB, EF/0164B/1, 30 May 1988. The same account was also published as a booklet (in Burmese) by the CPB's printing-press in Panghsang.
17. *The Working People's Daily*, 20 November 1989. A transcript of the entire discussion was published in the *Working People's Daily* of 18, 19, 20 and 21 November 1989. Surprisingly, the government published this in order to prove that the CPB was behind Burma's pro-democracy movement.
18. B. Lintner, *Outrage—Burma's Struggle for Democracy*, Hong Kong Review Publishing, 1989, pp. 203–4.
19. According to correspondence which I received from Panghsang in April 1989.
20. Hand-written minutes from this meeting were passed on to me during a visit to Kinghong, Unnan, China in May 1989.
21. According to numerous conversations between CPB soldiers overheard by myself during a visit to the CPB's base area from November 1986 to April 1987.
22. *The Working People's Daily*, 23 April 1989.
23. Interview with Sai Pao, Wa leader, Chiang Mai, 19 April 1990.
24. *Far Eastern Economic Review*, 28 December 1989.
25. Interviews with Western narcotics officials in Bangkok, April 1990, and US intelligence officers, Washington, January 1990.
26. Press release from the office of Senator Daniel P. Moynihan, 22 March 1990.
27. *Brief on Reactionary Organizations by the First Department of the Public Security Bureau*, Beijing, 1985 (in Chinese).
28. *Bangkok Post*, 14 July 1989.
29. *The Working People's Daily*, 14 February 1990.
30. Press release, 22 March 1990.
31. *The Nation*, 21 April 1990.
32. *Bangkok Post*, 16 April 1990.
33. *Far Eastern Economic Review*, 23 February 1989.
34. *Far Eastern Economic Review*, 15 June 1989.
35. C. Robinson, op. cit.

INDEX